Mastering Scheme Programming
From Basics to Expert Proficiency

Contents

1 Introduction to Scheme and Functional Programming **9**

1.1 History and Overview of Scheme 9

1.2 The Core Principles of Functional Programming 11

1.3 Getting Started with Scheme: Installation and Setup . . 13

1.4 Basic Scheme REPL Usage and Commands 16

1.5 The Simplicity and Power of Scheme Syntax 19

1.6 First Steps: Writing and Running Your First Scheme Program 21

1.7 Understanding Expressions and Evaluation in Scheme . 23

1.8 Introduction to Scheme Data Types 26

1.9 The Importance of Recursion in Functional Programming 27

1.10 Comparing Scheme with Other Functional Programming Languages 31

2 Scheme Syntax and Semantics **35**

2.1 Core Syntax and Structure of Scheme Programs 35

2.2 Identifiers and Naming Conventions 38

2.3 Scheme Reserved Keywords 41

2.4 Writing and Understanding Scheme Expressions 44

2.5 Defining and Using Variables 47

2.6 The Role of Parentheses in Scheme Syntax 49

2.7 Comments and Documentation in Scheme Code 51

2.8 Understanding the Scheme Evaluation Model 53
2.9 The Concept of Scoping and Binding 56
2.10 Literals and Self-Evaluating Expressions 58
2.11 Writing and Using Scheme Procedures 60
2.12 Introduction to Tail-Call Optimization 63

3 Variables, Data Types, and Structures 67
3.1 Introduction to Variables in Scheme 67
3.2 Defining and Using Variables: 'define' and 'set!' 69
3.3 Scope and Lifetime of Variables 72
3.4 Understanding Scheme Data Types 74
3.5 Booleans and Their Uses 76
3.6 Characters and Strings 78
3.7 Numbers: Integers, Rationals, and Real Numbers . . . 81
3.8 Symbols and Keywords in Scheme 83
3.9 Lists: The Core Data Structure 85
3.10 Pairs and Cons Cells 88
3.11 Vectors: Fixed-Size Collections 90
3.12 Hash Tables and Dictionaries 92
3.13 Working with Structs and Records 94

4 Control Structures and Recursion 97
4.1 Introduction to Control Structures in Scheme 97
4.2 Conditionals: 'if', 'cond', and 'case' 100
4.3 Boolean Logic: 'and', 'or', and 'not' 102
4.4 Loops and Iteration: 'do' and 'let' Constructs 103
4.5 Using 'begin' for Sequencing Expressions 105
4.6 The Concept of Recursion 108
4.7 Simple Recursive Functions 110
4.8 Tail Recursion and its Optimization 112

4.9 Mutual Recursion 114
4.10 Using Recursion for List Processing 115
4.11 Advanced Recursive Patterns 118
4.12 Combining Recursion with Higher-Order Functions . . . 120

5 Procedures and Higher-Order Functions 123

5.1 Introduction to Procedures in Scheme 123
5.2 Defining and Calling Procedures 125
5.3 Positional and Named Arguments 128
5.4 Procedures as First-Class Citizens 130
5.5 Anonymous Functions and 'lambda' Expressions 132
5.6 Introduction to Higher-Order Functions 134
5.7 Mapping Functions over Lists 136
5.8 Filtering and Reducing Lists 139
5.9 Composing Functions 141
5.10 Closures and Lexical Scoping 143
5.11 Recursive and Iterative Procedures 145
5.12 Memoization and Its Applications 147

6 Working with Lists and Pairs 151

6.1 Introduction to Lists and Pairs 151
6.2 Constructing Lists with 'cons' 153
6.3 Accessing List Elements: 'car' and 'cdr' 155
6.4 Basic List Operations: length, append, reverse 157
6.5 Nested Lists and Deep Recursion 159
6.6 Using 'list' to Create Lists 161
6.7 Constructing Pairs with 'cons' 163
6.8 Decomposing Pairs with 'car' and 'cdr' 165
6.9 Common List Processing Functions 167
6.10 Mapping and Filtering Lists 169

6.11 Association Lists 171
6.12 Advanced List Manipulation Techniques 173

7 Input and Output in Scheme 177
7.1 Introduction to Input and Output in Scheme 177
7.2 Basic I/O Functions: 'display', 'newline', and 'read' 180
7.3 Reading and Writing Characters 182
7.4 Working with Strings in I/O 184
7.5 File Handling: Opening and Closing Files 187
7.6 Reading from Files: 'read' and 'read-line' 189
7.7 Writing to Files: 'write' and 'write-line' 191
7.8 Binary I/O and Handling Byte Streams 193
7.9 Formatted I/O with format 194
7.10 Error Handling during I/O Operations 197
7.11 Using Ports in Scheme 199
7.12 Advanced I/O Techniques 201

8 Macros and Metaprogramming 205
8.1 Introduction to Macros and Metaprogramming 205
8.2 The Basics of Macro Definitions 208
8.3 Using 'define-syntax' and 'syntax-rules' 210
8.4 Hygienic Macros in Scheme 212
8.5 Creating Syntactic Sugar with Macros 215
8.6 Advanced Macro Patterns and Techniques 217
8.7 Macro Expansion and Transformation 219
8.8 Writing and Using Recursive Macros 221
8.9 Debugging Macros 223
8.10 The Role of Macros in Metaprogramming 226
8.11 Macros vs. Functions: When to Use Each 229
8.12 Case Studies: Practical Applications of Macros 232

9 Error Handling and Debugging 235
9.1 Introduction to Error Handling and Debugging in Scheme 235
9.2 Types of Errors in Scheme: Syntax, Runtime, and Logical 237
9.3 Using 'error' and 'raise' to Signal Errors 239
9.4 Catching and Handling Errors with 'guard' 242
9.5 Writing Robust Code with 'with-exception-handler' . . . 243
9.6 Common Debugging Techniques 246
9.7 Using the Scheme Debugger 248
9.8 Inspecting Stack Traces and Error Messages 251
9.9 Debugging Recursive Functions 253
9.10 Testing and Validating Scheme Code 256
9.11 Strategies for Preventing Common Errors 259
9.12 Case Studies: Debugging Real-World Scheme Programs 261

10 Advanced Topics in Scheme Programming 265
10.1 Introduction to Advanced Topics in Scheme Programming 265
10.2 Continuations and Their Uses 269
10.3 Understanding and Using Call/CC 271
10.4 Delimiters and Prompts with Continuations 274
10.5 Lazy Evaluation and Delayed Expressions 276
10.6 Streams and Infinite Lists 278
10.7 Functional Programming Techniques 280
10.8 Memory Management and Garbage Collection 283
10.9 Concurrency and Parallelism in Scheme 285
10.10 Interfacing with Other Languages 288
10.11 Building and Using Libraries and Modules 291
10.12 Advanced Metaprogramming Techniques 294
10.13 Case Studies: Advanced Scheme Applications 297

Introduction

Scheme is a distinguished member of the Lisp family of programming languages, characterized by its minimalist design and distinctive capability for powerful expression and abstraction. This book, *Mastering Scheme Programming: From Basics to Expert Proficiency*, is a comprehensive guide designed to usher readers from foundational concepts to advanced techniques in Scheme programming. Our aim is to facilitate a deep understanding of Scheme that will enable you to harness its full potential for practical applications.

Scheme embodies the core principles of functional programming—a paradigm emphasizing the evaluation of mathematical functions and avoiding state and mutable data. The language's simplicity in syntax, coupled with its powerful recursive and higher-order functions, makes it a preferred choice for enthusiasts of functional programming. Yet, Scheme's efficient nature and flexibility also make it a capable tool for a wide range of programming tasks, from academic research to practical software development.

Beginning with the roots of Scheme and the fundamentals of functional programming, we will guide you through the installation of Scheme on your development environment and introduce you to the Read-Eval-Print Loop (REPL), the interactive programming interface that is central to Scheme development. By the end of this introduction, you will have written and understood your first Scheme program, setting the stage for deeper exploration.

As we delve into the syntax and semantics of Scheme, you will learn the core structure of Scheme programs, including identifiers, reserved keywords, expressions, variables, and the Scheme evaluation model. This comprehensive overview will equip you with the necessary skills to write clear and efficient Scheme code, emphasizing the importance of scope and binding, as well as the unique role of parentheses in Scheme syntax.

A thorough understanding of variables, data types, and structures is essential for any programming language. This book covers defining and manipulating variables, exploring Scheme's diverse data types—including booleans, characters, strings, numbers, symbols, lists, pairs, vectors, and hash tables—and utilizing these to structure data effectively. Additionally, you will learn about the efficient construction and decomposition of lists and pairs, which are fundamental to Scheme's manipulation of data structures.

Control structures and recursion are pivotal in Scheme programming. Through detailed explanations and practical examples, we will explore conditionals, boolean logic, loops, and the significance of recursion. Emphasis will be placed on understanding and implementing tail-recursion optimization, enabling the creation of efficient and robust recursive functions.

Procedures, especially higher-order functions, form the backbone of Scheme. We will cover everything from defining simple procedures and utilizing positional and named arguments, to implementing anonymous functions with 'lambda' expressions. You will also learn to compose functions, leverage closures, and understand recursive and iterative procedures.

Input and output operations in Scheme are crucial for interacting with users and files. This book provides a detailed guide on basic I/O functions, reading and writing characters and strings, handling files, and utilizing ports. Special attention is paid to error handling during I/O operations, ensuring your programs are robust and user-friendly.

Macros offer a powerful tool for metaprogramming in Scheme. The book delves into designing macros with 'define-syntax' and 'syntax-rules', creating syntactic sugar, and implementing recursive macros. You will learn the distinction between macros and functions, understanding when to use each, along with practical applications of macros.

Effective error handling and debugging are critical for reliable software development. This book systematically addresses various error types, employing 'error' and 'raise' functions, utilizing 'guard' for handling errors, and debugging techniques including the use of the Scheme debugger, inspecting stack traces, and debugging recursive functions.

The advanced topics covered in this book, including continuations, lazy evaluation, streams, functional programming techniques, garbage collection, concurrency, interfacing with other languages, and advanced metaprogramming, will extend your knowledge and enable you to solve complex problems with elegance and efficiency.

Mastering Scheme Programming: From Basics to Expert Proficiency aims to be an indispensable resource in your programming library, providing both the theoretical foundation and practical skills required to excel in Scheme programming. Each chapter builds upon the previous, ensuring a cohesive and comprehensive learning experience, transforming you from a novice to an expert proficient in Scheme.

Chapter 1

Introduction to Scheme and Functional Programming

This chapter provides a foundational understanding of Scheme and the paradigm of functional programming. It begins with a historical overview of Scheme, followed by an exploration of the core principles that define functional programming. Practical steps for installing Scheme and using the REPL are included to get you started. The chapter introduces the simplicity and power of Scheme's syntax, guiding you through writing and running your first program, alongside an introduction to essential data types and the importance of recursion. The chapter concludes by comparing Scheme with other functional programming languages to contextualize its unique features and advantages.

1.1 History and Overview of Scheme

Scheme is a dialect of Lisp (LISt Processing), a programming language with roots stretching back to the 1950s. Lisp was conceived by John McCarthy at MIT and quickly became a staple of artificial intelligence research due to its symbolic expression capabilities. Scheme, developed in the 1970s, represents a significant branch in the Lisp family tree, designed with a minimalist philosophy emphasizing a small core of essential constructs.

The inception of Scheme can be traced back to 1975 when Guy L. Steele Jr. and Gerald Jay Sussman introduced it at the MIT AI Lab. Their objective was to create a simple, efficient dialect of Lisp that combined the powerful features of earlier Lisp systems with a new approach to language design. Unlike other Lisp variants, Scheme was designed to support a new paradigm of programming that combined functional and procedural paradigms.

A key motivation behind Scheme's development was the desire to better support a more advanced type of programming known as lexical scoping, which binds variables to the block structure of the code rather than the dynamic call sequence. This was a departure from the dynamic scoping prevalent in other Lisp dialects of the time. The lexical scoping mechanism provides a clearer, more predictable mapping of variables to their values, facilitating more reliable and maintainable code.

Scheme also introduced first-class continuations, a feature that allows the capture of the current state of program execution to be later resumed. This capability is achieved through the $call/cc$ (call-with-current-continuation) function. First-class continuations offer exceptional control over the flow of programs, enabling powerful constructs like coroutines, backtracking, and complex control structures.

The design philosophy of Scheme follows several guiding principles:

- **Minimalism:** Scheme strives to maintain a minimalistic language design with a small set of powerful constructs. This avoids the complexity and redundancy often found in larger languages.
- **Uniformity:** The syntax and semantics of Scheme aim for uniformity. This principle ensures that all expressions, whether simple constants or complex procedure applications, are treated uniformly.
- **Orthogonality:** Features of the language are designed to function independently of one another. This separation of concerns allows for building complex expressions from simpler, independent elements.

Scheme's simplicity and flexibility quickly led to its adoption in a variety of domains, including education, research, and application development. It serves as an excellent tool for teaching fundamental concepts in computer science, particularly due to its straightforward syntax and powerful abstraction mechanisms. Educational texts, including the esteemed *Structure and Interpretation of Computer Programs* (SICP) by Abelson and Sussman, utilize Scheme for its clear expression of computational ideas.

From an evolutionary perspective, Scheme paved the way for the development of various descendant languages and influenced numerous programming paradigms. The influence of Scheme can be seen in the design of other functional languages like Common Lisp, which adopts some of Scheme's innovations while maintaining compatibility with older Lisp systems.

Over the decades, standardization efforts for Scheme have led to the development of several versions of the Revised^n Report on the Algorithmic Language Scheme (RnRS), with the most current being the R7RS. Each revision reflects a community effort to refine and enhance the language while preserving its core principles.

The impact of Scheme on the understanding and development of programming language theory cannot be understated. By emphasizing concepts like recursion, higher-order procedures, and the manipulation of symbolic data, Scheme has enabled programmers to approach problem solving with unprecedented abstraction capabilities. Its minimalist design highlights the power of simplicity and elegance in programming language design.

Scheme's legacy endures, continuously inspiring new generations of programmers and serving as a research vehicle that bridges theory and practice. Through its enduring principles and influential design, Scheme remains a testament to the enduring power of Lisp's original vision of programmable programming languages.

1.2 The Core Principles of Functional Programming

Functional programming is a paradigm that treats computation as the evaluation of mathematical functions and avoids changing-state and mutable data. The core principles of functional programming can be summarized as follows: immutability, first-class functions, pure functions, higher-order functions, and avoidance of side effects. Understanding these principles is fundamental to mastering Scheme and functional programming in general.

Immutability is the concept that once a data structure is created, it cannot be changed. This is different from imperative programming, where data structures are often mutable. In Scheme, immutability means that values such as lists and numbers are not changed after their creation. Instead, new values are created as the results of functions, leaving the original values unchanged. This immutability makes reasoning about programs more straightforward because the state does not change unexpectedly.

First-Class Functions refer to the treatment of functions as first-class citizens. This means functions can be passed as arguments to other functions, returned as values from other functions, and assigned to variables. In Scheme, functions are indeed first-class objects, allowing for the creation of highly modular and reusable code. For instance, consider the following example where a function is assigned to a variable and then used:

```
(define square (lambda (x) (* x x)))
```

Here, square is a function that is assigned to a variable, demonstrating how functions can be treated as data.

Pure Functions are functions where the output value is only determined by its input values, without observable side effects. In other words, calling a pure function with the same arguments will always produce the same result and will not affect any state outside the function. Pure functions are essential in functional programming because they make programs more predictable and simpler to understand. For example:

```
(define add (lambda (a b) (+ a b)))
```

The function add is pure because it depends only on its arguments a and b and has no side effects.

Higher-Order Functions are functions that can take other functions as arguments and/or return functions as results. These are crucial for abstractions commonly used in functional programming such as map, reduce, and filter. Scheme provides powerful ways to manipulate functions, including creating higher-order functions. An example of a higher-order function is:

```
(define apply-twice
  (lambda (f x)
    (f (f x))))
```

apply-twice is a higher-order function that takes a function f and a value x, and applies f to x twice. This example showcases how functions can be composed and passed to other functions.

Avoidance of Side Effects is a principle that emphasizes the reduction or elimination of changes in state or mutable data. Side effects include any operations that modify some state or interaction with the outside world (e.g., input/output operations). By avoiding side effects, functional programs become easier to reason about, test, and debug. Scheme encourages writing functions that do not alter state or depend on mutable data, fostering safer and more predictable code.

The following Scheme code demonstrates how side effects can be avoided using purely functional techniques:

```
(define factorial
  (lambda (n)
    (if (= n 0)
        1
        (* n (factorial (- n 1))))))
```

The function factorial computes the factorial of a number recursively without any side effects. Each recursive call generates a new set of values without altering the state of the program.

Combining these principles, functional programming allows for the creation of clear, concise, and robust programs. These characteristics are achieved through the consistent application of immutability, first-class and higher-order functions, pure functions, and the avoidance of side effects. Scheme, as a representative of the functional programming paradigm, excels in providing the tools and structures necessary to implement these principles effectively.

1.3 Getting Started with Scheme: Installation and Setup

To begin programming in Scheme, the initial step is installing a Scheme interpreter and setting up your development environment. Scheme, being a dialect of Lisp, has various implementations, each with its own unique features and optimizations. For this section, we will focus on installing and setting up the Racket Scheme implementation, given its popularity and robust features suitable for both beginners and advanced users.

Racket is a general-purpose, multi-paradigm programming language in the Lisp-Scheme family. It aims to be a platform for programming language design and implementation. Racket includes a rich set of libraries and an integrated development environment (IDE) called DrRacket.

Downloading and Installing Racket

To download and install Racket, follow these steps:

- Navigate to the official Racket website at https://racket-lang.org.
- On the homepage, click on the "Download Racket" button.
- Select the appropriate installer for your operating system (Windows, macOS, or Linux).
- Once the installer is downloaded, open it and follow the on-screen instructions to complete the installation. The default settings are typically sufficient for most users.

Following the installation, you should have the racket command-line executable and the DrRacket IDE available on your system.

Verifying the Installation

After installation, it's important to verify that Racket was installed correctly. Open a terminal (or command prompt) and execute the following command to check the version of Racket installed:

```
$ racket --version
```

The expected output will display the installed version of Racket, ensuring that the installation was successful. For example:

```
Welcome to Racket v8.2 [cs].
```

Using DrRacket IDE

DrRacket is a powerful IDE that simplifies the development of Scheme programs. To start DrRacket:

- On Windows, you can find DrRacket in your Start Menu.
- On macOS, open DrRacket from the Applications folder.
- On Linux, use your distribution's application launcher or execute drracket from the terminal.

Once DrRacket is opened, you will be greeted with a two-pane interface. The top pane is for your program's source code, while the bottom pane is an interactive REPL for evaluating expressions.

Hello World in Scheme

After setting up the environment, a common practice is to write and run a "Hello, World!" program. In the source code pane of DrRacket, enter the following Scheme code:

```
#lang racket
(displayln "Hello, World!")
```

Click the "Run" button at the top-right corner of the window. The output pane (REPL) should display:

```
Hello, World!
```

This verifies that DrRacket and the Racket language installation are both working correctly.

Setting Up Racket with a Text Editor

While DrRacket is a comprehensive IDE, some developers prefer using text editors such as Emacs, Vim, or VSCode. To use these editors, ensure that racket is installed and added to your system's PATH.

Emacs: When using Emacs, you can enhance your Scheme development experience by installing the geiser-racket package:

- Install Geiser via MELPA:

```
M-x package-install [RET] geiser [RET]
```

- Configure Geiser to use Racket by adding the following line to your init.el or .emacs file:

```
(require 'geiser)
(setq geiser-active-implementations '(racket))
```

Vim: For Vim users, the racket.vim plugin offers syntax highlighting and other features:

- Install Pathogen or Vundle if not already installed.
- Add racket.vim to your plugin manager. For Vundle, add the following line to your .vimrc:

```
Plugin 'wlangstroth/vim-racket'
```

- Run :PluginInstall (Vundle) or restart Vim (Pathogen) to install the plugin.

VSCode: In Visual Studio Code, the Magic Racket extension provides excellent support:

- Open the Extensions view by clicking the square icon in the sidebar or pressing Ctrl+Shift+X.
- Search for "Magic Racket" and click "Install".
- Configure the extension to use your racket executable.

This concludes the installation and initial setup of the Racket Scheme environment. The following sections will guide you through using these tools to develop Scheme programs efficiently.

1.4 Basic Scheme REPL Usage and Commands

The Read-Eval-Print Loop (REPL) is an interactive programming environment essential for learning Scheme. The REPL enables users to enter Scheme expressions, evaluate them, and see the results immediately. This interactive feedback loop is invaluable for exploring the language and debugging code efficiently. Here, we delve into the fundamental mechanisms and commands within the Scheme REPL, ensuring a strong understanding of its functionalities.

The REPL operates as follows:

- **Read:** The REPL reads a user input, which can be an expression or command.

- **Eval:** The REPL evaluates the input, processing it according to the rules of the Scheme language.
- **Print:** The REPL prints the result of the evaluation, providing immediate feedback.

To access the Scheme REPL, open your terminal or command prompt and type the command to launch your Scheme interpreter (e.g., scheme, mzscheme, or guile depending on your installed Scheme variant). You should see a prompt indicating that the REPL is ready to accept input.

```
$ scheme
MIT/GNU Scheme running under GNU/Linux
Type '^C' (control-C) followed by 'H' (control-H) for help.
Type '^C' (control-C) followed by 'R' (control-R) to restart the Scheme top-level.
Type '^C' (control-C) followed by 'D' (control-D) to exit Scheme.

1 ]=>
```

The scheme prompt (1]=>) signifies that the REPL is awaiting input.

Evaluating Basic Expressions:

Scheme primarily supports numerical operations, symbolic expressions, and list manipulations. Here are some examples that you can type directly into the REPL:

```
1 ]=> (+ 2 3)
;Value: 5

1 ]=> (- 5 2)
;Value: 3

1 ]=> (* 4 7)
;Value: 28

1 ]=> (/ 10 2)
;Value: 5
```

Special Variables and Commands:

In the REPL, you can define variables and reuse them in subsequent expressions. For example:

```
1 ]=> (define x 10)
;Unspecified return value

1 ]=> (+ x 20)
;Value: 30
```

The define command introduces a variable or function. The interpreter does not explicitly return a value in some Scheme variants; instead, it may indicate its unspecified return status.

Defining Functions:

Scheme allows the creation of functions directly within the REPL. For instance, to define a function that adds two numbers:

```
1 ]=> (define (add-two-numbers a b) (+ a b))
;Unspecified return value

1 ]=> (add-two-numbers 3 5)
;Value: 8
```

Working with Lists:

Lists are a fundamental data structure in Scheme. Evaluate the following examples to gain familiarity:

```
1 ]=> (define lst '(1 2 3 4 5))
;Unspecified return value

1 ]=> (car lst)
;Value: 1

1 ]=> (cdr lst)
;Value: (2 3 4 5)

1 ]=> (cons 0 lst)
;Value: (0 1 2 3 4 5)
```

car, cdr, and cons are primitive operations for list manipulations in Scheme — retrieving the first element, the rest of the list, and constructing lists, respectively.

Control Commands:

Using the REPL efficiently includes knowing how to control the environment and handle errors. If you make a mistake, the REPL provides error messages:

```
1 ]=> (+ 1 'a)
;The object 'a, passed as the 2nd argument to +, is not the correct type.

1 ]=> (undefined-function)
;Unbound variable: undefined-function
```

If an expression is not well-formed or an evaluation error occurs, these messages help understand what went wrong and how to correct it.

Exiting the REPL:

To exit the REPL, the commands typically include special key combinations or commands like:

```
1 ]=> (exit)
```

or pressing Ctrl + D.

Understanding the basic commands and functionality of the Scheme REPL is critical for effective interaction with the language. This familiarity enables rapid testing and iteration of ideas, an essential skill for mastering Scheme programming.

1.5 The Simplicity and Power of Scheme Syntax

Scheme's syntax, characterized by its minimalistic and uniform structure, allows for expressive and readable code that is both simple and powerful. At its core, Scheme follows a few straightforward rules, making it easy to learn and apply but versatile enough to implement complex programming paradigms.

Scheme expressions, or S-expressions, adhere to a parenthesized prefix notation. This means that any operation or procedure call is made by placing the operator or function name first, followed by its arguments within parentheses. For example, the mathematical expression $1+2$ in Scheme syntax is written as:

```
(+ 1 2)
```

A key feature of Scheme is that everything is an expression, and thus every piece of code evaluates to a value. This consistent structure is a significant departure from other languages that distinguish between expressions and statements.

Scheme functions are first-class citizens, meaning they can be passed as arguments, returned from other functions, and assigned to variables. Here is an example of defining a function that takes two arguments and returns their sum:

```
(define (add a b)
  (+ a b))
```

In the example above, the define keyword is used to create a function named add, which takes two parameters, a and b, and returns their sum. Calling this function is straightforward:

```
(add 3 4)
```

This invocation returns 7, demonstrating the execution of the add function with the provided arguments.

Another powerful feature of Scheme syntax is the use of lambda expressions, which allow the creation of anonymous functions. This is particularly useful for short, throwaway functions that are not intended to be reused. A lambda expression is created using the lambda keyword, followed by the parameters and the expression:

```
(lambda (x y) (+ x y))
```

This lambda expression can be immediately applied to arguments:

```
((lambda (x y) (+ x y)) 5 6)
```

The result of the above code is 11, as the anonymous function is directly applied to the values 5 and 6.

Scheme's powerful macro system allows for syntax extensions and language modifications. Macros in Scheme are written using the define-syntax and syntax-rules constructs, enabling programmers to create new syntactic constructs in a way that integrates seamlessly with the language.

Consider the creation of a simple when macro, which executes a block of expressions only if a given condition is true:

```
(define-syntax when
  (syntax-rules ()
    ((when condition . body)
     (if condition
         (begin . body)))))
```

In this macro definition, - define-syntax and syntax-rules specify the macro. - The pattern (when condition . body) matches any usage of the when macro, capturing the condition and the expressions that constitute the body. - The if and begin constructs are then used to conditionally evaluate the body expressions if the condition holds true.

An example usage of the when macro would be:

```
(when (> 3 2)
  (display "3 is greater than 2")
  (newline))
```

This code evaluates the condition (>3 2), which is true. Consequently, it displays the string "3 is greater than 2" and starts a new line.

Scheme's syntax also includes powerful constructs for handling control flow and iteration, such as cond, let, do, and for-each. These constructs, though more complex in their full details, retain the overall simplicity and uniformity of Scheme syntax, enabling clear and well-structured code.

For instance, the cond expression provides a way to handle multiple conditions elegantly. It is akin to a series of if statements but more succinct:

```
(cond
  ((> x 0) 'positive)
  ((< x 0) 'negative)
  (else 'zero))
```

In the above cond expression: - If x is greater than 0, the result is positive. - If x is less than 0, the result is negative. - If neither condition is met, the result is zero.

Using let expressions allows for the creation of local bindings, facilitating the composition of more complex expressions without polluting the global namespace:

```
(let ((a 1)
      (b 2))
  (+ a b))
```

The let expression above binds a to 1 and b to 2 within its scope, and then computes their sum, resulting in 3.

Iteration over lists can be seamlessly accomplished using for-each:

```
(for-each (lambda (x) (display x) (newline))
          '(1 2 3 4))
```

This code iterates over each element in the list (1 2 3 4), displays each element, and starts a new line.

The simplicity and power of Scheme syntax lie in its emphasis on a small set of syntactic forms and the ability to build complex abstractions through first-class functions, macros, and cleanly integrated control structures. This gives Scheme its elegant, readable, and highly expressive nature, making it a powerful tool for both novices and seasoned programmers.

1.6 First Steps: Writing and Running Your First Scheme Program

The initial step in mastering Scheme is writing and running a basic program. This involves setting up the development environment, composing a simple Scheme program, and executing it to observe the behavior.

Consider the program:

```
(define (square x)
  (* x x))
```

This code defines a function called square that takes one argument, x, and returns the square of x. The function uses Scheme's prefix notation, where the operator * (multiplication) precedes its operands. To understand this fully, we need to break it down into smaller parts and analyze each component.

- define: This keyword is used to define variables and functions. In this case, it is defining a function.
- (square x): This part specifies the name of the function (square) and its parameter (x).
- (* x x): This is the body of the function. It multiplies x by x.

Next, to run this code, you'll need to follow these steps in your Scheme environment.

Step 1: Open the Scheme REPL To interactively execute Scheme code, you need to launch the REPL (Read-Eval-Print Loop). This can typically be done by running the scheme command in your terminal or command line interface.

Step 2: Define the Function Enter the function definition into the REPL. This can be done by typing the following at the prompt:

```
(define (square x)
  (* x x))
```

Once entered, the REPL should accept the definition with no immediate output, returning to the prompt.

Step 3: Call the Function To see the function in action, you can call it with various arguments. Type the following at the prompt:

```
(square 5)
```

The REPL then calculates the result:

```
25
```

The function correctly squares the number 5 to give 25.

Additionally, you may wish to save the function in a file and run the code from the file. This is especially useful for more complex programs. Create a new file called square.scm and include your function definition:

```
; square.scm
(define (square x)
  (* x x))

(display (square 5))
(newline)
```

The lines (display (square 5)) and (newline) are used to print the result of (square 5) followed by a new line. To execute this program, use the terminal or command line to navigate to the directory containing your square.scm file and run:

```
scheme --script square.scm
```

The output will be:

```
25
```

Writing and running Scheme programs in this manner is fundamental to becoming proficient in the language. The simplicity and clarity of Scheme's syntax allow for straightforward implementation of functions and immediate testing through the REPL, fostering an interactive and educational programming experience.

1.7 Understanding Expressions and Evaluation in Scheme

Expressions in Scheme are the fundamental building blocks of any program, serving as both the data and the code. An expression can be as simple as a constant or as complex as a nested procedure call. In Scheme, every piece of data and every transformation of that data is represented as an expression. Understanding how Scheme evaluates these expressions is crucial for mastering the language.

Scheme employs a uniform syntax known as S-expressions (Symbolic Expressions). An S-expression can be an atom or a list. Atoms are the simplest entities in Scheme and include numbers, symbols, and special syntactic keywords. Lists are collections of S-expressions enclosed in parentheses.

Consider the following example of a basic expression in Scheme:

```
(+ 2 3)
```

This expression is a list, with the first element being the operator (+) and the remaining elements the operands (2 and 3). Scheme evaluates this expression by applying the operator to the operands, yielding the result 5.

```
5
```

In Scheme, the evaluation of expressions follows these general rules:

- If an expression is an atom, it evaluates to its corresponding value.
- If an expression is a list, it is treated as a procedure call where the first element is the procedure and the subsequent elements are arguments to that procedure.

To illustrate, let's examine more detailed examples:

1. **Evaluating Constants** Constants like numbers and strings evaluate to themselves.

```
42
"hello world"
```

When evaluated, these expressions return their own values:

```
42
"hello world"
```

2. **Evaluating Symbols** Symbols represent either variable names or special constants. When evaluated, Scheme looks up the symbol value in the current environment.

```
(define x 10)
x
```

Here, x evaluates to 10 because it has been associated with this value.

3. **Procedure Calls** When a list is evaluated, the first element (the operator) is applied to the rest (the operands):

```
(+ 1 2)
```

This expression is evaluated by applying the + operator to 1 and 2, yielding 3.

4. **Nested Expressions** Scheme supports nesting of expressions, which follows the rules for evaluating lists recursively.

```
(+ 1 (* 2 3))
```

The sub-expression (* 2 3) is evaluated first, providing the result 6, which then becomes an operand to the outer addition expression resulting in 7.

7

5. **Function Definitions and Calls** Define functions using lambda expressions or the define keyword. Once defined, functions can be invoked just like primitive operations.

```
(define (square x)
  (* x x))

(square 4)
```

The above code defines a function square and then calls it with the argument 4. The result of (square 4) is 16.

16

6. **Conditional Expressions** Conditional expressions use if, cond, or case to select between alternate branches.

```
(if (> 5 3)
    "Greater"
    "Lesser")
```

The if expression evaluates the predicate (> 5 3), which is true, hence it returns "Greater".

"Greater"

7. **Quoting** Quoting an expression prevents its evaluation. Use the quote keyword or the shorthand '.

```
'(+ 1 2)
```

This expression evaluates to the list (+ 1 2) itself, not the sum.

(+ 1 2)

Understanding how these components fit together is key to writing effective Scheme programs. The rules of evaluation apply recursively, enabling the construction of complex expressions from simple ones. By practicing these concepts through various examples and exercises, gaining proficiency in Scheme's evaluation model becomes an achievable task.

1.8 Introduction to Scheme Data Types

Scheme, as a dialect of Lisp, adheres to the principles of simplicity and expressiveness regarding its data types. Understanding Scheme data types is crucial for effectively utilizing the language's capabilities in functional programming.

Scheme employs a variety of data types, each serving unique roles in the representation and manipulation of data. The fundamental data types include atoms (such as numbers, symbols, and booleans), pairs, lists, vectors, and strings.

Atoms in Scheme: Atoms are the simplest data types and include numbers, symbols, and booleans. These atomic values cannot be broken down into simpler components within the Scheme language.

- Numbers: Scheme supports various numeric types, including integers, rationals, reals, and complex numbers. An example of a numeric value is 42 or -3.14. Scheme handles arithmetic operations with these types effortlessly:

```
(+ 2 3) ; Adds two integers, resulting in 5
(- 7 2.5) ; Subtracts, resulting in 4.5
(* 3 4) ; Multiplies to give 12
(/ 8 2) ; Divides, resulting in 4
```

- Symbols: Symbols in Scheme are unique identifiers often used for variables or function names. They are case-sensitive and can include a variety of characters:

```
(define x 10) ; Defines symbol x with value 10
(define my-symbol 'y) ; Defines a symbol stored under the variable name my-
    symbol
```

- Booleans: Scheme boolean values are denoted by #t (true) and #f (false):

```
(if #t 1 0) ; Evaluates to 1
(if #f 1 0) ; Evaluates to 0
```

Pairs and **Lists**: Pairs are fundamental building blocks in Scheme, created using the cons function. A pair consists of two components, referred to as the car and cdr. Lists are recursively built using pairs.

- Pairs:

```
(define my-pair (cons 1 2)) ; Constructs a pair (1 . 2)
(car my-ppair) ; Returns the first element (1)
(cdr my-pair) ; Returns the second element (2)
```

- Lists: Lists are formed by nesting pairs where the cdr in the final pair is () (empty list):

```
(define my-list (list 1 2 3)) ; Constructs a list (1 2 3)
(car my-list) ; Returns the first element (1)
(cdr my-list) ; Returns the list (2 3)
```

  Concatenation and other operations on lists can be performed using built-in functions such as append, length, and map:

```
(append '(1 2) '(3 4)) ; Results in (1 2 3 4)
(length '(1 2 3)) ; Returns the length 3
(map (lambda (x) (* x 2)) '(1 2 3)) ; Results in (2 4 6)
```

Vectors: Vectors in Scheme are indexed collections of elements, allowing efficient access by position. They are designated using the #(...) notation:

```
(define my-vector #(1 2 3 4)) ; A vector with elements 1, 2, 3, 4
(vector-ref my-vector 2) ; Accesses the element at index 2 (3)
(vector-set! my-vector 0 10) ; Sets the element at index 0 to 10
```

Strings: Strings in Scheme are sequences of characters, enclosed in double quotes. They support standard operations like concatenation and length determination:

```
(define my-string "Hello, Scheme!")
(string-length my-string) ; Returns the length 14
(string-append my-string " Rocks!") ; Concatenates strings, resulting in "Hello, Scheme!
    Rocks!"
```

Understanding these data types and their manipulations is essential for programming in Scheme. The language's design fosters clarity and expressiveness, making it a powerful tool for functional programming.

1.9 The Importance of Recursion in Functional Programming

Recursion is a fundamental concept in functional programming and plays a critical role in Scheme. Unlike iterative approaches commonly used in imperative programming, recursion provides a way to solve problems by decomposing them into simpler subproblems. This aligns seamlessly with the functional programming paradigm where functions are the primary building blocks, and state changes are minimized or avoided.

Definition and Basic Example

Recursion occurs when a function calls itself as part of its execution. There are two essential components in any recursive function: the base case and the recursive case. The base case terminates the recursion and prevents infinite loops, while the recursive case breaks the problem into smaller instances of itself.

Consider the classic example of a function to calculate the factorial of a number n (denoted as $n!$):

```
(define (factorial n)
  (if (= n 0)
      1
      (* n (factorial (- n 1)))))
```

In this example:

- The base case is when n is 0, returning 1.
- The recursive case reduces the problem by multiplying n with the factorial of $n - 1$.

When this function is called with a positive integer, it repeatedly calls itself with decremented values of n until it reaches the base case.

Recursive vs. Iterative Approaches

Understanding the distinction between recursion and iteration is fundamental. Consider the iterative version of the factorial function:

```
(define (factorial-iter n)
  (define (fact-iter n result)
    (if (= n 0)
        result
        (fact-iter (- n 1) (* n result))))
  (fact-iter n 1))
```

In the iterative version, an auxiliary function fact-iter carries the accumulated result. This avoids the need for the function to call itself directly to reduce risk of stack overflow in languages or environments not optimized for recursion.

Tail Recursion

A special form of recursion, known as tail recursion, is particularly significant in functional programming. A function is tail-recursive if the recursive call is the last operation in the function. Scheme, like many functional languages, optimizes tail-recursive functions to prevent stack overflow and improve performance.

Transforming the factorial function to a tail-recursive version:

```
(define (factorial-tail n)
  (define (fact-tail n acc)
    (if (= n 0)
        acc
        (fact-tail (- n 1) (* n acc))))
  (fact-tail n 1))
```

Tail recursion converts the recursive call into a loop, allowing the Scheme interpreter to optimize it.

Example: Fibonacci Sequence

Another example of a recursive function is computing the n-th Fibonacci number. A naive recursive approach directly translates the mathematical definition into Scheme:

```
(define (fib n)
  (if (<= n 1)
      n
      (+ (fib (- n 1)) (fib (- n 2)))))
```

This version illustrates a common performance issue with naive recursion – redundant calculations. As n increases, the function recomputes values multiple times, leading to an exponential growth in computation.

To address this inefficiency, an iterative or tail-recursive approach is preferable:

```
(define (fib-iter n)
  (define (fib-helper a b count)
    (if (= count 0)
        a
        (fib-helper b (+ a b) (- count 1))))
  (fib-helper 0 1 n))
```

The tail-recursive version fib-iter uses an auxiliary function fib-helper, maintaining the progressive sum as parameters and efficiently computing the result iteratively.

Recursion in Data Structures

Recursion is also essential in handling recursive data structures such as lists and trees. Consider a function to sum elements of a list:

```
(define (sum-list lst)
```

```
  (if (null? lst)
      0
      (+ (car lst) (sum-list (cdr lst)))))
```

Here, the base case checks if the list is empty (null), returning 0. The recursive case adds the head (car) of the list to the result of summing the tail (cdr).

Algorithm Example: Merge Sort

To illustrate the power of recursion in sorting algorithms, consider Merge Sort, which divides a list into halves, recursively sorts each half, and then merges the sorted halves:

Algorithm 1: Merge Sort Algorithm in Pseudocode

```
Input: A list of numbers lst
Output: A sorted list
Function mergesort(lst):
    if length(lst) ≤ 1 then
        return lst;
    end
    Set middle = length(lst) / 2;
    Set left = lst[1:middle];
    Set right = lst[middle+1:];
    return merge(mergesort(left), mergesort(right));
Function merge(left, right):
    if left is empty then
        return right;
    end
    if right is empty then
        return left;
    end
    if first(left) ≤ first(right) then
        return concatenate(first(left), merge(rest(left), right));
    end
    else
        return concatenate(first(right), merge(left, rest(right)));
    end
```

In Scheme, the Merge Sort can be implemented as follows:

```
(define (merge-sort lst)
  (if (or (null? lst) (null? (cdr lst)))
      lst
      (let* ((middle (quotient (length lst) 2))
             (left (take lst middle))
```

```
        (right (drop lst middle)))
    (merge (merge-sort left) (merge-sort right)))))

(define (merge left right)
  (cond ((null? left) right)
        ((null? right) left)
        ((<= (car left) (car right))
         (cons (car left) (merge (cdr left) right)))
        (else
         (cons (car right) (merge left (cdr right))))))
```

The importance of recursion in functional programming cannot be overstated, offering an elegant, powerful means to solve problems. Mastery of recursion provides essential tools for effective functional programming, laying the groundwork for advanced topics and efficient code.

1.10 Comparing Scheme with Other Functional Programming Languages

Scheme, one of the prominent languages in the Lisp family, offers a unique approach within the realm of functional programming (FP). This section examines the distinguishing characteristics of Scheme when compared to other major functional programming languages, including Haskell, Erlang, OCaml, and Clojure. Analyzing these languages will highlight Scheme's strengths and help contextualize its usage in various applications.

Haskell vs. Scheme: Haskell is a statically-typed, purely functional programming language that emphasizes immutability and type safety. It uses lazy evaluation, meaning expressions are not evaluated until their results are needed. On the other hand, Scheme is dynamically-typed and allows both functional and imperative paradigms, thus being more flexible in its approach.

In Scheme, the distinction between expressions and statements is blurred, fitting well within the Lisp tradition of code as data and data as code. Haskell's type system ensures compile-time type checking, reducing runtime errors at the expense of flexibility. Here is an example to illustrate the difference in type declaration and usage:

```
-- Haskell function to calculate factorial
factorial :: Integer -> Integer
factorial 0 = 1
factorial n = n * factorial (n - 1)
```

In Scheme, the definition is more straightforward without implicit type constraints:

```
; Scheme function to calculate factorial
(define (factorial n)
  (if (= n 0)
      1
      (* n (factorial (- n 1)))))
```

Erlang vs. Scheme: Erlang is designed for concurrency, fault tolerance, and distributed systems. It employs an actor model for handling concurrent processes, making it highly suitable for telecom and real-time systems. While Scheme can support concurrency through libraries or extensions, it does not natively focus on it.

Erlang's syntax is concise for defining processes and message passing:

```
% Erlang spawn process example
process() ->
    receive
        {msg, Msg} -> io:format("Message: ~p~n", [Msg])
    end.
```

In Scheme, setting up concurrent processes might involve using SRFI-18 or other libraries, adding complexity:

```
; Scheme process example using SRFI-18
(let ((thread (thread-start!
                (lambda () (display "Concurrent Process\n")))))
  (thread-join! thread))
```

OCaml vs. Scheme: OCaml, part of the ML family, is a statically-typed functional language with a strong emphasis on performance and a mix of imperative features. It supports object-oriented programming, making it multifaceted. Scheme retains its minimalist nature, focusing on essential constructs without adding paradigms such as object orientation.

An OCaml function for list manipulation emphasizes the language's syntax and type annotations:

```
(* OCaml function to filter even numbers *)
let rec filter_evens lst =
  match lst with
  | [] -> []
  | hd :: tl -> if hd mod 2 = 0 then hd :: filter_evens tl else filter_evens tl
```

In Scheme, the equivalent operation is typeless but straightforward:

```
; Scheme function to filter even numbers
(define (filter-evens lst)
  (cond
    [(null? lst) '()]
```

```
    [(= 0 (mod (car lst) 2)) (cons (car lst) (filter-evens (cdr lst)))]
    [else (filter-evens (cdr lst))]))
```

Clojure vs. Scheme: Clojure, a modern Lisp dialect, runs on the Java Virtual Machine (JVM), which leverages Java libraries' robustness and ecosystem. Clojure emphasizes immutability and concurrency using Software Transactional Memory (STM). Scheme, while versatile, does not integrate as seamlessly with the JVM and does not have native STM support, depending instead on traditional mechanisms or third-party libraries.

A simple example in Clojure illustrates its emphasis on immutable data structures:

```
; Clojure function to add items to a list
(defn add-items [lst items]
  (conj lst items))
```

In Scheme, mutability is allowed and is more explicit:

```
; Scheme function to add items to a list
(define (add-items lst items)
  (append lst items))
```

The functional programming paradigms across these languages show diverse approaches to concurrency, type systems, and integration with other systems. Scheme's simplicity, flexibility, and Lisp heritage make it a powerful language for exploring core functional programming concepts, balancing conciseness and expressivity.

Chapter 2

Scheme Syntax and Semantics

This chapter delves into the fundamental syntax and semantics of Scheme, covering the core structure of programs, identifiers, naming conventions, and reserved keywords. You will learn to write and understand Scheme expressions, define and use variables, and grasp the critical role of parentheses. The evaluation model of Scheme is explored, along with the concepts of scoping, binding, literals, self-evaluating expressions, and the definition and use of procedures. An introduction to tail-call optimization rounds out the chapter, ensuring you have a solid grasp of Scheme's essential syntax and underlying semantics.

2.1 Core Syntax and Structure of Scheme Programs

Scheme is a minimalist, multi-paradigm programming language in the Lisp family with a simple yet powerful syntax. The structure of Scheme programs is centered around expressions and the proper use of parentheses, which are fundamental to the language's syntax and evaluation model. Scheme code is composed of forms, which are expressions enclosed in parentheses. The correct interpretation and evaluation of these forms are paramount in Scheme programming.

Expressions and Forms

In Scheme, everything is an expression. An expression can be a simple value such as a number or a more complex combination of symbols and values. The basic form is the expression enclosed in parentheses, also known as a list. Here, parentheses indicate function applications and grouping of expressions.

A simple example of a Scheme form is:

```
(+ 1 2 3)
```

This expression applies the + function to the arguments 1, 2, and 3, producing the result 6. The first item in the list, +, is the function or operator, and the remaining items are the arguments.

Function Application

Functions in Scheme are applied using prefix notation, meaning the function name or operator appears before the arguments it operates on. This form is consistent and simple:

```
(<operator> <arg1> <arg2> ... <argN>)
```

For example:

```
(* 2 3)
```

The above form multiplies the numbers 2 and 3. The operator * in Scheme denotes multiplication. Prefix notation is more regular than infix notation, where the operator is placed between operands, as seen in many other programming languages.

Nested Expressions

Scheme supports the nesting of expressions, allowing for the construction of more complex forms. Each sub-expression is itself a valid Scheme expression, which can be evaluated independently:

```
(+ (* 2 3) (- 5 2))
```

In this expression, (* 2 3) evaluates to 6 and (- 5 2) evaluates to 3. Then, the outer + function adds these results to produce 9. Scheme evaluates the innermost expressions first, then proceeds to evaluate the outer expressions.

Quoting Expressions

Sometimes it is necessary to refer to unevaluated expressions or symbols. Scheme allows expressions to be quoted, meaning their evaluation is deferred:

```
(quote (1 2 3))
```

This expression will yield the list (1 2 3) rather than attempting to evaluate it. The shorthand for quoting values is the single quotation mark:

```
'(1 2 3)
```

Quotation is essential when manipulating code as data, a common practice in Lisp-based languages.

Special Forms

Scheme includes a set of special forms that do not follow the regular rules for function application. These forms have unique syntax and semantics critical to Scheme programming. Examples include define, lambda, and if.

The define form is used to bind a value to a name:

```
(define x 10)
```

This expression binds the variable x to the value 10. Thereafter, x can be used to refer to 10.

The lambda form is used to create anonymous functions:

```
(lambda (x) (* x x))
```

This form defines a function that takes one argument, x, and returns x squared.

The if form is used for conditional evaluation:

```
(if (> 3 2)
    'true
    'false)
```

This expression evaluates the condition (> 3 2). If the condition is true, it returns 'true, otherwise, it returns 'false.

Let Binding Forms

Scheme provides the let construct for creating local bindings within a block of expressions. This enables more readable and manageable code:

```
(let ((x 2)
      (y 3))
  (+ x y))
```

The result of this expression is 5. The let form introduces local bindings x and y, and these bindings are used within the body of the let.

Comments

Comments enhance code readability and are ignored by the Scheme interpreter. A comment starts with a semicolon and continues to the end of the line:

```
; This is a single-line comment
```

Multi-line comments are enclosed between #| and |#:

```
#| This is a
   multi-line comment |#
```

Comments are crucial for documenting code and explaining logic.

Whitespace and Formatting

Whitespace (spaces, tabs, and newlines) is used to separate tokens in Scheme and is generally ignored beyond this purpose. Proper formatting and indentation are vital for readability. Functions and constructs are typically indented for clarity:

```
(define (square x)
  (* x x))
```

In this example, the function square is clearly defined, with the body indented appropriately.

Understanding the core syntax and structure of Scheme programs forms the foundation for effective programming in the language. Mastery of these concepts is essential as they underpin all subsequent programming activities in Scheme.

2.2 Identifiers and Naming Conventions

In Scheme, as in most programming languages, identifiers are names that refer to variables, functions, and other user-defined entities. Understanding the rules and conventions for naming identifiers is crucial for writing clear and maintainable code.

Identifiers in Scheme

Identifiers in Scheme consist of a sequence of characters. A valid identifier can include alphabets (both upper and lower case), digits, and special characters such as hyphens ('-'), underscores ('_'), plus ('+'), asterisk ('*'), and forward slash ('/'). However, identifiers must not start with a digit or a special character, and they cannot contain whitespace or delimiters such as parentheses.

Valid identifiers example:

```
total-sum, _counter, maxVal, average_2
```

Invalid identifiers example:

```
123total, +max, a b c, sum(total)
```

Scheme is case-insensitive when it comes to identifiers, meaning FOO, foo, and FoO are considered the same identifier. However, following a consistent convention, like using lowercase by default, is a good practice.

Keywords and Reserved Identifiers

Scheme has a set of reserved keywords that have special meaning and cannot be used as identifiers. These include control structures, primitive functions, and syntactic forms. Some commonly reserved identifiers are:

- lambda
- define
- if
- else
- let
- cond

Attempting to use any of these keywords for other purposes will result in a syntax error.

Scheme allows the usage of some special characters in identifiers, which can be useful for denoting specific functionalities. For example, an identifier ending with a ? is typically used to denote predicates (functions returning boolean values):

```
(define is-even? (lambda (n) (= (modulo n 2) 0)))
```

Similarly, an identifier ending with a ! usually indicates a procedure that performs side effects:

```
(define (increment! x) (set! x (+ x 1)))
```

Naming Conventions

Adhering to naming conventions is important for code readability and maintainability. Here are some commonly practiced conventions in Scheme:

- Use kebab-case for variables and functions, separating words with hyphens. For example:

  ```
  total-sum, calculate-average, number-of-students
  ```

- Use descriptive names that clearly indicate the purpose of the variable or function. Avoid single-letter names except for loop counters or very short-lived variables.
- Use camelCase for identifiers if the local convention prefers it, although this is less common in Scheme.
- Prefix helper functions with a tilde (~) or an underscore (_), although this is more a matter of personal or team preference.

  ```
  _helper-function, ~local-helper
  ```

- For constants, use uppercase letters separated by underscores ('_'). This is more a general programming practice, although not rigidly enforced in Scheme:

  ```
  MAX_VALUE, PI, TOTAL_COUNT
  ```

A standardized naming convention helps in distinguishing between different types of identifiers and makes the code comprehensible at a glance. This practice aids both the original author and any future programmers who may have to maintain or extend the code.

Example of a Well-Named Function in Scheme

Here is an example demonstrating good naming practices:

```
(define (calculate-factorial n)
  (define (factorial-iter k product)
    (if (> k n)
        product
        (factorial-iter (+ k 1) (* k product))))
  (factorial-iter 1 1))
```

In the above example, calculate-factorial is a descriptive name indicating the function's purpose. The inner function, factorial-iter, follows the same naming convention and is clearly distinguished as a helper function by its name.

Being consistent and descriptive with identifiers and following established conventions greatly improves the clarity and maintainability of Scheme programs. These practices form the foundation for effective communication of complex logic and ensure that code can be efficiently understood and modified.

2.3 Scheme Reserved Keywords

Scheme, being a dialect of Lisp, inherits many of its language constructs, including a specific set of reserved keywords. These keywords are predefined in the language and hold intrinsic meanings that cannot be redefined or used as variable names within the program. Understanding and correctly utilizing these reserved keywords is paramount for writing syntactically correct and semantically meaningful Scheme programs.

In Scheme, reserved keywords are utilized for defining syntax, establishing control flow, and constructing various types of expressions. Here, we will discuss the most commonly used reserved keywords and their uses.

- define: This keyword is employed to create variable bindings and to define functions. The general form for defining a variable is:

  ```
  (define <variable> <expression>)
  ```

  For example:

  ```
  (define x 10)
  ```

  This binds x to the value 10. For function definitions, define can be used as follows:

```
(define (square x) (* x x))
```

This creates a function named square that computes the square of its argument.

- lambda: The lambda keyword is utilized to create anonymous functions. An anonymous function is defined as:

  ```
  (lambda (arg1 arg2 ...) <body>)
  ```

  For instance, to create an anonymous function that adds two numbers:

  ```
  (lambda (a b) (+ a b))
  ```

- if: This keyword is used for conditional branching. The if expression takes the form:

  ```
  (if <test> <consequent> <alternate>)
  ```

  Here, if <test> evaluates to true, the <consequent> expression is evaluated, otherwise the <alternate> expression is evaluated. For example:

  ```
  (if (> x 0) 'positive 'non-positive)
  ```

  This checks if x is greater than zero, returning 'positive if true, otherwise 'non-positive.

- set!: The set! keyword is used to change the value of an already defined variable. Its usage is as follows:

  ```
  (set! <variable> <expression>)
  ```

  For example, to update the value of x to 20:

  ```
  (set! x 20)
  ```

- quote: The quote keyword prevents the evaluation of an expression. It is often abbreviated using the single quote character ('):

  ```
  (quote <datum>)
  ```

  For example:

  ```
  (quote (a b c))
  ```

  This returns the list '(a b c) without evaluating it. The abbreviated form is:

```
'(a b c)
```

- begin: The begin keyword is used to sequence multiple expressions, ensuring they are executed in order. Its form is:

```
(begin <expression1> <expression2> ...)
```

  For instance:

```
(begin
  (set! x 5)
  (set! y 10)
  (+ x y))
```

  This evaluates (set! x 5), then (set! y 10), and finally (+ x y), producing the result of 15.

- cond: This keyword serves as a more advanced conditional branching mechanism than if. It handles multiple conditions and takes the form:

```
(cond (<test1> <expression1>)
      (<test2> <expression2>)
      ...
      (else <default-expression>))
```

  For example:

```
(cond
  ((> x 0) 'positive)
  ((< x 0) 'negative)
  (else 'zero))
```

  This structure checks multiple conditions ensuring more complex decision-making.

- let, let*, letrec: These keywords are used for creating local bindings. The let form binds variables to expressions locally within a block:

```
(let ((var1 val1)
      (var2 val2))
  <body>)
```

  The let* expression allows sequential bindings where each binding can reference the previous ones:

```
(let* ((var1 val1)
       (var2 val2))
  <body>)
```

The letrec form is used for mutually recursive bindings:

```
(letrec ((var1 val1)
         (var2 val2))
  <body>)
```

Each of these forms supports various scenarios for local scoping.

Mastering these keywords and their appropriate usage is crucial for proficiency in Scheme programming. These reserved keywords form the backbone of Scheme's syntax and semantics, enabling complex program structures and efficient execution flow.

2.4 Writing and Understanding Scheme Expressions

In order to write and understand Scheme expressions, it is essential to grasp the basic structure and semantics of the language. Scheme expressions, or forms, are the building blocks of Scheme programs. Each expression can be either an atomic expression, such as numbers and symbols, or a compound expression, which is typically denoted by parentheses and consists of a combination of sub-expressions.

To elucidate these concepts, we shall examine several types of expressions supported by Scheme: literals, variable references, procedure calls, and special forms.

Literals
Literals in Scheme include numbers, strings, characters, and boolean values. They represent themselves directly and are self-evaluating expressions.

- Numbers: 42, -3, 3.14
- Strings: "hello, world"
- Characters: #\a, #\newline
- Booleans: #t (true), #f (false)

```
42 ; evaluates to 42
"hello, world" ; evaluates to "hello, world"
#\a ; evaluates to the character 'a'
#t ; evaluates to true
```

```
42
"hello, world"
#\a
#t
```

Variable References

A variable reference expression returns the value bound to the variable. If a variable named x is bound to the value 10, referencing x yields 10.

```
(define x 10)
x
```

```
10
```

Procedure Calls

The essence of Scheme expressions lies in procedure calls, denoted by a list where the first element is the procedure and the subsequent elements are the arguments passed to that procedure.

```
(+ 3 4) ; Addition procedure
(* 2 5) ; Multiplication procedure
```

```
7
10
```

The syntax of a procedure call follows the form:

```
(<operator> <operand1> <operand2> ...)
```

Special Forms

Scheme provides several special forms for fundamental programming constructs such as control-flow, variable binding, and defining functions. Special forms are distinct from procedure calls as they have special evaluation rules:

- quote: Avoids evaluation of its argument.
- if: Conditionally evaluates one of two expressions.
- lambda: Creates anonymous functions.
- define: Binds a variable to a value or defines a function.

Quote

The quote form returns its argument without evaluating it. The shorthand for quote is the apostrophe (').

```
(quote (1 2 3)) ; Explicit form
'(1 2 3) ; Equivalent shorthand
```

```
(1 2 3)
(1 2 3)
```

If

The if form evaluates a given condition and branches to one of the two alternatives based on its truth value.

```
(if (< 2 3)
    'yes
    'no) ; Conditional branching
```

```
yes
```

Lambda

The lambda form creates anonymous functions, enabling higher-order function definitions and functional programming paradigms.

```
(lambda (x)
  (* x x)) ; Defines an anonymous function that squares its argument
```

```
#<procedure>
```

Define

The define form assigns values to variables or introduces function definitions.

```
(define y 5) ; Variable binding
(define (square x)
  (* x x)) ; Function definition
```

```
#<undefined>
(square 4)
16
```

By understanding and practicing these fundamental expressions, one gains the ability to read, interpret, and write Scheme code proficiently. Scheme's simplicity in expression evaluation and consistency in syntax supports the construction of complex procedures and programs with ease.

2.5 Defining and Using Variables

In Scheme, variables are used to store values that can be referenced and manipulated throughout a program. The process of defining and using variables involves several key concepts and functions, which we will explore in detail.

To define a variable in Scheme, the define keyword is utilized. The syntax for defining a variable is as follows:

```
(define variable-name value)
```

The variable-name is the identifier used to reference the variable, while value is the data assigned to the variable. The value can be any valid Scheme expression, including numbers, strings, lists, or even the result of a function call.

For example, to define a variable x with the value 10, you would write:

```
(define x 10)
```

This command assigns the integer value 10 to the variable x. You can then use x in other expressions. For instance:

```
(+ x 5)
```

This expression evaluates to 15 because the value of x is 10, and adding 5 to it yields 15.

Scheme allows for variables to be redefined, a process known as reassignment. Reassignment is achieved by using set! followed by the variable name and the new value:

```
(set! x 20)
```

After this reassignment, the variable x now holds the value 20. Any subsequent references to x will use this new value.

It is important to distinguish between define and set!. The define keyword is used for the initial creation and assignment of a variable, whereas set! changes the value of an already defined variable.

Variables can also store the results of expressions. Consider the following example where a variable y is defined to be the product of x and 2:

```
(define y (* x 2))
```

If x is 20 (from our previous reassignment), then y will be evaluated as 40. The expression (* x 2) computes the product of x, which is 20, and 2, resulting in 40.

Scheme supports lexical scoping, meaning the visibility of variables is restricted to the block where they are defined. We can observe this more clearly through the use of local variables. The let expression allows for the creation of local variables within a specific block of code. The syntax for a let expression is:

```
(let ((variable1 value1)
      (variable2 value2)
      ...
      (variableN valueN))
  body)
```

Each variableN is initialized to the corresponding valueN. The body is an expression or set of expressions where these variables can be used. For example:

```
(let ((a 3)
      (b 4))
  (+ a b))
```

In this example, a is assigned the value 3, and b is assigned the value 4. The body of the let expression adds a and b, resulting in 7.

Local variables defined within a let expression cannot be accessed outside of the block, enforcing scoping rules. This property helps to prevent conflicts and unintended interference between different parts of the code.

To return a value from a let block, the last expression evaluated within the body is used. This can be leveraged to create more complex variable bindings:

```
(let ((x 5)
      (y (+ 2 3)))
  (* x y))
```

Here, x is assigned 5, and y is assigned the result of the expression (+ 2 3), which is 5. The body then multiplies x and y, returning 25.

Variables in Scheme are fundamental for constructing more intricate programs and managing state efficiently. Proper usage and understanding of variable binding, scope, and mutability are critical for writing robust Scheme code.

2.6 The Role of Parentheses in Scheme Syntax

In Scheme, parentheses play a pivotal role in defining the structure and execution order of expressions. Unlike some other programming languages where parentheses are often used to group expressions or enforce precedence, in Scheme, parentheses indicate the beginning and end of expressions, functions, and various syntactic constructs. Understanding how to correctly use parentheses is essential for writing syntactically valid and logically correct Scheme programs.

Scheme is a dialect of Lisp, and like all Lisp dialects, it is known for its extensive use of parentheses. Each set of parentheses denotes a list, and within these lists, Scheme code is written. This section will explore the various contexts and constructs in which parentheses are used in Scheme and provide detailed examples to solidify your understanding.

Basic Expression Syntax: At its core, a Scheme expression is written using parentheses in a prefix notation style. The general format for an expression is:

```
(operator operand1 operand2 ... operandN)
```

Here, the operator is a function or procedure, and the operand values are the arguments passed to this operator. For instance, to add two numbers:

```
(+ 3 5)
```

In this example, the operator is $+$, and 3 and 5 are the operands. Scheme evaluates this expression to produce the result 8.

Nested Expressions: Scheme allows for nesting of expressions, which means an expression can contain other expressions as operands. For example:

```
(+ 3 (* 2 4))
```

In this case, the expression $(* \ 2 \ 4)$ is nested within the outer $+$ expression. Scheme first evaluates the inner expression $(* \ 2 \ 4)$ to 8, and then the outer expression $(+ \ 3 \ 8)$, which results in 11.

Defining Functions: One of the most common uses of parentheses in Scheme is in the definition and invocation of functions. For defining a function, the define keyword is used, and the function body is enclosed within its own set of parentheses:

```
(define (square x)
  (* x x))
```

Here, the function square takes one argument x and returns the result of (* x x). To invoke this function, parentheses are used again:

```
(square 5)
```

Scheme evaluates this function call to produce the result 25.

Conditional Expressions: Parentheses are critical in the structure of conditional expressions in Scheme. A common conditional form is the if expression, which follows the format:

```
(if condition
    consequence
    alternative)
```

This can be exemplified by the following:

```
(if (> 3 2)
    'yes
    'no)
```

Scheme evaluates the condition (> 3 2) to #t (true) and thus returns 'yes. The parentheses clearly define the boundaries of the if expression and its components.

Let Binding: Scheme provides mechanisms for local bindings using the let construct. Parentheses serve to encapsulate the binding list and the body of the let expression:

```
(let ((x 2)
      (y 3))
  (+ x y))
```

In this example, x and y are locally bound to 2 and 3, respectively, and their sum is calculated within the body of the let expression, which results in 5.

Lists and Quotation: Parentheses are also used to denote literal lists. In conjunction with the quote operator ('), a list can be created as follows:

```
'(1 2 3 4)
```

This expression is evaluated to the list (1 2 3 4). Note the difference between quoted and unquoted lists; an unquoted list is evaluated as a function call:

```
(1 2 3 4)
```

Scheme would attempt to interpret 1 as a function, leading to an error since 1 is not a valid operator.

Correctly using parentheses is fundamental to writing functional and syntactically correct Scheme code. By mastering the placement and purpose of parentheses, you ensure that your Scheme programs are well-structured and that the interpreter can correctly parse and evaluate the code.

2.7 Comments and Documentation in Scheme Code

Comments and proper documentation play an integral role in ensuring that Scheme code is understandable, maintainable, and reusable. While Scheme is designed for terseness and power, code readability should not be sacrificed. Documenting the intent, logic, and structure of your code using comments can aid both your future self and other developers who may work with your code.

Scheme supports two types of comments: single-line comments and block comments.

Single-line comments begin with a semicolon (;) and continue until the end of the line. These are typically used for short explanations or annotations. For example:

```
; This is a single-line comment
(define x 10) ; Define variable x with value 10
```

Block comments or multi-line comments are enclosed between #| and |#. These allow for more extensive documentation, which can span multiple lines. This is useful for providing detailed descriptions or temporarily disabling chunks of code. For example:

```
#|
This is a block comment.
It can span multiple lines.
|#
(define y 20)
```

It is important to use comments judiciously to improve clarity without overwhelming the code. Here are some best practices for using comments and documentation effectively in Scheme:

- **Explain the why, not the what**: Focus on explaining why a certain piece of code exists or why a particular approach was taken rather than describing what the code does, which should be clear from the code itself.
- **Maintain consistency**: Use a consistent style of commenting throughout the codebase. This includes using the same symbols for single-line comments and structuring block comments uniformly.
- **Document complex logic**: Where the logic is not immediately apparent, or the code is particularly complex, provide detailed explanations. This can include describing algorithms, edge cases, and specific design decisions.
- **Update comments as code evolves**: Ensure that comments are kept up-to-date with the code they describe. Outdated comments can be misleading and more harmful than no comments at all.

Consider this example, which includes succinct single-line comments and a more detailed block comment:

```
; Initialize an empty list to hold results
(define results '())

; Define a function to compute the factorial of a number
(define (factorial n)
  (if (= n 0)
      1
      (* n (factorial (- n 1)))))

#|
Factorial computation involves a recursive process.
1. If n is 0, return 1 (base case).
2. Otherwise, return n multiplied by the factorial of (n - 1).
This utilizes Scheme's recursion capabilities effectively.
|#
; Calculate and store factorials of numbers from 0 to 5
(for-each (lambda (x) (set! results (cons (factorial x) results)))
          (list 0 1 2 3 4 5))

; Output the results list - should contain factorials of 5, 4, 3, 2, 1, 0
results ; Expected output: (120 24 6 2 1 1)
```

The above code snippet starts with single-line comments to explain variable initialization and function definition. The block comment then provides an in-depth explanation of the recursive factorial computation.

Such use of comments enhances readability and aids in understanding, especially for developers unfamiliar with the code.

While Scheme and other Lisp dialects often rely on their syntax to convey structure, well-placed comments bridge any gaps in readability. Consequently, they are not just optional but vital to writing professional, sustainable code.

2.8 Understanding the Scheme Evaluation Model

Scheme, like many other Lisp dialects, follows a precise and systematic evaluation model that ensures expressions are executed in a predictable manner. Understanding this evaluation model is crucial for mastering Scheme, as it underpins how expressions are interpreted, executed, and how results are produced. This section details the sequential steps taken by the Scheme interpreter when it evaluates expressions.

When a Scheme expression is evaluated, the interpreter follows these steps:

- If the expression is a self-evaluating expression, such as a number or a string, the value of the expression is the expression itself.
- If the expression is a variable reference, the interpreter looks up the variable in the current environment and returns its corresponding value.
- If the expression is a procedure call, the interpreter applies the procedure to the arguments by evaluating the operand expressions in a specific order.
- If the expression is a special form, it is evaluated according to the rules of that specific form.

Each of these steps will be elaborated below with examples and illustrations.

Self-Evaluating Expressions

Self-evaluating expressions are the simplest type of expressions in Scheme. These include numbers, strings, and booleans. When the interpreter encounters a self-evaluating expression, it immediately returns the expression as its value without further processing. For instance:

```
42
"Hello, World!"
#t
#f
```

Evaluating any of these expressions will yield the expression itself, i.e., 42, "Hello, World!", #t, and #f.

Variable References

When an expression is a variable, the interpreter must determine the value bound to that variable in the current scope. This is a fundamental operation in Scheme and involves looking up the variable in the environment. Consider the following example:

```
(define x 10)
x
```

In this case, evaluating x will return 10, because x is bound to 10 in the current environment.

Procedure Calls

Procedure calls in Scheme involve more complex evaluation rules. A procedure call expression typically consists of an operator and one or more operands. The steps to evaluate a procedure call are:

1. Evaluate the operator to obtain the procedure. 2. Evaluate each operand to obtain the argument values. 3. Apply the procedure to the argument values.

Consider the following example:

```
(+ 3 5)
```

To evaluate this, the interpreter first evaluates the operator + to obtain the addition procedure. Then, it evaluates the operands 3 and 5, yielding the values 3 and 5, respectively. Finally, the addition procedure is applied to these values, resulting in 8.

Special Forms

Special forms have unique evaluation rules defined within the Scheme language. These forms control aspects of the evaluation process, such as conditional execution and scope definition. Common special forms include if, define, lambda, and quote.

if **Special Form** The if form evaluates conditionally, based on a predicate. The syntax of if is:

```
(if predicate consequent alternative)
```

To evaluate an if expression, the interpreter evaluates the predicate. If the result is true (non-#f), the consequent expression is evaluated; otherwise, the alternative expression is evaluated.

```
(if (< 3 5)
    "3 is less than 5"
    "3 is not less than 5")
```

In this example, (< 3 5) evaluates to true, so the consequent "3 is less than 5" is the result.

define **Special Form** The define form binds a symbol to a value or procedure within the current environment. A variable definition takes the form:

```
(define var expr)
```

The interpreter evaluates the expr and binds its value to var. For example:

```
(define radius 10)
```

Here, radius is bound to 10.

lambda **Special Form** The lambda form creates procedures. The syntax is:

```
(lambda (parameters) body)
```

This form does not immediately evaluate the body; instead, it creates a procedure that can be called later. For instance:

```
(define add-two
  (lambda (x) (+ x 2)))
```

This defines add-two, a procedure that adds 2 to its argument.

quote **Special Form** The quote special form returns its argument without evaluation, useful for handling literals like lists. The syntax is:

```
(quote expr)
```

For convenience, Scheme provides a shorthand using an apostrophe:

```
'(a b c)
```

This evaluates to the list (a b c) without evaluating a, b, or c.

These fundamental concepts of Scheme's evaluation model form the bedrock upon which more complex behaviors and optimizations, such as tail-call optimization, are built. Proper understanding ensures precise control over program execution and reliable use of the language's features.

2.9 The Concept of Scoping and Binding

In Scheme programming, understanding scoping and binding is fundamental to mastering the language's syntax and semantics. Scoping determines the visibility and lifetime of variables, while binding refers to the association between variables and their values or procedures. Scheme, like many other programming languages, utilizes lexical scoping and has specific rules for variable binding that govern how code is interpreted and executed.

Lexical scoping, also known as static scoping, means that the scope of a variable is determined by the structure of the program text. In other words, where a variable is declared in the code dictates its scope and lifespan. Scheme adheres strictly to this principle, allowing for predictability and clarity in variable management.

Consider the following example illustrating lexical scoping and variable binding in Scheme:

```
(define x 10)

(define (example-scope)
  (let ((x 20)
        (y 30))
    (+ x y)))

(example-scope)
```

In this snippet, the global variable x is initially bound to the value 10. Within the example-scope procedure, a local environment is created using let, which temporarily binds x to 20 and y to 30. The let construct introduces new bindings within the scope of the let expression, and these bindings are active only within this local scope.

Upon evaluating (example-scope), the local bindings are used, hence the result is:

50

The global binding of x remains unaffected outside the example-scope procedure. To illustrate this further:

```
x
```

This results in:

```
10
```

Scheme's lexical scoping ensures that the binding of any variable can be determined by examining the program's text without executing the program. This aspect creates a clear and predictable environment, as seen in nested scopes:

```
(define a 5)

(define (outer)
  (define b 10)
  (define (inner)
    (define a 20)
    (+ a b))
  (inner))

(outer)
```

Here, the procedure outer defines a variable b with a binding of 10. Inside outer, another procedure inner is defined, creating a nested scope. Within inner, the variable a is locally redefined to 20. Invoking (outer) calls inner within its scope, resulting in:

```
30
```

The value of a in inner shadows the global binding, and b retains its binding from outer due to nested scoping.

Binding in Scheme involves more than just variables; it also extends to procedure names and their definitions. The define form is crucial for creating bindings. When a procedure is defined, its name is bound to a lambda expression in the current environment:

```
(define (square x)
  (* x x))
```

This creates a binding where square refers to a lambda expression that squares its argument.

To understand variable binding further, consider the concepts of let, let*, and letrec. Each introduces bindings differently and is useful in various scenarios.

let creates a parallel binding environment, where all expressions are evaluated in the outer scope before the actual binding occurs:

```
(let ((a 1)
      (b (+ a 1)))
  (list a b))
```

This results in an error since a is not yet bound when b is being defined. Instead, let* evaluates and binds sequentially:

```
(let* ((a 1)
       (b (+ a 1)))
  (list a b))
```

This results in:

```
(1 2)
```

letrec is used when mutually recursive definitions are needed, ensuring that all names are accessible within the bindings:

```
(letrec ((even?
          (lambda (n)
            (if (zero? n)
                #t
                (odd? (- n 1)))))
         (odd?
          (lambda (n)
            (if (zero? n)
                #f
                (even? (- n 1))))))
  (even? 4))
```

This evaluates to:

```
#t
```

Understanding scoping and binding in Scheme is essential for writing clear and maintainable code. The predictability of lexical scoping allows precise control over variable lifetimes and environments, while the various forms of let facilitate flexible binding strategies tailored to different coding needs.

2.10 Literals and Self-Evaluating Expressions

Literals in Scheme are data objects that evaluate to themselves. These include numbers, characters, strings, booleans, and symbols. An understanding of literals and self-evaluating expressions is fundamental to mastering the execution of Scheme programs.

Numbers: Scheme supports several numeric types, including integers, real numbers (both rational and irrational), and complex numbers. Scheme's numeric tower adheres to the IEEE floating-point standard, ensuring cross-platform consistency.

```
> (define int-literal 42)
> (define real-literal 3.14)
> (define complex-literal #c(1.5 -2.3))
```

```
#| Evaluations |
int-literal ; 42
real-literal ; 3.14
complex-literal ; #c(1.5 -2.3)
```

Characters: Characters in Scheme are denoted with ##backslash followed by a character. The Scheme standard predefines several escape sequences for commonly used characters.

```
> (define char-literal #\a)
> (define newline-literal #\newline)
> (define space-literal #\space)
```

```
#| Evaluations |
char-literal ; #\a
newline-literal ; #\newline
space-literal ; #\space
```

Strings: String literals are sequences of characters enclosed in double quotation marks. Strings are immutable in Scheme, and any operation that appears to modify a string returns a new string instead.

```
> (define str-literal "Hello, Scheme!")
```

```
#| Evaluation |
str-literal ; "Hello, Scheme!"
```

Booleans: Boolean literals in Scheme are represented as #t for true and #f for false. Every value in Scheme can be used in a boolean context, with all values except #f evaluating to true.

```
> (define bool-true #t)
> (define bool-false #f)
```

```
#| Evaluations |
bool-true ; #t
bool-false ; #f
```

Symbols: Symbols are unique identifiers in Scheme and are utilized extensively in the language. They can be created explicitly using the quote syntax or implicitly by referring to an identifier.

```
> (define sym-literal 'example)
> (define sym-literal-2 (quote example2))
```

```
#| Evaluations |
sym-literal ; 'example
sym-literal-2 ; 'example2
```

Pairs and Lists: Pairs are fundamental building blocks in Scheme, created using the cons function. Lists, a specific type of pair, are widely used to store sequences of elements. Lists can be created using the list function.

```
> (define pair-literal (cons 1 2))
> (define list-literal (list 1 2 3))
```

```
#| Evaluations |
pair-literal ; (1 . 2)
list-literal ; (1 2 3)
```

Vectors: Vectors in Scheme are similar to lists but store data in a contiguous memory block, allowing for constant-time access. Vectors are mutable.

```
> (define vec-literal '#(1 2 3 4))
```

```
#| Evaluation |
vec-literal ; #(1 2 3 4)
```

Self-evaluating expressions are expressions that evaluate to themselves without the need for further interpretation. Literals such as numbers and strings are prime examples. This property allows them to be used directly in expressions without requiring further processing.

```
> (+ 1 2) ; Numbers are self-evaluating
> (string-append "Hello, " "World!") ; Strings are self-evaluating
```

```
#| Evaluations |
(+ 1 2) ; 3
(string-append "Hello, " "World!") ; "Hello, World!"
```

In Scheme, the structure and evaluation of literals and self-evaluating expressions form the bedrock of program construction, impacting the way we define, use, and manipulate data.

2.11 Writing and Using Scheme Procedures

In Scheme, procedures (also known as functions or subroutines in other programming languages) are foundational elements that allow us to encapsulate functionality and reuse code efficiently. Understanding how to write and use Scheme procedures is crucial for mastering this functional programming language.

A procedure in Scheme is defined using the texttdefine keyword combined with the texttlambda keyword. The general syntax for defining a procedure is as follows:

```
(define (procedure-name arg1 arg2 ... argN)
  (expression-body))
```

Here, texttprocedure-name is the identifier for the procedure, and texttarg1, texttarg2, ..., texttargN are the arguments that the procedure will take. The texttexpression-body contains the expressions that make up the body of the procedure, which defines the actions that the procedure will perform when called.

For example, consider a simple procedure that calculates the square of a number:

```
(define (square x)
  (* x x))
```

In this example, the procedure, texttsquare, takes one argument, texttx, and returns the result of multiplying texttx by itself. To use this procedure, we simply call it with a numeric argument:

```
(square 5)
```

The expected output of this expression is:

```
25
```

When defining a procedure, the texttlambda keyword is essential. It creates an anonymous procedure that is then given a name using texttdefine. The syntax for an anonymous procedure is:

```
(lambda (arg1 arg2 ... argN)
  (expression-body))
```

For instance, the texttsquare procedure can also be defined using texttlambda as follows:

```
(define square
  (lambda (x)
    (* x x)))
```

Calling an anonymous procedure directly is less common but possible in Scheme. For example:

```
((lambda (x) (* x x)) 5)
```

This expression will yield the same output as calling texttsquare with 5:

25

Higher-Order Procedures

Scheme procedures are first-class citizens. This means they can be passed as arguments to other procedures, returned as values from other procedures, and assigned to variables. Procedures that take other procedures as arguments or return procedures as results are known as higher-order procedures.

Consider a procedure that applies a given procedure twice to its argument:

```
(define (apply-twice proc x)
  (proc (proc x)))
```

We can use texttapply-twice to apply the texttsquare procedure twice:

```
(apply-twice square 2)
```

This will apply the texttsquare procedure to textttx (which is 2) and then apply texttsquare again to the result:

16

Procedures with Variable Arity

Scheme allows the definition of procedures that can accept a variable number of arguments. This is done using a dot (.) before the last parameter in the parameter list, which collects all remaining arguments into a list.

Here is an example of a procedure that sums all its arguments:

```
(define (sum . numbers)
  (apply + numbers))
```

When we call texttsum with various numbers of arguments:

```
(sum 1 2 3 4 5)
```

The result will be:

15

Recursive Procedures

Recursion is a common technique in functional programming where a procedure calls itself to solve a problem. Scheme supports recursion naturally, and many problems are elegantly solved using recursive procedures.

Consider the classic example of calculating the factorial of a number:

```
(define (factorial n)
  (if (= n 0)
      1
      (* n (factorial (- n 1)))))
```

Calling textttfactorial with an argument of 5:

```
(factorial 5)
```

The output will be:

```
120
```

The textttfactorial procedure works by checking if texttttn is zero, in which case it returns 1, the base condition. Otherwise, it multiplies texttttn by the result of textttfactorial called with texttttn-1.

Procedures in Scheme are a powerful abstraction mechanism that enables code reuse, modularity, and clarity. Mastering the creation and usage of procedures is integral to proficient Scheme programming.

2.12 Introduction to Tail-Call Optimization

Tail-call optimization (TCO) is an important optimization technique in Scheme and many other functional programming languages. It allows for certain kinds of function calls, specifically tail calls, to be executed more efficiently, often converting what would be a recursive process into an iterative one. This can significantly reduce the amount of stack space required for function calls, enabling the handling of deeply recursive procedures without the risk of stack overflow errors.

A tail call occurs when a function calls another function as its final action. For example, consider the following Scheme code:

```
(define (factorial n)
  (if (<= n 1)
      1
      (* n (factorial (- n 1)))))
```

In the factorial function, the call to factorial is not in tail position because the multiplication operation (* n ...) follows it. To transform this function to use tail-call optimization, an accumulator parameter can be introduced to carry the result of the multiplication.

Here is the tail-recursive version of the factorial function:

```
(define (factorial n)
  (define (fact-iter n acc)
    (if (<= n 1)
        acc
        (fact-iter (- n 1) (* n acc))))
  (fact-iter n 1))
```

In this version, fact-iter is a helper function that accumulates the result of the multiplication in the acc parameter. The call to fact-iter is in tail position since it is the last action in its own execution path.

Scheme implementations are required by the standard to perform tail-call optimization. This means that the scheme runtime will reuse the current function's stack frame for the tail call instead of creating a new one, thereby optimizing memory usage. Here's how tail-call optimization fundamentally works:

- When the Scheme interpreter or compiler encounters a tail call, it recognizes that the current function call's stack frame is no longer needed.
- Instead of adding a new stack frame on top of the current one, the interpreter or compiler reuses the existing stack frame for the tail call.
- This reuse of the stack frame allows the recursion to continue with constant stack space, effectively converting a recursive call into a loop in terms of memory usage.

Consider another practical example - the calculation of the greatest common divisor (GCD) using Euclid's algorithm. Here is the non-tail-recursive version:

```
(define (gcd a b)
  (if (= b 0)
      a
      (gcd b (mod a b))))
```

Even though gcd appears to be in tail position, tail call optimization can truly be observed when the language's semantics guarantee that the stack frame is reused. This guarantees that gcd can be computed for very large inputs without consuming additional stack space.

To further clarify the mechanics, the following algorithm outlines a standard approach to detect and apply tail-call optimization during the interpretation or compilation phase:

Algorithm 2: tailCallOptimize

```
Function tailCallOptimize(func, args):
    while current function call is tail-recursive do
        // Replace current frame with the next call
        replace current frame with args for next call;
    return result from the tail call;
```

Physically, this algorithm would be integrated into the interpreter's runtime routine, where function calls are evaluated. Whenever a tail call is detected, the current function frame is replaced by the next call's arguments.

The benefits of using tail-call optimization are:

- **Reduced Memory Usage:** By reusing stack frames, memory consumption remains constant, which is critical for recursive algorithms.
- **Performance Enhancement:** Decreases the overhead associated with function calls by eliminating the need to push and pop frames from the call stack.
- **Infinite Recursion Handling:** Allows certain recursive processes to run indefinitely without running into stack overflow errors.

The correct application and understanding of tail-call optimization will enable writing efficient recursive algorithms in Scheme. Analyzing function calls to identify if they are in tail position and restructuring recursive functions to leverage TCO will greatly enhance both the performance and the reliability of Scheme programs.

Chapter 3

Variables, Data Types, and Structures

This chapter covers the essential aspects of defining and using variables in Scheme, including scope and lifetime considerations. It provides a comprehensive overview of Scheme's data types, such as booleans, characters, strings, numbers, and symbols. Additionally, the chapter delves into core data structures like lists, pairs, vectors, hash tables, and structs, offering practical guidance on constructing and manipulating these structures to effectively organize and manage data in your programs.

3.1 Introduction to Variables in Scheme

Variables in Scheme act as symbolic names that reference specific values or data objects. They provide a way to store data that can be retrieved and manipulated throughout the course of a program. The binding of variables to values is fundamental in Scheme and forms the cornerstone for more complex programming constructs.

```
(define x 10)
```

In the above example, x is a variable that is bound to the value 10. The define keyword is used to create this association. Once defined, x can be used wherever its value is needed in the program.

Variables in Scheme are typically categorized by their scope, which determines where in the program the variable is accessible, and their lifetime, which determines how long the variable exists in memory. This creates a structure for understanding how variables behave and interact within different parts of a Scheme program.

```
(define y 20)
(define (add-to-y n)
  (+ y n))
```

In this snippet, y is accessible inside the add-to-y function because it is defined in the same scope. When add-to-y is called with an argument, it will add that argument to the value of y and return the result.

Scheme supports both global and local variable scopes. A global variable is defined outside any function or block and is accessible from any part of the program.

```
(define global-var 100)

(define (access-global)
  global-var)
```

```
> (access-global)
100
```

Here, global-var is defined as a global variable and can be accessed from within the access-global function, demonstrating its global scope.

To create local variables, Scheme provides constructs such as let, let*, and letrec. These constructs are used to bind variables to values within a specific block of code.

```
(let ((a 30)
      (b 40))
  (+ a b))
```

In this example, a and b are local variables defined within the let block. The variables a and b exist only within this block and cannot be accessed outside it.

```
> (let ((a 30)
        (b 40))
    (+ a b))
70
```

The output 70 indicates the sum of a and b within the local scope defined by let.

For more dynamic scoping, Scheme allows the use of let*, which is a variant of let that permits sequential bindings. This means each successive binding can reference the values of the previous bindings within the same let* block.

```
(let* ((x 1)
       (y (+ x 1))
       (z (+ x y)))
  z)
```

```
> (let* ((x 1)
        (y (+ x 1))
        (z (+ x y)))
    z)
3
```

The output 3 demonstrates how let* allows y to depend on x and z to depend on both x and y sequentially.

letrec is used for defining mutually recursive local variables, ensuring every variable in the block is accessible within the same block, making it particularly useful for defining recursive functions.

```
(letrec ((even? (lambda (n)
                  (or (zero? n)
                      (odd? (- n 1)))))
         (odd? (lambda (n)
                 (and (not (zero? n))
                      (even? (- n 1))))))
  (even? 10))
```

```
> (letrec ((even? (lambda (n)
                  (or (zero? n)
                      (odd? (- n 1)))))
          (odd? (lambda (n)
                  (and (not (zero? n))
                      (even? (- n 1))))))
    (even? 10))
#t
```

This example defines two mutually recursive functions, even? and odd?, using letrec, demonstrating that even? 10 returns #t (true).

Understanding the declaration and manipulation of variables in Scheme is crucial for writing effective and robust programs. The scoping rules and constructs available provide a flexible and powerful way to manage variable lifetimes and their accessibility, enabling complex program logic to be implemented with clarity.

3.2 Defining and Using Variables: 'define' and 'set!'

In Scheme, variables play a central role in the construction and manipulation of data. The primary mechanisms for defining and manipulating variables include the define and set! special forms. This section explores these mechanisms with illustrative examples and detailed explanations.

Variable Definition with define

The define form is used to create new variables and bind them to values. The syntax of define is straightforward:

```
(define variable-name expression)
```

This form evaluates expression and binds the result to variable-name. For example:

```
(define x 5)
```

In this example, the variable x is bound to the value 5. The following elements are crucial when using define:

- variable-name: The name of the variable to be defined. In Scheme, variable names can contain letters, digits, and special characters such as !, ?, -, but they should not start with a digit.
- expression: Any valid Scheme expression whose value will be assigned to variable-name.

Scheme programming emphasizes immutability initially; thus, once defined, it is encouraged not to change the value of the variable unless necessary. This practice helps maintain functional programming principles.

Variable Assignment with set!

While define introduces new variables, the set! form is used to modify the value of an existing variable. The syntax for set! is as follows:

```
(set! variable-name new-expression)
```

Here, variable-name refers to a previously defined variable, and new-expression is the new value to be assigned to that variable. For example:

```
(set! x 10)
```

Given the previous definition of x, this statement reassigns x to the value 10. It's important to note that set! operates only on previously defined variables. Attempting to use set! with an undefined variable will result in an error.

```
; Example error using set! on an undefined variable
(set! y 15) ; Error: reference to undefined identifier y
```

Combining define and set!

Often, define and set! are used together in programs where it is necessary to initialize a variable and later modify its value based on certain conditions or within iterative processes. Consider the following example:

```
(define total 0)
(define numbers '(1 2 3 4 5))

(define (sum-list lst)
  (begin
    (for-each
      (lambda (n) (set! total (+ total n)))
      lst)
    total))

(sum-list numbers)
```

In this example:

- The variable total is initialized to 0.
- A function sum-list is defined to sum the elements of the list numbers.
- The for-each procedure iterates over each element of the list, applying the lambda function.
- Inside the lambda, set! updates the value of total by adding the current element n.
- After the loop, the final value of total is returned.

The correct implementation of define and set! helps effectively manage variable states, ensuring that the program calculates the intended results.

Best Practices

To ensure clean and maintainable Scheme code, consider the following best practices:

- Favor immutability: Use define to introduce variables and minimize the use of set! to promote a functional programming style.
- Avoid global state mutations: Limit the scope of variable modifications to local contexts when possible to mitigate side effects and improve code readability.

- Use meaningful variable names: Choosing descriptive names for variables enhances code readability and maintainability.
- Validate variable existence before using set!: Ensure the variable being modified with set! has been previously defined to avoid runtime errors.

Understanding and correctly applying define and set! forms the foundation for effective variable management in Scheme.

3.3 Scope and Lifetime of Variables

Understanding the scope and lifetime of variables is crucial for effective programming in Scheme. These concepts determine where and for how long a variable is accessible in a program.

Scope refers to the region of the program where a variable can be accessed. Scheme supports several kinds of scope, including lexical (or static) scope and dynamic scope. Lexical scope is the default in Scheme and is determined by the physical structure of the code, while dynamic scope is determined at runtime.

Consider the following example to illustrate lexical scoping:

```
(define x 10)
(define (example-scope)
  (define x 20)
  (display x)) ; Outputs 20
(example-scope)
(display x) ; Outputs 10
```

In this example, the x inside the example-scope function shadows the global x. The variable x, when displayed inside the function, refers to the function-local x and outputs 20. Outside the function, it refers to the global x and outputs 10. The scope of the local variable x extends only within the {example-scope} function.

Lexical scope is managed by the function definitions and the blocks of code where the variables are defined using define or let. Here is an example using let:

```
(let ((x 5))
  (define (inner-func)
    (display x))
  (inner-func)) ; Outputs 5
(display x) ; Error: Reference to undefined identifier: x
```

The let form creates a new scope for the variable x. The x is only accessible within the {let} form.

Lifetime refers to the duration for which a variable retains its value during program execution. In Scheme, the lifetime of a variable is usually tied to its scope.

If a variable is defined in a global scope using define, its lifetime lasts for the entire duration of the program execution. For example:

```
(define global-var 42)
; global-var is accessible throughout the program
```

On the other hand, if a variable is defined using let or within a function, its lifetime is limited to the execution of that particular scope or function. For instance:

```
(define (example-lifetime)
  (let ((local-var 100))
    (display local-var))) ; Outputs 100
(example-lifetime)
(display local-var) ; Error: Reference to undefined identifier: local-var
```

In this example, local-var is only alive during the execution of example-lifetime. Once the function execution is complete, local-var is no longer accessible.

Scheme also supports closures, which can extend the lifetime of a variable beyond the scope in which it was defined. A closure is an instance of a function along with a reference to its lexical environment. This allows the function to access non-local variables even after the block that defines those variables has finished executing:

```
(define (make-counter)
  (let ((count 0))
    (lambda ()
      (set! count (+ count 1))
      count)))
(define counter (make-counter))
(display (counter)) ; Outputs 1
(display (counter)) ; Outputs 2
```

In this example, count is a local variable within the {let} block inside make-counter. However, the returned lambda function (closure) keeps a reference to count, extending its lifetime beyond the make-counter execution.

Dynamic scope is occasionally used for certain programming tasks, but its use can lead to unpredictable behavior and is generally not recommended due to the complexity it introduces.Wisely managing scope and lifetime of variables in Scheme enhances not only the readability but also the efficiency and maintainability of the codebase.

3.4 Understanding Scheme Data Types

Scheme, a dialect of Lisp, provides a rich set of data types that are essential for the implementation of diverse algorithms and data structures. Understanding these data types is fundamental to mastering Scheme programming. This section will cover the primary data types in Scheme, focusing on their properties, usage, and relevance in various computational contexts.

Booleans in Scheme are represented by the literals #t and #f, corresponding to true and false, respectively. These are used in conditional expressions and form the basis of control structures such as if, cond, and case. Scheme treats any value other than #f as true in conditional contexts.

Characters are represented using the prefix #\. For instance, the character 'a' is written as #\a, and a space character is written as #\space. Characters are useful for text processing and can be compared using procedures like char=?, char<?, char>?, among others.

Strings are sequences of characters enclosed in double quotes, such as "Hello, World!". Strings in Scheme are versatile and support a variety of operations such as concatenation, substring extraction, and length determination using procedures like string-append, substring, and string-length. Here is an example of string manipulation:

```
(define str1 "Hello")
(define str2 "World")
(define result (string-append str1 ", " str2 "!"))
```

To extract a substring from a string, use the substring function:

```
(substring result 0 5) ; returns "Hello"
```

Numbers in Scheme are divided into several categories: integers, rationals, and real numbers. Integers are whole numbers without a fractional component, while rationals can be any fraction represented as a ratio of two integers. Real numbers cover the broad spectrum of floating-point numbers. Scheme supports arithmetic operations across these numerical types using procedures like +, -, *, and /. Here's a simple arithmetic example:

```
(define a 10)
(define b 3)
(define sum (+ a b)) ; Addition, returns 13
(define diff (- a b)) ; Subtraction, returns 7
(define prod (* a b)) ; Multiplication, returns 30
(define quot (/ a b)) ; Division, returns 10/3
```

Symbols in Scheme are unique identifiers that are often used as keys in associative data structures or to represent specific concepts within the code. Symbols are created using the quote prefix, e.g., 'example-symbol, or the symbol procedure. Each symbol is guaranteed to be unique, ensuring that identity comparisons are straightforward.

```
(define sym1 'example)
(define sym2 'example)
(eq? sym1 sym2) ; returns #t
```

Lists are the primary data structure in Scheme, representing ordered collections of elements. Lists are created using the cons function, and standard list operations include car, cdr, list, and append. Lists can be processed recursively or iteratively, making them extremely flexible for various applications. Here's a simple example of list manipulation:

```
(define lst1 (list 1 2 3 4))
(define lst2 (list 5 6))
(define combined (append lst1 lst2)) ; returns (1 2 3 4 5 6)
```

Vectors are similar to lists but provide constant-time access and update capabilities. Vectors are fixed-size collections created with the vector procedure, and individual elements can be accessed with vector-ref and modified using vector-set!.

```
(define vec (vector 1 2 3 4))
(vector-ref vec 2) ; returns 3
(vector-set! vec 2 10) ; modifies vec to #(1 2 10 4)
```

Hash tables provide efficient key-value associations and are suitable for fast lookups and updates. They are created using the make-hash, hash, and hash-set! procedures. Hash tables are widely used in situations where quick access to data is critical.

To summarize the functional methods of Scheme data types, you apply specific procedures for verification, manipulation, and traversal. Understanding these core principles and practices enables you to write efficient and effective Scheme programs. This knowledge is foundational, as the proper application and manipulation of data types enhance the overall robustness and readability of your code.

Each data type serves a distinct purpose and, when used appropriately, can significantly streamline your programming endeavors. By leveraging the full spectrum of Scheme's data types, you can develop solutions that are both elegant and computationally efficient.

3.5 Booleans and Their Uses

The boolean data type is one of the most fundamental in Scheme, representing the two possible truth values: true and false. Scheme provides two literal constants for these values: #t for true and #f for false. This section explores the use of booleans, their syntactic representation, and their role in control structures, comparisons, and logical operations.

Booleans are integral to controlling the flow of programs. They are used extensively in conditional expressions, loops, and as return values for predicates. Predicates are functions that return a boolean value, answering yes/no questions about data.

- **True and False**: The boolean constants in Scheme are #t (true) and #f (false). Anything not explicitly false (i.e., #f) is considered true in a conditional context. This includes all the other standard data types such as numbers, strings, lists, and even the empty list '().

Using Scheme's built-in predicates, one can perform various tests and comparisons. For example:

```
(equal? 'apple 'apple) ; This returns #t
(equal? 5 10) ; This returns #f
(null? '()) ; This returns #t
(pair? '(a . b)) ; This returns #t
```

In the above examples, equal? checks for structural equality, null? checks if a list is empty, and pair? checks if an object is a pair (a combination of two values).

Booleans also play a critical role in Scheme's control structures:

- if Expression: It is used to choose between two possible outcomes based on a condition.

```
(if (> 3 2)
    (display "3 is greater than 2")
    (display "3 is not greater than 2"))
; This prints "3 is greater than 2"
```

In this expression, the condition (> 3 2) evaluates to #t, so the consequent expression (display "3 is greater than 2") is executed.

- cond Expression: Useful for multiple conditional branches, akin to a switch statement in other languages.

```
(cond ((< 3 2) (display "3 is less than 2"))
      ((= 3 2) (display "3 is equal to 2"))
      (else (display "3 is greater than 2")))
; This prints "3 is greater than 2"
```

In this case, all preceding conditions are false, so the else branch is executed.

Logical operations can manipulate boolean values. Scheme supports standard logical operators such as and, or, and not:

```
(and #t #t) ; This returns #t
(and #t #f) ; This returns #f
(or #f #t) ; This returns #t
(or #f #f) ; This returns #f
(not #t) ; This returns #f
(not #f) ; This returns #t
```

The and operator returns true if all arguments are true. The or operator returns true if at least one argument is true. The not operator inverts the boolean value.

Logical operators can also be applied to custom predicates, facilitating complex logical operations. For instance:

```
(define (positive-even? x)
  (and (even? x) (> x 0)))

(positive-even? 4) ; This returns #t
(positive-even? -4) ; This returns #f
```

Here, the positive-even? predicate checks if a number is both even and positive by combining the built-in even? predicate with a greater-than comparison using and.

Additionally, using boolean values can simplify the readability and maintenance of complex conditional expressions:

```
(define (leap-year? year)
  (or (and (= (mod year 4) 0) (not (= (mod year 100) 0)))
      (= (mod year 400) 0)))

(leap-year? 2000) ; This returns #t
(leap-year? 1900) ; This returns #f
(leap-year? 2024) ; This returns #t
```

The leap-year? function checks if a given year is a leap year. The condition relies on the and and or operators to ensure that a leap year is either divisible by 400 or divisible by 4 but not by 100.

Understanding and effectively using booleans in Scheme allows for more concise, expressive, and powerful programs. They are foundational for implementing algorithms that require decision-making and control flow.

3.6 Characters and Strings

Characters and strings are fundamental data types in Scheme that represent text. Understanding these data types and how to manipulate them is essential for tasks involving text processing, user interaction, or displaying messages.

In Scheme, a character is denoted by the prefix #\ followed by the character itself. For example, #\a, #\tab, and #\space represent the character 'a', the tab character, and the space character, respectively.

To check for character data types, Scheme provides several predicates, such as char?.

```
(char? #\a)
```

The above expression returns

```
#t
```

Comparing characters can be done using a variety of procedures such as char=?, char<?, char>?, char<=?, and char>=?. These functions compare characters based on their Unicode values.

```
(char<? #\a #\b)
```

The above expression returns

```
#t
```

Scheme also provides case-insensitive versions of these comparison functions, like char-ci=?.

```
(char-ci=? #\a #\A)
```

The above expression returns

```
#t
```

Strings in Scheme are sequences of characters enclosed in double quotes, such as "hello world". Strings are mutable; you can change their contents after creation. Functions for creating and manipulating strings include string constructors and accessors, and various utilities for string comparison and conversion.

To create a string, use the string procedure, which takes any number of characters as arguments.

```
(string #\h #\e #\l #\l #\o)
```

The above expression returns

"hello"

Access individual characters in a string using the string-ref procedure, which takes a string and an index (starting from 0) as arguments:

```
(string-ref "hello" 1)
```

The above expression returns

#\e

To determine the length of a string, use the string-length procedure:

```
(string-length "hello")
```

The above expression returns

5

Strings can be modified using the string-set! procedure. For instance, to change the second character of a string:

```
(define my-string "hello")
(string-set! my-string 1 #\a)
my-string
```

The above code will modify my-string to be "hallo".

Scheme also provides utility procedures for string manipulation such as substring, string-append, and string->list.

```
(substring "hello world" 0 5)
```

The above expression returns

"hello"

```
(string-append "hello" " " "world")
```

The above expression returns

"hello world"

```
(string->list "hello")
```

The above expression returns

(#\h #\e #\l #\l #\o)

It is possible to convert between strings and other data types. To convert a string to a list of characters, use string->list. Conversely, to convert a list of characters back to a string, use list->string.

```
(list->string '(#\h #\e #\l #\l #\o))
```

The above expression returns

"hello"

String comparison is an essential task, often needed in programs. Scheme provides various procedures for this purpose, including string=?, string<?, string>?, string<=?, and string>=?. These compare strings lexicographically.

```
(string=? "hello" "hello")
```

The above expression returns

#t

```
(string<? "hello" "world")
```

The above expression returns

#t

```
(string>? "world" "hello")
```

The above expression returns

#t

For case-insensitive comparisons, Scheme provides similar procedures prefixed with string-ci, such as string-ci=?.

```
(string-ci=? "hello" "HELLO")
```

The above expression returns

#t

Using characters and strings effectively in Scheme requires familiarity with various procedures and their functionalities. Their usage allows for sophisticated text manipulation, data entry validation, and more, contributing significantly to the development of robust Scheme programs.

3.7 Numbers: Integers, Rationals, and Real Numbers

Scheme supports a rich set of numeric types that cater to various computational needs, including exact and inexact representations. Understanding these numeric types and how to manipulate them forms a core component of effective Scheme programming.

Numbers in Scheme are divided into several categories:

- Integers
- Rationals
- Real Numbers

Each of these categories has unique properties and usage scenarios, which we will explore in detail.

Integers: Integers in Scheme are whole numbers that can be either positive, negative, or zero. Scheme distinguishes between exact integers, which have an exact mathematical value, and inexact integers, which may be subject to precision errors due to their representation in a computer.

Here is an example of working with integers in Scheme:

```
(define a 42) ; Exact integer
(define b -7) ; Negative integer
(define c 0) ; Zero

; Simple arithmetic operations
(+ a b) ; Addition
(* a b) ; Multiplication
(- a b) ; Subtraction
(quotient a b) ; Integer division
```

The output of the above operations is as follows:

```
35
-294
49
-6
```

It is important to note that the quotient function performs integer division, which discards any remainder.

Rationals: Rationals in Scheme are numbers that can be expressed as the quotient of two integers, p/q, where p and q are integers and q is non-zero. Rationals include integers, since any integer can be represented as a fraction with a denominator of one.

Here is an example of working with rationals:

```
(define r1 (/ 3 4)) ; 3/4
(define r2 (/ 5 2)) ; 5/2

; Arithmetic operations on rationals
(+ r1 r2) ; Addition
(- r1 r2) ; Subtraction
(* r1 r2) ; Multiplication
(/ r1 r2) ; Division
```

The output of the above operations is as follows:

```
17/8
-7/8
15/8
6/20 (simplifies to 3/10)
```

Scheme automatically reduces rational numbers to their simplest form.

Real Numbers: Reals in Scheme cover both rational numbers and irrational numbers – those which cannot be expressed as a quotient of two integers. Real numbers can be either exact or inexact. Inexact reals are typically represented as floating-point numbers and may be subject to rounding errors.

Here is an example illustrating exact and inexact reals:

```
(define r3 3.14) ; Inexact real number (floating-point)
(define c2 (sqrt 2)) ; Inexact irrational number, square root of 2

; Arithmetic operations on reals
(+ r3 c2)
(- r3 c2)
(* r3 c2)
(/ r3 c2)
```

The output of these operations is as follows:

```
4.555442
1.724558
4.444561200000001
1.307189542483660
```

The floating-point representation can introduce small precision errors, especially noticeable in complex calculations. Scheme provides functions to distinguish between exact and inexact numbers, essential for ensuring numerical accuracy where required:

```
(exact? r1) ; Checks if r1 is exact (returns #t for true)
(inexact? r3) ; Checks if r3 is inexact (returns #t for true)
```

The output of these functions is as follows:

```
#t
#t
```

Precise handling of these numeric types allows for robust mathematical operations and ensures that computational tasks that depend on numeric accuracy are implemented correctly. Scheme's extensive numeric functionality, combined with its exact and inexact distinction, provides a powerful toolkit for complex number manipulations and analyses, crucial for advanced programming and scientific computing purposes.

3.8 Symbols and Keywords in Scheme

Symbols and keywords are fundamental elements in Scheme, serving as key building blocks for creating and managing identifiers, variables, and constant expressions. Understanding how to define, manipulate, and utilize symbols and keywords effectively is essential for efficient Scheme programming.

In Scheme, symbols are atomic, immutable data types that are primarily used as identifiers for variables, functions, and other named entities in your programs. They play a crucial role in the metaprogramming capabilities of Scheme, allowing programmers to treat names as first-class objects. A symbol is defined by any sequence of characters that does not begin with a number and does not contain any spaces or special characters. Symbols can be written directly by preceding the name with a single quote.

```
(define sym 'mySymbol)
```

In this example, mySymbol is a symbol, and using define, it can be bound to a variable, thereby making sym a reference to the symbol mySymbol.

To check if a given entity is a symbol, we use the symbol? function, which returns #t if the argument is a symbol and #f otherwise.

```
(symbol? 'example) ; Returns #t
(symbol? 42) ; Returns #f
(symbol? "example") ; Returns #f
```

Symbols are frequently used in Scheme for comparison and lookup operations due to their unique and efficient nature. The eq? function is often employed to test the identity of two symbols:

```
(eq? 'symbol1 'symbol1) ; Returns #t
(eq? 'symbol1 'symbol2) ; Returns #f
```

It's important to distinguish symbols from variables even though they can sometimes be visually similar. Unlike variables, which hold values, symbols are self-evaluating and represent constant names.

Keywords in Scheme, on the other hand, are usually employed to refer to specific argument names in functions or syntactic constructs. Keywords follow strict syntactic rules and often appear in special forms or macro definitions. A keyword is typically defined using the define-syntax form.

Here is an example where define-syntax is used to create a custom macro, demonstrating the usage of keywords within.

```
(define-syntax mymacro
  (syntax-rules (:do :then)
    [(_ :do action :then consequence)
     (begin action consequence)]))

(mymacro :do (display "Executing action") :then (display " followed by consequence"))
```

In this case, :do and :then serve as keywords to separate different parts of the macro definition. The macro mymacro evaluates the action followed by the consequence, showcasing a clear application of keywords to structure and extend syntax.

Scheme provides several built-in functions tailored for creating and manipulating symbols. Two of the most commonly used are string->symbol and symbol->string, which convert strings to symbols and symbols back to strings, respectively.

Consider the following example:

```
(define sym1 (string->symbol "newSymbol"))
(define str1 (symbol->string 'anotherSymbol))
```

In this code, string->symbol is used to turn a string into a symbol, while symbol->string does the reverse, retrieving the string representation of a symbol.

Due to their immutable nature, symbols can be especially useful in situations where constant lookups or references are required. They are distinct from strings not only in their usage but also in their performance characteristics. Symbols are interned, meaning each occurrence of a symbol with the same name refers to the exact same object in memory, which makes comparisons very efficient.

Given the significant role of symbols and keywords in Scheme, particularly in the context of macros and metaprogramming, a solid grasp of their properties and behavioral aspects is beneficial for leveraging the full power of the language.

3.9 Lists: The Core Data Structure

In Scheme, lists are one of the most fundamental and versatile data structures. They are used extensively due to their simplicity and power in representing various data collections. A list in Scheme is an ordered collection of elements, which can be of any data type, including numbers, symbols, strings, other lists, and more. This section will explore how to create, manipulate, and utilize lists in Scheme programming.

Creating Lists: The primary way to define a list in Scheme is using the quote special form or its shorthand notation: the single quote (').

```
(define my-list '(1 2 3 4 5))
```

The above example creates a list containing the numbers 1 through 5 and binds it to the variable my-list. Note that the single quote before the parentheses indicates that we are creating a literal list. Alternatively, the list procedure can be used to construct lists.

```
(define another-list (list 'a 'b 'c 'd 'e))
```

Accessing List Elements: Scheme provides various procedures to access elements within a list. The car and cdr procedures are used to retrieve the first element and the rest of the list, respectively.

```
(define first-element (car my-list)) ; first-element now holds the value 1
(define rest-of-list (cdr my-list)) ; rest-of-list now holds the list (2 3 4 5)
```

car returns the first element of my-list, while cdr returns a list consisting of all elements except the first. For deeper access, we can use nested car and cdr calls.

```
(define second-element (car (cdr my-list))) ; Extracts the second element
```

Constructing Lists: To create more complex lists, the cons procedure is used. cons constructs a new pair (a cons cell) from its two arguments—an element and a list.

```
(define new-list (cons 0 my-list)) ; new-list is now (0 1 2 3 4 5)
```

cons is fundamental in building lists by prepending elements to existing lists.

List Predicates: To determine if an object is a list, Scheme provides the list? predicate. Additionally, to check if a list is empty, the null? predicate is used.

```
(list? my-list) ; Returns #t (true)
(null? my-list) ; Returns #f (false)
(null? '()) ; Returns #t (true)
```

Common List Operations: Scheme includes many built-in procedures for common list manipulations such as length, append, reverse, list-tail, and list-ref.

```
(length my-list) ; Returns 5
(append my-list '(6 7)) ; Returns (1 2 3 4 5 6 7)
(reverse my-list) ; Returns (5 4 3 2 1)
(list-tail my-list 3) ; Returns (4 5)
(list-ref my-list 2) ; Returns 3
```

Each of these procedures has its specific utility for list-based operations, such as obtaining the length of a list, combining lists, reversing the elements of a list, getting a sublist starting at a specific index, or retrieving an element at a given position.

Mapping Over Lists: One of the powerful features of Scheme is the ability to apply a procedure to each element of a list using the map procedure.

```
(define incremented-list (map (lambda (x) (+ x 1)) my-list)) ; (2 3 4 5 6)
```

Here, map applies the provided anonymous function (lambda expression) to each element of my-list, resulting in a new list where each element is incremented by one.

Algorithm 3: Recursive List Sum

Data: my-list: A list of integers
Result: sum_list: Sum of elements in my-list

```
Function recursive-sum(lst):
    if (null? lst) then
        return 0
    else
        return (+ (car lst) (recursive-sum((cdr lst))))
    end
```

Recursively Processing Lists: Lists in Scheme are well-suited for recursive processing. Here, an example algorithm demonstrates summing all elements in a list using recursion.

```
(define (recursive-sum lst)
  (if (null? lst)
      0
      (+ (car lst) (recursive-sum (cdr lst)))))
```

Executing the recursive-sum procedure with my-list:

```
(recursive-sum my-list) ; Returns 15
```

This procedure uses a simple recursive base case (empty list) and recursive step (sum of the first element and the recursion on the rest of the list).

Higher-Order List Procedures: Scheme also supports other higher-order procedures such as filter, fold-left, and fold-right.

```
(define evens (filter even? my-list)) ; Returns (2 4)
```

```
(define sum-left (fold-left + 0 my-list)) ; Returns 15
(define sum-right (fold-right + 0 my-list)) ; Returns 15
```

These procedures provide powerful tools for functional list processing, allowing the programmer to effectively traverse, transform, and reduce lists.

Understanding and mastering lists is paramount for efficient Scheme programming. They serve as the backbone for numerous algorithms and data manipulation techniques. By practicing the creation and manipulation of lists, you can harness their full potential in solving a wide array of computational problems.

3.10 Pairs and Cons Cells

In Scheme, pairs form the foundational building blocks for constructing lists and complex data structures. A pair is a compound data object consisting of two components, referred to as the *car* and the *cdr*. The terminology originates from the early days of Lisp, where *car* and *cdr* represent the "contents of the address register" and the "contents of the decrement register," respectively.

The primary procedure to create pairs in Scheme is cons. This procedure takes two arguments and returns a newly allocated pair:

```
(cons 1 2)
```

This will produce a pair where the car is 1 and the cdr is 2. To access the components of the pair, we use the car and cdr procedures:

```
(car (cons 1 2)) ; Returns 1
(cdr (cons 1 2)) ; Returns 2
```

Pairs can be nested to create more complex structures. For instance, (cons 1 (cons 2 3)) creates a pair where the car is 1 and the cdr is another pair (2 . 3). This nested structure can be visualized as:

```
+---+---+  +---+---+
| 1 | o--->| 2 | 3 |
+---+---+  +---+---+
```

Scheme provides a more concise way to visualize and work with pairs and lists. The dot notation (1 . 2) represents a single pair. Lists, which are sequences of pairs, can be represented without explicit dots once the pattern is recognized. For example:

```
(cons 1 (cons 2 (cons 3 nil)))
; Can be written as
(list 1 2 3)
```

This usage of nil (often written as '() in Scheme) is crucial, as nil signifies the end of a list. The list (list 1 2 3) internally is equivalent to:

```
(cons 1 (cons 2 (cons 3 '())))
```

Visual representation:

```
+---+---+  +---+---+  +---+---+
| 1 | o--->| 2 | o--->| 3 | / |
+---+---+  +---+---+  +---+---+
```

Scheme includes a suite of procedures for constructing and manipulating pairs and lists. For example, cons, car, and cdr are complemented by set-car! and set-cdr!, which mutate the car and cdr fields of pairs, respectively. Consider the following example to change components of a pair:

```
(define pair (cons 1 2))
(set-car! pair 3) ; The pair is now (3 . 2)
(set-cdr! pair 4) ; The pair is now (3 . 4)
```

While mutation can be powerful, it should be used with caution as it introduces state and can complicate reasoning about code.

When examining or debugging lists and pairs, the pair? and list? predicates prove invaluable. They determine whether an object is a pair or a list:

```
(pair? (cons 1 2)) ; Returns #t
(list? (cons 1 2)) ; Returns #f
(list? (list 1 2)) ; Returns #t
```

Cons cells are versatile and can represent various data structures beyond simple lists, such as trees. For example, a binary tree can be built using nested pairs:

```
(define tree (cons (cons 1 2) (cons 3 4)))
```

This expression represents a tree where the left subtree is (1 . 2) and the right subtree is (3 . 4). Traversing such structures involves recursive application of car and cdr:

Algorithm 4: Traversal of a binary tree

```
Input: tree - A binary tree as nested pairs
Function traverse(tree):
    if pair? tree then
        traverse(car tree);
        traverse(cdr tree);
    end
    else
        print(tree);
    end
```

To traverse the tree nodes, we recursively apply traverse to both the left and right subtrees. The base case of the recursion occurs when the subtree is not a pair, where we then print the element.

Pairs and cons cells are fundamental to understanding more complex data structures in Scheme. They allow for the creation of lists, trees, and custom data structures, underscoring the flexibility and power of Scheme's minimalist design. Properly mastering the use of pairs and cons cells is critical for leveraging Scheme's full potential in data manipulation and organization.

3.11 Vectors: Fixed-Size Collections

Vectors in Scheme represent fixed-size collections of elements, providing an indexed structure that enables efficient random access and update. Unlike lists, where accessing an element requires traversal from the beginning, vectors allow direct access to any element using an index, yielding an efficient and scalable means for handling collections with known sizes.

Vectors are defined using the vector keyword, which initializes a vector with a set of elements. The elements can be of any type, including numbers, strings, symbols, or even other vectors. Here's a simple example of vector initialization and usage:

```
(define vec (vector 1 2 3 4 5))
```

In this example, vec is a vector containing five integers. You can access elements in vectors using the vector-ref procedure. The index is zero-based, meaning the first element is at index 0:

```
(vector-ref vec 0) ; => 1
(vector-ref vec 2) ; => 3
(vector-ref vec 4) ; => 5
```

To modify an element in a vector, use the vector-set! procedure. This procedure takes three arguments: the vector, the index, and the new value:

```
(vector-set! vec 1 10)
(vec) ; => #(1 10 3 4 5)
```

Vectors can also be created with a pre-defined size and elements initialized to a specific value using the make-vector procedure. This is useful when the size of the vector is known but the initial values are not:

```
(define vec (make-vector 5 0))
(vec) ; => #(0 0 0 0 0)
```

In the above example, vec is a vector of size 5 where all elements are initialized to 0.

Several built-in procedures are available for vectors, aiding in tasks like conversion between lists and vectors, obtaining the length of a vector, or filling a vector with a particular value. Below is a concise list of these procedures and their purposes:

- vector->list - Converts a vector to a list.

```
(vector->list vec) ; => (0 0 0 0 0)
```

- list->vector - Converts a list to a vector.

```
(list->vector '(1 2 3 4 5)) ; => #(1 2 3 4 5)
```

- vector-length - Returns the number of elements in a vector.

```
(vector-length vec) ; => 5
```

- vector-fill! - Sets all elements in a vector to a specified value.

```
(vector-fill! vec 7)
(vec) ; => #(7 7 7 7 7)
```

Vectors can be iterated over using loops. Here's a simple example of iterating over a vector using the do loop:

```
(do ((i 0 (+ i 1)))
    ((= i (vector-length vec)))
  (printf "Element at index ~a: ~a\n" i (vector-ref vec i)))
```

In this loop, i is the loop variable initialized to 0 and incremented by 1 on each iteration. The loop continues until i equals the length of the vector. During each iteration, the current element of the vector is accessed and printed.

Using vectors in Scheme is particularly useful in scenarios where quick access and updates are essential. Their fixed size characteristic enables certain optimizations over lists, especially in situations involving large datasets where constant-time access to elements is paramount. Understanding how to manipulate and apply vectors effectively can significantly enhance the performance and readability of Scheme programs.

3.12 Hash Tables and Dictionaries

In Scheme, hash tables provide a powerful and flexible way to manage collections of key-value pairs, much like dictionaries in other high-level programming languages. Hash tables offer efficient average-case performance for insertion, deletion, and lookup operations, making them a preferred choice for many applications where rapid access to data is critical.

Hash tables are characterized by their use of a hash function to compute an index into an array of buckets or slots, where the desired value can be found. The primary advantage of hash tables is their ability to handle large amounts of data with minimal performance degradation.

Creating Hash Tables

To work with hash tables in Scheme, we use the built-in procedures for creating and manipulating these data structures. The following example illustrates how to create an empty hash table:

```
(define ht (make-hash-table))
```

The make-hash-table procedure returns a new, empty hash table. By default, this creates a hash table with a predefined hashing mechanism and size. For more control over the hash table's behavior, additional parameters can be specified, including the hash function and the equality predicate.

Adding and Accessing Elements

Elements are added to a hash table using the hash-set! procedure, which associates a key with a value. Here is an example of adding key-value pairs to our hash table:

```
(hash-set! ht 'name "Alice")
(hash-set! ht 'age 30)
(hash-set! ht 'occupation "Engineer")
```

In this example, we have inserted three key-value pairs into the hash table ht. The keys are symbols ('name, 'age, and 'occupation), and the values are of different data types (a string, an integer, and another string, respectively).

To access the value associated with a particular key, we use the hash-ref procedure:

```
(define name (hash-ref ht 'name))
(display name) ; Output: Alice
```

If the specified key does not exist in the hash table, hash-ref can also take an optional third argument that provides a default return value:

```
(define height (hash-ref ht 'height 'unknown))
(display height) ; Output: unknown
```

Removing Elements

To remove an entry from the hash table, the hash-remove! procedure is used:

```
(hash-remove! ht 'occupation)
```

After calling hash-remove!, the key 'occupation and its associated value are deleted from the hash table. Attempting to reference 'occupation afterward will yield the default return value if specified, or an error if not.

Checking for Keys

One can check if a key exists in the hash table using the hash-has-key? procedure:

```
(if (hash-has-key? ht 'age)
    (display "Key 'age' is present.")
    (display "Key 'age' is not present."))
```

This procedure returns a boolean indicating whether the provided key is present in the hash table.

Iterating over Hash Tables

Scheme supports iteration over the key-value pairs in a hash table using the hash-map procedure, which applies a given function to each key-value pair in the hash table. Here is an example that prints all keys and values:

```
(hash-map ht
    (lambda (key value)
        (display key)
        (display ": ")
        (display value)
        (newline)))
```

The specified lambda function is called for each key-value pair in the hash table, allowing you to process each entry as needed.

Advanced Hash Table Usage

For more advanced use cases, Scheme allows specifying custom comparison procedures and hash functions when creating a hash table. This can optimize the hash table for specific types of keys or usage patterns:

```
(define custom-hash (make-hash-table
                     (lambda (key) (string-length key))
                     string=?))
```

In this example, custom-hash is created with a custom hash function that computes the hash based on the length of the key strings and uses string=? for key comparison.

Scheme hash tables effectively manage key-value collections, offering efficient access, manipulation, and flexibility. Using hash tables can significantly optimize applications that require frequent and rapid data lookups.

3.13 Working with Structs and Records

In Scheme, structs and records are essential for representing complex data structures. They provide a more organized and modular way to manage related data than using multiple lists or vectors. Structs are collections of related fields that can be treated as a single unit. This section delves into defining, constructing, and manipulating structs and records in Scheme.

Defining Structs

To define a struct, Scheme provides the define-struct form, which allows you to specify the name of the struct and its fields. The following is an example of how to define a struct for a simple point with two fields, x and y:

```
(define-struct point (x y))
```

This definition creates several related functions automatically:

- make-point - a constructor function that creates a new point.
- point-x - a selector function that retrieves the x field from a point.
- point-y - a selector function that retrieves the y field from a point.
- point? - a predicate function that checks whether a given argument is of type point.

Creating Instances of Structs

To create an instance of a struct, you use the constructor function. For the point struct defined above, you can create a new point as follows:

```
(define p1 (make-point 3 4))
```

The variable p1 now holds a point with x equal to 3 and y equal to 4.

Accessing Fields

To access the fields of a struct, you use the selector functions. Continuing with the previous example:

```
(define x-value (point-x p1))
(define y-value (point-y p1))
```

This will assign the x value of p1 to x-value and the y value of p1 to y-value.

Modifying Fields

While structs offer a convenient means of bundling related data, Scheme supports immutable structs by default. To create mutable structs, you need to specify it in the define-struct definition:

```
(define-struct point (x y) #:mutable)
```

Once a struct is mutable, you can modify its fields with the corresponding set-struct-field! procedure:

```
(set-point-x! p1 5)
(set-point-y! p1 6)
```

After these operations, p1 will have x equal to 5 and y equal to 6.

Struct Predicate Functions

The predicate function generated by define-struct checks if a given instance is of the specified struct type. Predicate functions return #t if the argument is of the respective struct type and #f otherwise:

```
(if (point? p1)
    (display "p1 is a point")
    (display "p1 is not a point"))
```

In this example, the check point?(p1) returns #t, and p1 is a point is displayed.

Nested Structs

Structs can contain other structs as fields. To illustrate, consider the following nested struct definitions:

```
(define-struct date (day month year))
(define-struct person (name birthdate))
```

You can create a person struct with a date as the birthdate field:

```
(define birth (make-date 14 3 1990))
(define person1 (make-person "Alice" birth))
```

Accessing the fields of the nested structs involves chaining the selector functions:

```
(define birth-year (date-year (person-birthdate person1)))
```

This code assigns 1990 to birth-year.

Record Types

Records in Scheme provide a lower-level and more customizable mechanism to define data structures compared to structs. The mechanism of records provides greater flexibility in terms of field names and behaviors. It is implemented using the R⁶RS define-record-type syntax.

The following is an example of defining and using records:

```
(define-record-type point
  (fields (mutable x) (mutable y)))

(define p1 (make-point 'x 1 'y 2))

(protocol (getter (opt 1) getter-name)
(read p1 'x)) ;=> 1

(protocol (setter (opt 1) setter-name)
(set! (read p1 'x) 3)
(read p1 'x)) ;=> 3
```

The example demonstrates the creation of a point record with x and y fields. Field access and modification are straightforward, achieving mutable semantics for those fields.

Schemes's struct and record facilities provide powerful and flexible ways to encapsulate and manage related data. Proper use of these abstractions can lead to code that is easier to maintain and understand. Ensuring that the structures appropriately encapsulate behavior related to the data they manage helps in maintaining clear, modular, and reusable code.

Chapter 4

Control Structures and Recursion

This chapter introduces the control structures in Scheme, focusing on conditionals like 'if', 'cond', and 'case', as well as boolean logic operations such as 'and', 'or', and 'not'. It covers loops and iterative constructs like 'do' and 'let', and the sequencing of expressions using 'begin'. The concept and implementation of recursion are thoroughly explored, including simple and tail-recursive functions, mutual recursion, and advanced recursive patterns. Practical applications of recursion for list processing and its combination with higher-order functions are also discussed.

4.1 Introduction to Control Structures in Scheme

Control structures are fundamental components of any programming language, determining the flow of execution within a program. Scheme, a dialect of Lisp, provides a rich set of control structures that allow for powerful and flexible programming paradigms. The primary control structures in Scheme include conditionals, loops, and recursive constructs.

Scheme uses a minimalist approach to control structures, favoring a small number of powerful constructs over a large number of specialized ones. This approach aligns with the language's design philosophy of simplicity and elegance, enabling programmers to construct sophisticated control flows through composition and abstraction.

Conditionals in Scheme are primarily managed through the if, cond, and case expressions. Each of these has unique characteristics and use-cases, yet they all serve the purpose of directing the program to execute certain expressions based on specified conditions.

The if expression is the simplest form of conditional control in Scheme. It takes a predicate (a boolean expression) and two branches: one to execute if the predicate is true, and another (optional) branch if the predicate is false. The syntax for if is as follows:

```
(if predicate
    consequent
    alternative)
```

If the predicate evaluates to true, the consequent expression is evaluated; otherwise, the alternative expression (if provided) is evaluated.

The cond expression is more powerful and versatile. It allows for multiple conditional branches, enabling more complex decision-making processes. The cond expression evaluates a series of predicate-expression pairs in sequence and executes the expression corresponding to the first true predicate. The syntax of cond is as follows:

```
(cond ((predicate1) expression1)
      ((predicate2) expression2)
      ...
      (else default-expression))
```

The else clause is a catch-all that executes if none of the preceding predicates evaluate to true. This makes cond an essential construct for handling more elaborate conditional logic in Scheme programs.

The case expression is used for multi-way branching based on the value of a single expression. Unlike cond, case matches the evaluated expression against a series of possible values, executing the corresponding expression for the first matching value. The case syntax is:

```
(case key
  ((value1) expression1)
  ((value2) expression2)
  ...
  (else default-expression))
```

Boolean Logic in Scheme involves the use of and, or, and not operators to combine or invert boolean expressions. These operators are essential in constructing complex predicates that control the flow of conditional expressions.

Looping constructs in Scheme include do and let, which facilitate iterative execution of expressions. The do loop provides a comprehensive mechanism for iteration with initialization, termination, and update expressions. Its syntax is complex but powerful:

```
(do ((var1 init1 update1)
     ...
     (varN initN updateN))
   (test result)
  body ...)
```

The let bindings, although primarily used for creating local variables, can be leveraged to construct loops, particularly through recursive function calls.

The begin expression allows for sequencing multiple expressions, evaluating them in order, and returning the value of the last expression. This is invaluable in scenarios where side-effects (e.g., I/O operations) require precise ordering.

Recursion is a cornerstone of Scheme programming, enabling the definition of functions that call themselves, either directly or indirectly. Simple recursion involves functions that solve problems by reducing them to smaller instances of the same problem. Tail recursion optimization in Scheme is a significant feature, enabling functions to call themselves without growing the call stack, making recursive patterns efficient and scalable.

Here is an example of a simple recursive function, which calculates the factorial of a number:

```
(define (factorial n)
  (if (= n 0)
      1
      (* n (factorial (- n 1)))))
```

In Scheme, mutual recursion occurs when two or more functions are defined in terms of each other, offering a robust mechanism for dealing with problems that naturally decompose into interrelated parts.

These elements form the foundation of control structures in Scheme. Mastery of these constructs is essential for leveraging the full power of the language, enabling the development of concise, expressive, and efficient programs.

4.2 Conditionals: 'if', 'cond', and 'case'

In Scheme, control structures are fundamental for decision-making processes within a program. The primary conditional constructs are if, cond, and case. Understanding these constructs is essential for implementing logic that varies based on the evaluation of conditions.

if **Construct**

The if construct in Scheme is a basic conditional expression. It evaluates a provided condition and executes one of two possible branches based on the condition's result. The general syntax of the if construct is as follows:

```
(if condition then-expression else-expression)
```

Here, condition is an expression that evaluates to either #t (true) or #f (false). If condition evaluates to true, the then-expression is executed; otherwise, the else-expression is executed.

Consider the following example, which determines if a number is positive:

```
(if (> x 0)
    'positive
    'non-positive)
```

If x is greater than 0, the expression evaluates to 'positive; otherwise, it evaluates to 'non-positive.

cond **Construct**

For more complex decision-making requiring multiple conditions, the cond construct is used. It provides a way to express a sequence of condition-action pairs. The general syntax of the cond construct is:

```
(cond
  (condition1 expression1)
  (condition2 expression2)
  ...
  (else default-expression))
```

Each condition is evaluated in sequence. When a condition evaluates to true, the corresponding expression is executed, and the cond construct terminates. The else clause is optional and serves as a default action if none of the conditions are true.

Consider the following example, which categorizes an integer into positive, negative, or zero:

```
(cond
  ((> x 0) 'positive)
  ((< x 0) 'negative)
  (else 'zero))
```

Here, cond evaluates the conditions in order. If x is greater than 0, 'positive is returned. If x is less than 0, 'negative is returned. If neither condition is true, the else clause is executed, returning 'zero.

case Construct

The case construct is utilized for scenarios where an expression is compared against a set of potential values. It is analogous to the switch statement in other programming languages. The general syntax for the case construct is:

```
(case key
  ((datum1 datum2 ...) expression1)
  ((datum3 datum4 ...) expression2)
  ...
  (else default-expression))
```

The key expression is evaluated once and compared against the provided datums. When a match is found, the corresponding expression is executed. The else clause is optional and serves as a fallback if no matches are found.

Consider the following example, which assigns a color based on an integer code:

```
(case color-code
  ((1 2 3) 'red)
  ((4 5 6) 'green)
  ((7 8 9) 'blue)
  (else 'unknown))
```

If color-code evaluates to 1, 2, or 3, the expression returns 'red. If color-code is 4, 5, or 6, 'green is returned. If color-code is 7, 8, or 9, 'blue is returned. If none of these cases match, the else clause returns 'unknown.

Overall, using if, cond, and case constructs allows a Scheme programmer to implement sophisticated decision-making logic within their programs, enhancing both readability and functionality.

4.3 Boolean Logic: 'and', 'or', and 'not'

Boolean logic is a critical component of control structures in Scheme, providing the foundation for making decisions and controlling the flow of execution based on logical conditions. The primary logical operators in Scheme are and, or, and not. Each of these operators is essential for constructing complex logical expressions and implementing conditional logic.

The and operator evaluates multiple expressions and returns #f (false) as soon as one of the expressions evaluates to #f; otherwise, it returns the value of the last expression if all expressions are true. The or operator evaluates multiple expressions and returns the value of the first expression that is not #f; if all expressions are false, it returns #f. The not operator returns #t (true) if the expression evaluates to #f, and #f if the expression evaluates to #t.

```
(and expr1 expr2 ... exprN)
(or expr1 expr2 ... exprN)
(not expr)
```

The and Operator

The and operator is used to ensure that multiple conditions are all true. If any of the conditions are false, the entire expression evaluates to false.

```
(and (> 5 3) (< 10 20)) ; Returns #t because both expressions are true
(and (> 5 3) (< 10 5)) ; Returns #f because the second expression is false
(and) ; Returns #t since there are no expressions to evaluate
```

In the above examples: - The first and expression evaluates to #t because both conditions (> 5 3) and (< 10 20) are true. - The second and expression evaluates to #f because the condition (< 10 5) is false. - The third and expression evaluates to #t by default, as an empty and returns true.

The or Operator

The or operator evaluates a series of expressions and returns true as soon as any expression evaluates to true.

```
(or (> 5 3) (< 10 20)) ; Returns #t because the first expression is true
(or (< 5 3) (> 10 20)) ; Returns #f because both expressions are false
(or) ; Returns #f since there are no expressions to evaluate
```

In these examples: - The first or expression evaluates to #t because (> 5 3) is true. - The second or expression evaluates to #f because both conditions $(< 5\ 3)$ and $(> 10\ 20)$ are false. - The third or expression evaluates to #f by default, as an empty or returns false.

The not Operator

The not operator negates the truth value of its single argument, making true values false and false values true.

```
(not #t) ; Returns #f
(not #f) ; Returns #t
(not (> 5 3)) ; Returns #f because (> 5 3) is true
```

In these examples: - The first not expression evaluates to #f because the original value is #t. - The second not expression evaluates to #t because the original value is #f. - The third not expression evaluates to #f because $(> 5\ 3)$ is true.

Combining Boolean Operators

Scheme allows combining and, or, and not to form more complex logical expressions.

```
(and (or (> 5 3) (< 1 0)) (not (= 3 4))) ; Returns #t
```

In this complex expression: - The or expression $(> 5\ 3)$ $(< 1\ 0)$ evaluates to #t because $(> 5\ 3)$ is true. - The not expression $(= 3\ 4)$ evaluates to #t because $(3\ 4)$ is false. - Therefore, the and expression combining these results evaluates to #t.

4.4 Loops and Iteration: 'do' and 'let' Constructs

Scheme supports iterative processes through constructs such as do and let. Both constructs enable the implementation of loops, which are a fundamental aspect of control flow in programming. This section delves into the syntax and practical applications of these constructs, illustrating their versatility and efficiency.

The do construct in Scheme provides a flexible way to implement loops with an explicit form for initialization, termination, and iterative step expressions.

```
(do ((<variable1> <init1> <step1>)
     (<variable2> <init2> <step2>)
     ...)
   (<test> <result>)
  <body>)
```

Explanation of the do construct syntax:

- The loop begins with the do keyword.
- The variables $variable1, variable2, \ldots$ are initialized with $init1, init2, \ldots$.
- On each iteration, each variable is updated with the corresponding step expression.
- The loop terminates when the test expression evaluates to true. If the test returns true, the loop returns the result expression.
- The body contains the expressions executed on each loop iteration.

Consider an example where we calculate the sum of the first n integers using the do loop:

```
(define (sum-n n)
  (do ((i 0 (+ i 1))
       (sum 0 (+ sum i)))
      ((> i n) sum)))
```

```
> (sum-n 5)
15
```

In this example:

- The variables i and sum are initialized to 0.
- i is incremented by 1 and sum is incremented by i in each iteration.
- The loop terminates when i exceeds n, returning the sum.

The let construct, while primarily a binding construct, can also facilitate iteration through recursion. The named-let or let loop pattern is especially useful for this purpose. The syntax is as follows:

```
(let loop ((<variable1> <init1>)
           (<variable2> <init2>)
           ...)
  (if <test>
      <result>
      (loop <step1> <step2> ...)))
```

The named let introduces a local function named loop (or any name chosen), which can be recursively called to simulate iteration.

Consider an example where we calculate the factorial of a number using the let construct:

```
(define (factorial n)
  (let fact ((i n)
             (acc 1))
    (if (= i 0)
        acc
        (fact (- i 1) (* acc i)))))
```

```
> (factorial 5)
120
```

In this example:

- The function fact is defined using let.
- The variables i (initially n) and acc (initially 1) are iteratively updated.
- The loop continues until i is zero, at which point the accumulator acc holds the factorial.

Combining do and let, you can create more complex iterative processes. For instance, consider the task of computing the greatest common divisor (GCD) using Euclid's algorithm with iteration:

```
(define (gcd a b)
  (do ((x a (abs (- x y)))
       (y b (min x y)))
     ((= y 0) x)))
```

```
> (gcd 48 18)
6
```

Here, x and y are iteratively updated using Euclid's algorithm until y is zero, at which point x is the GCD.

Understanding and utilizing do and let constructs effectively equips programmers with powerful tools for crafting iterative processes in Scheme. They add to the flexibility and capability of Scheme, complementing the language's functional paradigms.

4.5 Using 'begin' for Sequencing Expressions

The begin construct in Scheme is used for sequencing multiple expressions, ensuring they are evaluated in the specified order. This sequencing is essential in scenarios where the order of operations affects the program's behavior or where side-effects occur, such as printing output or modifying variables. The begin expression evaluates its subexpressions in sequence and returns the value of the last expression.

begin follows the syntax:

```
(begin expr1 expr2 ... exprn)
```

Here, expr1 through exprn represent the expressions to be executed sequentially. Consider an example where multiple arithmetic operations and a variable assignment are performed within a single begin expression:

```
(define x 0)
(begin
  (set! x (+ x 1))
  (set! x (* x 2))
  x)
```

In this example: 1. set! x (+ x 1) increments x by 1, making x equal to 1. 2. set! x (* x 2) then multiplies x by 2, resulting in x equal to 2. 3. x returns the final value of x, which is 2.

The entire begin expression above would evaluate to 2, demonstrating how each subexpression is executed in sequence.

The begin construct becomes particularly useful when combined with control structures and other expressions that need to be evaluated in a specific order. For example, when using conditionals with side-effecting operations:

```
(if (> 5 3)
    (begin
      (display "Condition is true\n")
      (set! x 10))
    (begin
      (display "Condition is false\n")
      (set! x -10)))
```

In this example, if the condition > 5 3 is true, the subexpressions within the first begin block are executed, printing "Condition is true" and setting x to 10. If the condition was false, the subexpressions within the second begin block would execute, printing "Condition is false" and setting x to -10. This illustrates how begin can be used to sequence side-effecting operations in branches of conditionals.

begin also plays a significant role in function definitions, especially when defining helper procedures or performing initialization steps before returning a result. Suppose a function needs to compute and print intermediate results before returning the final value:

```
(define (process-and-sum a b)
  (begin
    (display "Processing the first argument\n")
    (let ((result-a (* a 2)))
      (display (string-append "Result-A: " (number->string result-a) "\n")))
    (display "Processing the second argument\n")
    (let ((result-b (+ b 3)))
      (display (string-append "Result-B: " (number->string result-b) "\n")))
    (+ (* a 2) (+ b 3))))
```

In this process-and-sum example: 1. "Processing the first argument" is printed. 2. result-a is calculated and printed. 3. "Processing the second argument" is printed. 4. result-b is calculated and printed. 5. Finally, the function returns the sum of result-a and result-b.

To demonstrate the output, evaluating the function with arguments 3 and 4 yields:

```
Processing the first argument
Result-A: 6
Processing the second argument
Result-B: 7
13
```

Each step is performed in the sequence specified by begin, ensuring the correct order of operations.

Another practical application of begin is within loops and iterative constructs. For instance, using the do loop:

```
(define (iterate-over-list lst)
  (do ((n 0 (+ n 1)))
      ((>= n (length lst)))
    (begin
      (display "Element: ")
      (display (list-ref lst n))
      (newline))))

(iterate-over-list '(10 20 30))
```

This loop iterates over each element in the list lst, printing each element in sequence. The begin expression ensures that both the display and newline operations are executed for each iteration.

Evaluating iterate-over-list with the list (10 20 30) gives:

```
Element: 10
Element: 20
Element: 30
```

The begin construct is essential for scenarios where expressions must be executed sequentially, ensuring side-effects occur in the correct order and enabling complex operations to be structured logically. This functionality enhances the control and readability of Scheme programs, facilitating precise execution flow management and effective debugging.

4.6 The Concept of Recursion

In computer science, recursion is a fundamental concept that plays a crucial role in both algorithm design and the functional programming paradigm. Recursion occurs when a function calls itself directly or indirectly, allowing problems to be defined in terms of simpler subproblems. This section delves into the concept of recursion in Scheme, illustrating its syntax, mechanics, and practical applications.

A recursive function consists of two essential components: the base case and the recursive step. The base case provides a condition under which the recursion terminates, preventing infinite recursion. The recursive step breaks the problem into smaller instances of the same problem, progressively moving towards the base case.

Consider the simple example of a factorial function defined recursively. The factorial of a non-negative integer n, denoted $n!$, is defined as:

$$n! = \begin{cases} 1 & \text{if } n = 0 \\ n \times (n-1)! & \text{if } n > 0 \end{cases}$$

The corresponding Scheme implementation of the factorial function is as follows:

```
(define (factorial n)
  (if (= n 0)
      1
      (* n (factorial (- n 1)))))
```

In this example, the base case is $n = 0$, returning 1. The recursive step reduces the problem by calling factorial with $n - 1$.

To understand the flow of a recursive function, consider the evaluation of $(\text{factorial } 3)$:

1. $(\text{factorial } 3)$ results in: $3 \times (\text{factorial } 2)$ 2. $(\text{factorial } 2)$ results in: $2 \times (\text{factorial } 1)$ 3. $(\text{factorial } 1)$ results in: $1 \times (\text{factorial } 0)$ 4. $(\text{factorial } 0)$ results in: 1

Combining these results, we get:

$$3 \times (2 \times (1 \times 1)) = 6$$

Recursion is not limited to numerical computations; it can be effectively used for list processing. For instance, consider a function that sums the elements of a list:

```
(define (sum-list lst)
  (if (null? lst)
      0
      (+ (car lst) (sum-list (cdr lst)))))
```

In this function, the base case is (null? lst), where an empty list returns 0. The recursive step adds the first element of the list (car lst) to the sum of the remaining elements (sum-list (cdr lst)).

Evaluating (sum-list '(1 2 3)), the function steps are:

1. (sum-list '(1 2 3)) results in: $1 + $(sum-list '(2 3)) 2. (sum-list '(2 3)) results in: $2+$(sum-list '(3)) 3. (sum-list '(3)) results in: $3+$(sum-list '()) 4. (sum-list '()) results in: 0

Thus, the result is $1 + (2 + (3 + 0)) = 6$.

Recursive functions can be designed efficiently by ensuring they meet the base case correctly and by correctly structuring the recursive step to approach the base case. Recursive thinking often provides elegant solutions, especially in functional programming languages like Scheme.

The principle of recursion can also be visualized through the concept of a call stack, where each recursive call adds a new frame to the stack, maintaining the state of the computation. Once the base case is reached, these frames are popped off the stack in reverse order, completing the computation.

Considerations for the efficient implementation of recursion involve recognizing when to use tail recursion. Tail recursion is a special case of recursion where the recursive call is the final action in the function. Tail-recursive functions are optimized by Scheme compilers to reuse stack frames, improving performance and preventing stack overflow.

Understanding and correctly applying recursion in Scheme allows for solving complex problems with simplicity and clarity, embracing the functional programming paradigm's core principles.

4.7 Simple Recursive Functions

Scheme, as a functional programming language, heavily relies on recursive functions to solve problems that might otherwise require iterative approaches. Recursive functions are defined in terms of themselves and typically consist of a base case and a recursive call. The base case provides a terminating scenario that prevents infinite loops, while the recursive call processes the data by reducing its size or complexity step by step until reaching the base case.

A fundamental example of a simple recursive function is the calculation of the factorial of a number. The factorial of a non-negative integer n, denoted as $n!$, is the product of all positive integers less than or equal to n. Mathematically, this is defined as:

$$n! = \begin{cases} 1 & \text{if } n = 0, \\ n \times (n-1)! & \text{if } n > 0. \end{cases}$$

This definition translates naturally into a Scheme function:

```
(define (factorial n)
  (if (= n 0)
      1
      (* n (factorial (- n 1)))))
```

Here, the base case is when n equals 0, for which the function returns 1. Otherwise, it multiplies n by the factorial of $n - 1$, thus reducing the problem size with each recursive call until the base case is reached.

Another classical example of a recursive function is the computation of Fibonacci numbers. The Fibonacci sequence is defined as follows:

$$F(n) = \begin{cases} 0 & \text{if } n = 0, \\ 1 & \text{if } n = 1, \\ F(n-1) + F(n-2) & \text{if } n > 1. \end{cases}$$

Expressing the above in Scheme results in:

```
(define (fibonacci n)
  (cond ((= n 0) 0)
        ((= n 1) 1)
        (else (+ (fibonacci (- n 1))
                 (fibonacci (- n 2))))))
```

This implementation uses the cond conditional structure to handle the multiple base cases (when n is 0 or 1) and the recursive case (when n is greater than 1).

Recursion is particularly advantageous when processing lists. For example, consider a function that computes the length of a list. The base case for an empty list returns 0, while for a non-empty list, the function reduces the problem by recursively computing the length of the tail (rest of the list) and adding one:

```
(define (list-length lst)
  (if (null? lst)
      0
      (+ 1 (list-length (cdr lst)))))
```

In the above example, (null? lst) checks if the list is empty. If it is, the function returns 0. Otherwise, it adds 1 to the length of the rest of the list, which is obtained by recursively calling list-length on (cdr lst) (where cdr retrieves the tail of the list).

Recursive functions can also be used to perform transformations on lists. Consider a function that doubles each element in a list:

```
(define (double-list lst)
  (if (null? lst)
      '()
      (cons (* 2 (car lst))
            (double-list (cdr lst)))))
```

This function checks if the list is empty. If it is, it returns an empty list. Otherwise, it constructs a new list (cons) where the head is twice the first element of the original list (car lst) and the tail is the result of recursively doubling the rest of the list (double-list (cdr lst)).

Recursion can also be applied to more complex data structures. For example, consider computing the depth of a nested list, where the depth of an atom is 0, and the depth of a list is 1 plus the maximum depth of its elements:

```
(define (depth lst)
  (if (atom? lst)
      0
      (+ 1 (apply max (map depth lst)))))
```

Here, the base case checks if the list is an atom using (atom? lst); if it is, it returns 0. Otherwise, it uses map to apply the depth function to each element of the list and apply to find the maximum depth among those elements, adding 1 to account for the current list level.

The examples provided demonstrate how recursion in Scheme simplifies problem-solving for various data structures and computations.

When implementing recursive functions, careful attention must be given to defining base cases properly and ensuring recursive calls move towards these base cases to prevent infinite recursion.

4.8 Tail Recursion and its Optimization

Tail recursion is an essential concept in Scheme programming and functional programming in general. A function is tail-recursive if the recursive call is the last operation in the function. This means that the function does not need to perform any additional work after the recursive call returns. This characteristic allows the Scheme interpreter to optimize tail-recursive functions by reusing the current function's stack frame for the recursive call, thereby saving memory and preventing stack overflow errors.

Tail Recursion can be elucidated with a detailed Scheme example. Consider the simple case of calculating the factorial of a number. A non-tail-recursive version of the factorial function is written as follows:

```
(define (factorial n)
  (if (= n 0)
      1
      (* n (factorial (- n 1)))))
```

In this version, the multiplication operation (* n ...) needs to be performed after the recursive call to factorial, meaning it is not tail-recursive. This can lead to deep recursion and potentially a stack overflow for large values of n.

To convert this into a tail-recursive version, consider using an auxiliary function with an accumulator argument that carries the result of the calculations through the recursive calls:

```
(define (factorial n)
  (define (iter n acc)
    (if (= n 0)
        acc
        (iter (- n 1) (* n acc))))
  (iter n 1))
```

In this tail-recursive version, the recursive call to iter is the last operation performed in the iter function. The Scheme interpreter can optimize this version by reusing the current stack frame, making it significantly more memory efficient.

The concept of Tail Call Optimization (TCO) is crucial for understanding how tail recursion benefits performance. TCO refers to the process by which an interpreter or compiler recognizes a function call as tail-recursive and optimizes it, typically by eliminating the need to allocate a new stack frame for the call. Because of this, tail-recursive functions can run in constant stack space, allowing for potentially infinite recursion without growing the stack.

It is essential to identify tail-recursive patterns and refactor functions accordingly. Here's another example involving the summation of a list of numbers:

```
(define (sum-list lst)
  (if (null? lst)
      0
      (+ (car lst) (sum-list (cdr lst)))))
```

This version is not tail-recursive because the addition operation occurs after the recursive call to sum-list. To refactor it into a tail-recursive version, introduce an auxiliary function with an accumulator:

```
(define (sum-list lst)
  (define (iter lst acc)
    (if (null? lst)
        acc
        (iter (cdr lst) (+ (car lst) acc))))
  (iter lst 0))
```

Here, the recursive call to iter is the last operation performed, making it tail-recursive. The accumulator acc accumulates the total sum through each iteration, and once the list is fully traversed, the accumulated value is returned.

Understanding and applying tail recursion and its optimization is essential when working with large data sets or when recursion depth can be significantly deep. Language implementations like Scheme inherently support TCO, but it is still the programmer's responsibility to write functions in a tail-recursive manner to leverage this powerful feature fully.

Conventionally, identifying candidate functions for tail recursion involves checking for operations that rely on the results of the recursive calls and then restructuring such functions to pass intermediate states through accumulator parameters. The benefits include enhanced performance and avoidance of stack overflow errors, making tail recursion a cornerstone technique in efficient Scheme programming.

4.9 Mutual Recursion

Mutual recursion occurs when two or more functions are defined in terms of each other. This technique is essential in scenarios where the problem domain can be naturally divided into distinct, yet interdependent, parts. In Scheme, mutual recursion can be implemented by defining functions that call each other in their bodies, leveraging the language's support for nested function definitions.

Consider two simple functions, even? and odd?, which determine the parity of a number. Here, even? determines if a number is even by checking if subtracting 1 makes it odd, and odd? checks if subtracting 1 makes it even. These functions are classic examples of mutual recursion:

```
(define (even? n)
  (if (= n 0)
      #t
      (odd? (- n 1))))

(define (odd? n)
  (if (= n 0)
      #f
      (even? (- n 1))))
```

In this example, even? calls odd? and vice versa. This mutual calling continues until the base case is reached, where n is zero. If n is zero, even? returns true because zero is even, and odd? returns false because zero is not odd.

The core idea of mutual recursion is prevalent in various algorithms, including those dealing with grammatical parsing and state transitions in finite automata. To further illustrate the concept, let's consider a more complex mutual recursion scenario involving a pair of functions to check for balanced parentheses in a string.

First, let's define a function balanced? which determines if an entire string contains balanced parentheses. This function will call another helper function bal-helper, which processes the string recursively:

```
(define (balanced? str)
  (bal-helper str 0))

(define (bal-helper str depth)
  (cond ((null? str) (= depth 0))
        ((char=? (car str) #\() (bal-helper (cdr str) (+ depth 1)))
        ((char=? (car str) #\)) (and (> depth 0) (bal-helper (cdr str) (- depth 1))))
        (else (bal-helper (cdr str) depth))))
```

In this example, mutually recursive calls are not strictly between distinct functions but rather between the initial function balanced? and its helper bal-helper. The helper function bal-helper manages the state depth, representing the number of unclosed '('. When depth becomes negative or nonzero at the end of the string, the parentheses are unbalanced.

To deepen our understanding, let's consider an additional example involving mutual recursion for navigating binary trees. Assume we have two functions, traverse-left and traverse-right, that navigate the left and right subtrees of a binary tree:

```
(define (traverse-left tree)
  (if (null? tree)
      '()
      (cons (car tree)
            (traverse-right (cdr tree)))))

(define (traverse-right tree)
  (if (null? tree)
      '()
      (cons (car tree)
            (traverse-left (cdr tree)))))
```

Here, traverse-left moves to the right after processing the current node, and traverse-right moves to the left. This mutual recursion ensures that both subtrees are traversed completely.

Care must be taken when using mutual recursion to ensure that termination conditions are well-defined to avoid infinite loops. Proper base cases must be included in all mutually recursive functions.

Finally, it's worth highlighting the power of mutual recursion in depicting complex relationships via function interdependence. With practice, this programming technique can become an invaluable tool in any Scheme programmer's arsenal, enabling elegant and efficient solutions to multifaceted problems.

4.10 Using Recursion for List Processing

In Scheme programming, recursion is a fundamental technique used extensively for list processing. Scheme's elegant handling of lists and its powerful support for recursive definitions enable succinct and expressive solutions to common problems.

When working with lists, recursive functions often exhibit a similar pattern: processing the head (the first element) of the list and then recursively processing the tail (the rest of the list). This section explores various list processing techniques using recursive functions.

Basic List Traversal

Consider a simple task of calculating the sum of all elements in a list. The recursive approach can be outlined as follows: 1. If the list is empty, the sum is 0. 2. If the list is not empty, the sum is the first element plus the sum of the rest of the list.

Using Scheme, this can be implemented as:

```
(define (sum-list lst)
  (if (null? lst)
      0
      (+ (car lst) (sum-list (cdr lst)))))
```

This function works by first checking if the list is null (empty). If it is, it returns 0. Otherwise, it returns the sum of the first element (obtained using car) and the recursive call on the rest of the list (obtained using cdr).

Mapping Functions

Another common operation on lists is mapping a function over each element of the list to produce a new list. For example, doubling each element in a list can be performed using recursion:

```
(define (double-list lst)
  (if (null? lst)
      '()
      (cons (* 2 (car lst)) (double-list (cdr lst)))))
```

In this function, if the list is empty, it returns an empty list. Otherwise, it constructs a new list with the first element doubled and recursively processes the rest of the list. The cons function constructs a new list by combining the doubled first element and the result of the recursive call.

Filtering Lists

Filtering elements from a list based on a predicate function is another important list operation. For example, extracting even numbers from a list can be done as follows:

```
(define (filter-even lst)
  (cond
    ((null? lst) '())
    ((even? (car lst)) (cons (car lst) (filter-even (cdr lst))))
    (else (filter-even (cdr lst)))))
```

This function uses cond to handle multiple conditions. If the list is empty, it returns an empty list. If the first element is even, it adds it to the result of recursively filtering the rest of the list. Otherwise, it continues filtering the rest of the list without including the current element.

Flattening Nested Lists

Flattening a nested list structure (a list containing other lists) into a single list can be achieved recursively. Here is an example function:

```
(define (flatten lst)
  (cond
    ((null? lst) '())
    ((list? (car lst)) (append (flatten (car lst)) (flatten (cdr lst))))
    (else (cons (car lst) (flatten (cdr lst))))))
```

In this function, if the list is empty, it returns an empty list. If the first element is a list, it flattens both the first element and the rest of the list and then appends them. If the first element is not a list, it is added to the result of flattening the rest of the list.

Advanced Applications: Folding (Reducing) Lists

Folding, or reducing, is a powerful higher-order function that applies a binary operation recursively to a list, effectively reducing the list to a single value. Scheme provides a built-in fold function, but it can also be implemented using recursion:

```
(define (fold f initial lst)
  (if (null? lst)
      initial
      (f (car lst) (fold f initial (cdr lst)))))
```

Here, fold takes a function f, an initial value, and a list. It recursively applies f to the current element and the result of folding the rest of the list. For instance, summing a list can be redefined using fold:

```
(define (sum-list lst)
  (fold + 0 lst))
```

The power and flexibility of recursion in list processing become evident when considering complex data manipulations, wherein these recursive patterns can be nested and combined to perform intricate computations efficiently.

4.11 Advanced Recursive Patterns

Understanding advanced recursive patterns opens up numerous possibilities for efficient and elegant problem-solving in Scheme. This section explores sophisticated techniques such as accumulative recursion, continuation-passing style, and the Y-combinator, providing users with tools to implement complex operations effectively.

Accumulative Recursion:

Accumulative recursion, also recognized as *accumulative parameter recursion*, involves passing an additional parameter, commonly known as an accumulator, that aggregates information as the recursion progresses. This technique builds upon the idea of tail recursion, often making recursive algorithms more efficient.

Consider the problem of finding the sum of elements in a list. A naive recursive approach would involve a straightforward function that traverses the list:

```
(define (sum-list lst)
  (if (null? lst)
      0
      (+ (car lst) (sum-list (cdr lst)))))
```

However, this approach is not tail-recursive. To convert it into an accumulative recursive form, we introduce an accumulator parameter:

```
(define (sum-list-acc lst acc)
  (if (null? lst)
      acc
      (sum-list-acc (cdr lst) (+ acc (car lst)))))
```

We must now provide an initial call to our function with the accumulator initialized to 0:

```
(sum-list-acc '(1 2 3 4) 0)
```

resulting in:

```
10
```

Continuation-Passing Style (CPS):

Continuation-passing style (CPS) transforms traditional function calls to accept an additional argument—the continuation—which represents the rest of the computation. This style is essential for various advanced techniques, such as implementing backtracking algorithms and handling asynchronous operations.

To illustrate CPS, we first define a simple factorial function, then convert it to CPS.

Standard factorial function:

```
(define (factorial n)
  (if (zero? n)
      1
      (* n (factorial (- n 1)))))
```

Transforming the factorial function into CPS involves adding a continuation parameter cont:

```
(define (factorial-cps n cont)
  (if (zero? n)
      (cont 1)
      (factorial-cps (- n 1)
                     (lambda (result)
                       (cont (* n result))))))
```

We call our CPS function with an identity continuation:

```
(factorial-cps 5 (lambda (x) x))
```

producing:

```
120
```

Y-Combinator:

The Y-combinator is a fixed-point combinator enabling the definition of recursive functions without self-references. The concept relies on higher-order functions and is a core feature in lambda calculus. Implementing the Y-combinator in Scheme provides a profound understanding of how recursion can be framed purely in functional terms.

The Y-combinator can be defined as follows:

```
(define Y
  (lambda (r)
    ((lambda (x) (r (lambda (v) ((x x) v))))
     (lambda (x) (r (lambda (v) ((x x) v)))))))
```

We can now use the Y-combinator to define a recursive factorial function:

```
((Y (lambda (fact)
      (lambda (n)
        (if (zero? n)
            1
            (* n (fact (- n 1)))))))
 5)
```

producing:

The Y-combinator is particularly useful in environments where direct recursive definitions are restricted, emphasizing the power of fixed-point combinators in theoretical computer science.

Advanced recursive patterns such as accumulative recursion, CPS, and the Y-combinator are pivotal for developing complex algorithms, offering efficient and versatile approaches to problem-solving in Scheme.

4.12 Combining Recursion with Higher-Order Functions

In Scheme, higher-order functions are a powerful feature that allows functions to be passed as arguments or returned as results. When combined with recursion, higher-order functions enable the creation of highly expressive and modular code. This section delves into various aspects of combining recursion with higher-order functions, with illustrative examples to demonstrate key concepts.

A higher-order function is any function that takes one or more functions as arguments or returns a function. Examples of common higher-order functions include map, filter, and fold (also known as reduce). The combination of these higher-order functions with recursive functions allows for the elegant expression of complex computations.

```
(define (map f lst)
  (if (null? lst)
      '()
      (cons (f (car lst)) (map f (cdr lst)))))
```

In the map function defined above, f is a function that is applied to each element of the list lst. The function is recursive: it processes the head of the list with the function f, then recursively maps the rest of the list. This is a straightforward example of combining recursion with a higher-order function.

```
(define (filter pred lst)
  (if (null? lst)
      '()
      (let ((rest (filter pred (cdr lst))))
        (if (pred (car lst))
            (cons (car lst) rest)
            rest))))
```

The filter function applies a predicate function pred to each element of the list lst, returning a list of elements for which the predicate holds true. The recursion is evident in the way filter calls itself to process the rest of the list.

Consider a more advanced example where we use foldl (left fold) and foldr (right fold) functions. These are higher-order functions that accumulate a result by iterating over a list and applying a function.

```
(define (foldl f acc lst)
  (if (null? lst)
      acc
      (foldl f (f acc (car lst)) (cdr lst))))

(define (foldr f acc lst)
  (if (null? lst)
      acc
      (f (car lst) (foldr f acc (cdr lst)))))
```

foldl takes a function f, an accumulator acc, and a list lst. It applies the function from the left, each time updating the accumulator until the list is empty. Conversely, foldr applies the function from the right.

```
(define (sum lst)
  (foldl + 0 lst))

(define (product lst)
  (foldr * 1 lst))
```

Here, the sum function uses foldl to compute the sum of a list, starting with an initial accumulator of 0. Similarly, the product function uses foldr to compute the product of all elements in the list, starting with an accumulator of 1.

Combining recursion with higher-order functions can lead to the creation of efficient and compact code. This is particularly useful in functional programming paradigms. For instance, consider the problem of mapping a function over a nested list structure:

```
(define (map-nested f lst)
  (map (lambda (elm)
         (if (list? elm)
             (map-nested f elm)
             (f elm)))
       lst))
```

In this function, map-nested recursively maps the function f to each element of a possibly nested list. The lambda function checks if an element is a list. If so, it recursively maps f to the nested list; otherwise, it simply applies f to the element.

The expressive power of combining recursion with higher-order functions is vast. As an exercise, consider writing a flatten function that flattens a nested list into a single list of elements. This not only enhances the understanding of recursion but also provides hands-on experience with higher-order functions.

```
(define (flatten lst)
  (foldr (lambda (x acc)
           (if (list? x)
               (append (flatten x) acc)
               (cons x acc)))
         '()
         lst))
```

In the flatten function, foldr accumulates elements from the right, and if an element is a list, it recursively flattens it and appends it to the accumulator. If the element is not a list, it simply conses the element to the accumulator.

The crucial aspect of learning to combine recursion with higher-order functions lies in understanding both the recursive process and the role of higher-order functions in abstracting common patterns of computation. This enables the creation of robust, reusable code constructs that can be effectively leveraged in a variety of programming contexts.

Chapter 5

Procedures and Higher-Order Functions

This chapter explores the definition and use of procedures in Scheme, including positional and named arguments. It delves into the concept of procedures as first-class citizens, enabling the creation of anonymous functions with 'lambda' expressions. The chapter introduces higher-order functions, covering their use in mapping, filtering, and reducing lists, as well as function composition. Additionally, it examines closures, lexical scoping, and the distinctions between recursive and iterative procedures, concluding with an overview of memoization techniques and their practical applications.

5.1 Introduction to Procedures in Scheme

In Scheme, procedures (also referred to as functions or subroutines in other programming languages) serve as fundamental building blocks for constructing programs. They allow for the encapsulation of code within a reusable and portable unit, facilitating abstraction and modularity.

At the core of Scheme procedures lies the concept of applying a sequence of expressions to a set of arguments to yield a computational result. Scheme treats procedures as first-class entities, meaning they can be passed as arguments, returned as values, and assigned to variables.

define is the primary means by which procedures are declared in Scheme. The syntactic structure involves specifying the procedure name followed by its parameter list and the body containing expressions to be evaluated.

```
(define (procedure-name parameter1 parameter2 ... parameterN)
  expression1
  expression2
  ...
  expressionM)
```

A simple example to illustrate the definition and usage of a procedure in Scheme is a function to compute the square of a number:

```
(define (square x)
  (* x x))
```

In this example, the procedure square takes a single parameter x and returns the result of multiplying x by itself. This procedure can then be invoked by passing an argument:

```
(square 4)
```

16

It is crucial to note that the parentheses in Scheme denote both procedure invocation and scoping rules. In the case of procedure calls, the parentheses enclose the procedure name followed by its arguments.

Scheme procedures can also handle multiple parameters. For instance, a procedure to calculate the area of a rectangle:

```
(define (rectangle-area length width)
  (* length width))
```

Invoking rectangle-area with the arguments 5 and 3 yields:

```
(rectangle-area 5 3)
```

15

This demonstrates how Scheme procedures can accept more than one parameter to perform more complex computations.

Consider the use of local bindings within procedures, which can be achieved using the let keyword. This allows for temporary variables and makes the code more readable:

```
(define (sum-of-squares x y)
  (let ((square-x (* x x))
        (square-y (* y y)))
    (+ square-x square-y)))
```

Here, sum-of-squares computes the sum of the squares of two numbers by introducing local bindings square-x and square-y. Invoking this procedure:

```
(sum-of-squares 3 4)
```

25

Lambda calculus underpins the theoretical foundation of Scheme procedures. A lambda expression in Scheme defines an anonymous function (a function without a name). Here's how one might define the square procedure using a lambda expression:

```
(define square
  (lambda (x)
    (* x x)))
```

Invoking square with an argument behaves identically to the previous definition:

```
(square 5)
```

25

Higher-order functions, which will be covered in a subsequent section, leverage this property of functions being first-class. Scheme's concise syntax and powerful abstractions make it an effective language for composing intricate procedures from simple building blocks.

In this context, the procedural abstraction enables encapsulating repetitive logic within reusable units. This design encourages code reuse, maintainability, and a clear structure, integral to crafting robust programs in Scheme.

5.2 Defining and Calling Procedures

In Scheme, a procedure is a fundamental construct that encapsulates computations and can be invoked, or called, with a set of arguments. Procedures are defined using the define syntax alongside *lambda* expressions, which elucidate the parameters and the body of the procedure.

Procedure Definition Syntax

To define a procedure in Scheme, we use the define keyword followed by a procedure name and a lambda expression that specifies the parameters and the body. The general form is:

```
(define <procedure-name>
  (lambda (<param1> <param2> ... <paramN>)
    <procedure-body>))
```

For instance, consider a procedure to compute the square of a number:

```
(define square
  (lambda (x)
    (* x x)))
```

Invoking Procedures

Once a procedure is defined, it can be invoked by specifying its name followed by the arguments within parentheses. The general form for calling a procedure is:

```
(<procedure-name> <arg1> <arg2> ... <argN>)
```

To invoke the square procedure with an argument of 5, we write:

```
(square 5)
```

This invocation evaluates to 25 as shown:

```
25
```

Example: Defining and Calling a Procedure

Here is an example that defines a procedure to compute the greatest common divisor (GCD) using Euclid's algorithm and demonstrates how to call it:

```
(define gcd
  (lambda (a b)
    (if (= b 0)
        a
        (gcd b (mod a b)))))
```

To compute the GCD of 56 and 98, we invoke the gcd procedure:

```
(gcd 56 98)
```

The resulting output is:

```
14
```

An Alternative Notation for Procedure Definition

Scheme provides a syntactic sugar to define procedures more succinctly without explicitly using lambda. The alternative form integrates the parameters directly into the define statement:

```
(define (<procedure-name> <param1> <param2> ... <paramN>)
  <procedure-body>)
```

The square procedure using this notation becomes:

```
(define (square x)
  (* x x))
```

To calculate square(5) using the alternative notation:

```
(square 5)
```

which yields:

```
25
```

Both notations are equivalent and interchangeable, offering flexibility depending on personal preference or style guidelines.

Variadic Procedures

Scheme allows the definition of variadic procedures that can accept an arbitrary number of arguments. This is denoted by a period (.) separating required parameters from the rest arguments, which are captured as a list.

For example, a procedure to compute the sum of any number of arguments is defined as:

```
(define (sum . nums)
  (apply + nums))
```

Here, nums is a list containing all the additional arguments. To call sum with arguments 1, 2, 3, 4:

```
(sum 1 2 3 4)
```

The resulting output is:

```
10
```

Parameter Passing Mechanisms

Scheme supports positional parameters, where arguments are passed by position according to the order specified in the procedure definition. Consider a procedure to concatenate first name and last name:

```
(define (full-name first last)
  (string-append first " " last))
```

Calling the above procedure with positional arguments:

```
(full-name "John" "Doe")
```

produces the output:

```
"John Doe"
```

Understanding these elements of procedure definition and invocation lays the groundwork for advanced concepts such as higher-order functions and closure in subsequent sections.

5.3 Positional and Named Arguments

In Scheme, procedures can accept a variety of arguments that provide flexibility in how functions are defined and invoked. Understanding the mechanisms for passing these arguments—whether they are positional or named—is crucial for effective Scheme programming.

Positional Arguments

Positional arguments are the most straightforward type, where each argument is passed to the procedure in a specific order. The parameters of the procedure are defined in a list, and the actual arguments are matched to these parameters by their positions. Consider a simple example:

```
(define (add x y)
  (+ x y))
```

In this definition, x and y are positional arguments. When calling the function, the first argument provided goes to x, and the second to y:

```
(add 3 5)
```

The above call results in the value 8, as the arguments 3 and 5 are matched to x and y, respectively.

Variadic Functions

Scheme procedures can also handle a varying number of arguments using a "rest" parameter, indicated by a dot before the final parameter. This parameter collects all additional arguments into a list. For instance:

```
(define (sum . numbers)
  (apply + numbers))
```

Calling sum with any number of arguments results in their summation:

```
(sum 1 2 3 4) ; Returns 10
(sum 5 10 15) ; Returns 30
```

This shows the flexibility of positional arguments in managing multiple inputs through variadic functions.

Named Arguments (Keyword Arguments)

Named arguments, or keyword arguments, provide a means to explicitly associate values with parameters, improving readability and flexibility. While Scheme does not natively support keyword arguments as some other languages do, we can achieve similar functionality using association lists (alist) or property lists (plist).

One common approach is using an alist to simulate named arguments. Below is an example of a procedure that processes named arguments:

```
(define (make-person . args)
  (let* ((args-alist (pairlis '(:name :age :email) args))
         (name (or (assoc-ref args-alist :name) "Anonymous"))
         (age (or (assoc-ref args-alist :age) 0))
         (email (or (assoc-ref args-alist :email) "none@example.com")))
    (list :name name :age age :email email)))
```

In this function, args are converted into an association list where keywords are paired with their corresponding values. The assoc-ref function retrieves values by their keys, and or provides default values if any keys are missing.

This procedure can be called as follows:

```
(make-person "Alice" 30 "alice@example.com")
; Returns (:name "Alice" :age 30 :email "alice@example.com")

(make-person "Bob")
```

```
; Returns (:name "Bob" :age 0 :email "none@example.com")
```

The use of keyword arguments enhances the readability of function calls by clearly associating values with parameter names.

Parameter Passing Techniques

To further elucidate the usage of positional and named arguments, let's delve into an example that combines both techniques. Consider a procedure that calculates the volume of a rectangular prism, with positional arguments for mandatory dimensions and named arguments for optional parameters:

```
(define (volume length width height . optional-args)
  (let ((args-alist (pairlis '(:unit) optional-args))
        (unit (or (assoc-ref args-alist :unit) "cm^3")))
    (list :volume (* length width height) :unit unit)))
```

The mandatory dimensions (length, width, height) are passed positionally, while the optional parameter (:unit) is handled through an association list:

```
(volume 2 3 4)
; Returns (:volume 24 :unit "cm^3")

(volume 2 3 4 "m^3")
; Returns (:volume 24 :unit "m^3")
```

In this example, the volume procedure calculates the product of the dimensions and incorporates an optional unit parameter, using a default value if none is provided.

The nuanced use of positional and named arguments in Scheme thus provides powerful tools for designing flexible and expressive procedures. This versatility is further amplified when combined with higher-order functions and other advanced features in Scheme, enabling programmers to craft highly reusable and readable code.

5.4 Procedures as First-Class Citizens

In Scheme, procedures are treated as first-class citizens. This concept allows for procedures to be passed as arguments to other procedures, returned as values from procedures, and assigned to variables. By enabling such powerful abstractions, Scheme facilitates the creation of more modular and reusable code. This section details the facets of first-class procedures and how to leverage them effectively in Scheme programming.

First-class means that procedures behave like any other data type, providing flexibility and expressiveness in program design. To illustrate this, consider an example where a procedure is assigned to a variable:

```
(define (square x)
  (* x x))

(define sq square)
(sq 4) ; Returns 16
```

In this code, the square procedure is assigned to the variable sq. Invoking sq with an argument of 4 correctly returns 16, demonstrating that sq is a valid alias for the square procedure.

Procedures can also be passed as arguments to other procedures. This capability is fundamental for higher-order functions, which we discuss in subsequent sections. Here is an example showcasing passing a procedure as an argument:

```
(define (apply-twice f x)
  (f (f x)))

(apply-twice square 3) ; Returns 81
```

In this example, the apply-twice procedure takes a procedure f and a value x, then applies f to x twice. Passing square and 3 yields 81, as square(3) is 9 and square(9) is 81.

Returning procedures from other procedures is another powerful feature. This allows for the creation of function generators, which can produce customized procedures based on input parameters. For example:

```
(define (make-adder n)
  (lambda (x) (+ x n)))

(define add5 (make-adder 5))
(add5 10) ; Returns 15
```

Here, make-adder returns a new procedure that adds n to its argument. add5 is thus a procedure that adds 5 to any given number, demonstrated by add5(10), which returns 15.

Scheme's support for first-class procedures also enables the creation of procedural data structures. These structures can represent concepts and operations more abstractly. For example, creating a list of procedures:

```
(define procedures (list (lambda (x) (+ x 1))
```

```
                    (lambda (x) (* x 2))
                    (lambda (x) (- x 3))))

(map (lambda (f) (f 5)) procedures) ; Returns (6 10 2)
```

This code defines a list of anonymous procedures, each performing a different operation on its input. The map function applies each procedure in the list to the number 5, resulting in a list where each value is the result of the corresponding procedure's application.

Heuristic use of first-class procedures involves the combination of procedures to form new, composite procedures. This is often done using function composition, which enables the chaining of multiple operations into a single procedure:

```
(define (compose f g)
  (lambda (x) (f (g x))))

(define increment (lambda (x) (+ x 1)))
(define double (lambda (x) (* x 2)))

(define increment-then-double (compose double increment))
(increment-then-double 4) ; Returns 10
```

In this example, compose takes two procedures f and g, and returns a new procedure that first applies g to its input and then f to the result. The composed function increment-then-double demonstrates this composition, producing a value of 10 for an input of 4.

First-class procedures empower Scheme programmers to express a wide variety of computational patterns succinctly and elegantly. Leveraging this facility simplifies the creation of complex abstractions and promotes code reuse. The next section extends these concepts to anonymous functions and lambda expressions, elucidating their role in functional programming within Scheme.

5.5 Anonymous Functions and 'lambda' Expressions

In Scheme, functions can exist without being bound to a specific name, which are referred to as anonymous functions. These anonymous functions are defined using lambda expressions. The lambda keyword introduces a function definition and is directly tied to the concept of higher-order functions, as it allows the creation, manipulation, and use of functions within other functions.

A basic lambda expression consists of the lambda keyword, followed by a list of parameters, and then the body of the function. For instance, to create a function that adds two numbers x and y, we can write:

```
(lambda (x y) (+ x y))
```

This lambda expression produces a function that can be invoked with two arguments, and it will return their sum. Given that the function is anonymous, it is not directly named but can be used immediately where needed or passed as an argument to other functions.

To demonstrate the use of anonymous functions, consider the map function, which applies a given function to each element of a list. In the following example, we use lambda to create an anonymous function that squares each element in a list:

```
(map (lambda (x) (* x x)) '(1 2 3 4 5))
```

The output of this code will be:

```
(1 4 9 16 25)
```

Anonymous functions prove useful when a function is needed temporarily and will not be reused. Writing such functions directly where they are invoked eliminates the need to bind them to a name, thus requiring fewer lines of code and reducing potential namespace pollution.

Consider another example where we filter a list to keep only the even numbers, again using an anonymous function within the filter function:

```
(filter (lambda (x) (= 0 (mod x 2))) '(1 2 3 4 5 6))
```

The output here will be:

```
(2 4 6)
```

Anonymous functions can also serve as arguments for higher-order functions that may require more complex functionality. For instance, when sorting a list of numbers in descending order, an anonymous function can be used to define the sorting criteria:

```
(sort '(3 1 4 1 5 9 2 6 5) (lambda (a b) (> a b)))
```

The result of this operation is:

```
(9 6 5 5 4 3 2 1 1)
```

One may also define multi-line lambda expressions. Made possible by the inclusion of multiple expressions within the body of the lambda function, where the last expression determines the return value. Consider a lambda expression that calculates the factorial of a number:

```
(lambda (n)
  (if (= n 0)
      1
      (* n (fact (- n 1)))))
```

This lambda function can be immediately used by employing a method such as let to bind it to a temporary name within a local scope:

```
(let ((fact (lambda (n)
              (if (= n 0)
                  1
                  (* n (fact (- n 1)))))))
  (fact 5))
```

Evaluating this code returns:

```
120
```

Using lambda expressions effectively allows Scheme programmers to write concise, powerful, and readable code. They facilitate functional programming by enabling function composition, high-level operations on data structures, and greater abstraction capabilities without the syntactic overhead of naming every intermediary function.

5.6 Introduction to Higher-Order Functions

Higher-order functions are a fundamental concept in functional programming languages like Scheme. These functions operate on other functions by either taking them as arguments or returning them as results. This capability allows for more abstract and flexible programming paradigms, enhancing code reusability and modularity.

A higher-order function can be defined in Scheme as follows:

```
(define (apply-twice f x)
  (f (f x)))
```

In this example, apply-twice is a higher-order function because it accepts another function f as its parameter and applies f twice to the argument x. To see it in action, consider the following:

```
(define (square x)
  (* x x))

(apply-twice square 2)
```

The function square is passed to apply-twice, which then returns:

```
(apply-twice square 2)  ; evaluates to (square (square 2)) which is (square 4) resulting in 16
```

Higher-order functions are particularly useful for constructing generic operations that can work with any supplied function. An example is the map function, which applies a given function to each element of a list, creating a new list with the results:

```
(define (map f lst)
  (if (null? lst)
      '()
      (cons (f (car lst)) (map f (cdr lst)))))
```

To use the map function to square all elements in a list, you would do:

```
(map square '(1 2 3 4)) ; returns (1 4 9 16)
```

Here, map applies the square function to each element of the list (1 2 3 4), resulting in a new list (1 4 9 16).

Another common higher-order function is filter, which selects elements from a list that satisfy a predicate:

```
(define (filter pred lst)
  (cond
    ((null? lst) '())
    ((pred (car lst)) (cons (car lst) (filter pred (cdr lst))))
    (else (filter pred (cdr lst)))))
```

To filter out even numbers from a list, use the filter function with an appropriate predicate:

```
(define (even? x)
  (= (remainder x 2) 0))

(filter even? '(1 2 3 4 5 6)) ; returns (2 4 6)
```

In this case, the filter function applies the even? predicate to each element of the list, returning a new list containing only the even numbers (2 4 6).

Higher-order functions are also essential in defining more complex operations like reduce (or fold), which combines the elements of a list using a binary operation:

```
(define (reduce f init lst)
  (if (null? lst)
      init
      (reduce f (f init (car lst)) (cdr lst))))
```

To sum all elements of a list:

```
(define (add x y)
  (+ x y))

(reduce add 0 '(1 2 3 4 5)) ; returns 15
```

Here, reduce takes the add function, an initial value of 0, and the list (1 2 3 4 5), producing the sum 15.

Function composition is another powerful concept facilitated by higher-order functions. It allows combining multiple functions into a single function:

```
(define (compose f g)
  (lambda (x)
    (f (g x))))
```

To compose a square function and an add1 function (which increments a number by 1), and then apply it to 3:

```
(define (add1 x)
  (+ x 1))

((compose square add1) 3) ; returns 16
```

The compose function creates a new function that, when applied to 3, first applies add1 to get 4, then applies square to get 16.

The utility of higher-order functions extends throughout functional programming, providing powerful abstractions for performing repeated, generalized operations on data structures, encapsulating control patterns, and facilitating code reuse.

5.7 Mapping Functions over Lists

Mapping functions over lists is a fundamental concept in functional programming, allowing us to transform each element of a list using a specified function. Scheme provides built-in procedures to facilitate this process, most notably the map procedure. The map procedure takes a function and one or more lists as arguments and applies the function to each element of the lists, producing a new list with the results.

The syntax for the map procedure is as follows:

```
(map proc list1 list2 ...)
```

Here, proc is the function to be applied, and list1, list2, etc., are the lists over which the function is mapped. Each element of the resulting list is obtained by applying proc to the corresponding elements from the input lists.

Let's consider an example where we define a simple function to square a number and then map this function over a list of numbers.

```
(define (square x)
  (* x x))

(map square '(1 2 3 4 5))
```

The output of this expression is:

```
(1 4 9 16 25)
```

The map procedure applies the square function to each element of the list (1 2 3 4 5), producing a new list containing the squares of the original elements.

Mapping with Anonymous Functions

We can also use anonymous functions (created with lambda expressions) in the map procedure, eliminating the need to define named functions when the transformation is simple or used only once. The previous example can be rewritten using an anonymous function:

```
(map (lambda (x) (* x x)) '(1 2 3 4 5))
```

The output remains the same:

```
(1 4 9 16 25)
```

Mapping functions with multiple lists allows for element-wise operations, assuming the lists are of equal length. If provided lists are of different lengths, map will terminate as soon as the shortest list is exhausted. Let's illustrate this with an example that adds corresponding elements of two lists:

```
(map + '(1 2 3) '(4 5 6))
```

The output is:

```
(5 7 9)
```

In this case, the + function is applied to each pair of corresponding elements from the two lists, producing a new list with the sums.

Higher-Order Functions with map

The map procedure can be combined with other higher-order functions to perform more complex tasks. For example, consider a scenario where we want to filter, map, and reduce the elements of a list. Let's define a procedure that doubles each element of a list and then keeps only the results that are even.

```
(map (lambda (x) (* 2 x)) (filter even? '(1 2 3 4 5 6)))
```

Here, the filter procedure first selects the even numbers from the input list (1 2 3 4 5 6), resulting in (2 4 6). Then, map doubles each element of this filtered list, producing:

```
(4 8 12)
```

Practical Applications

Mapping functions are not confined to numerical operations. They can be applied to any data types or structures, enabling versatile transformations. For instance, we can define a procedure to convert a list of strings to uppercase:

```
(map string-upcase '("hello" "world" "scheme"))
```

The output will be:

```
("HELLO" "WORLD" "SCHEME")
```

Similarly, associating mappings with more complex data structures like lists of lists, allows us to flatten and manipulate nested data. Let's define a procedure that flattens a list of lists into a single list, capitalizing each element.

```
(define (flatten lst)
  (apply append lst))

(map string-upcase (flatten '(("cat" "dog") ("bird" "fish") ("ant" "bee"))))
```

This will yield:

```
("CAT" "DOG" "BIRD" "FISH" "ANT" "BEE")
```

By harnessing the power of map, we can efficiently transform complex and nested structures. The ability to use both named and anonymous functions provides flexibility, supporting a wide range of functional programming paradigms in Scheme. This approach not only ensures concise and readable code but also leverages the principles of functional abstraction and composability.

5.8 Filtering and Reducing Lists

Filtering and reducing lists are fundamental operations in the functional programming paradigm. These operations allow for concise, expressive, and efficient transformations and aggregations of data structures such as lists. In Scheme, these concepts are implemented through higher-order functions that take other functions as arguments, enabling a flexible approach to data manipulation.

The filter function selectively includes elements from a list that satisfy a given predicate. The predicate is a procedure that returns a boolean value, determining whether an element should be included in the resulting list.

```
(define (filter pred lst)
  (cond
    ((null? lst) '())
    ((pred (car lst)) (cons (car lst) (filter pred (cdr lst))))
    (else (filter pred (cdr lst)))))
```

In this implementation of filter, the function pred is applied to each element of the list lst. If pred returns #t, the element is included in the output list. Otherwise, the element is excluded. Consider an example where we filter out odd numbers from a list:

```
(define (odd? x) (= (modulo x 2) 1))
(filter odd? '(1 2 3 4 5 6 7 8 9))
```

The output of this code will be:

```
(1 3 5 7 9)
```

Reduction, also known as folding, involves combining the elements of a list to produce a single accumulated value. The fold function, also known as reduce, applies a binary operation recursively across the elements of the list, accumulating the result. Scheme provides two primary variants: fold-left and fold-right.

The fold-left function processes the list from left to right:

```
(define (fold-left op init lst)
  (if (null? lst)
      init
      (fold-left op (op init (car lst)) (cdr lst))))
```

The fold-right function, on the other hand, processes the list from right to left:

```
(define (fold-right op init lst)
```

```
  (if (null? lst)
      init
      (op (car lst) (fold-right op init (cdr lst)))))
```

The choice between fold-left and fold-right depends on the properties of the operation op and the structure of the data. For associative operations, either form will yield the same result.

Consider the example of summing a list of numbers using fold-left and fold-right:

```
(define (sum lst)
  (fold-left + 0 lst))

(sum '(1 2 3 4 5))
```

The output will be:

15

Alternatively, using fold-right:

```
(define (sum lst)
  (fold-right + 0 lst))

(sum '(1 2 3 4 5))
```

The result is identical:

15

Reduction is highly versatile and can be used for various purposes, such as finding the product of a list of numbers, concatenating lists, or computing logical operations.

```
; Product of numbers
(define (product lst)
  (fold-left * 1 lst))
(product '(1 2 3 4 5))
```

120

```
; Concatenate lists
(define (concatenate lst-of-lists)
  (fold-right append '() lst-of-lists))
(concatenate '((1 2) (3 4) (5 6)))
```

(1 2 3 4 5 6)

Combining filtering and reducing operations can provide powerful data transformations. For example, consider filtering out even numbers from a list and then summing the remaining elements:

```
; Define a predicate for even numbers
```

```
(define (even? x) (= (modulo x 2) 0))

; Filter and sum odd numbers
(define (sum-odd lst)
  (sum (filter odd? lst)))

(sum-odd '(1 2 3 4 5 6 7 8 9))
```

The output will be:

```
25
```

Using these functions in combination encourages the development of modular, reusable code, enhancing both maintainability and readability.

5.9 Composing Functions

Function composition is a crucial technique in Scheme and functional programming more broadly. It entails combining multiple functions to create a new function, enabling modular, readable, and reusable code. In Scheme, function composition is achieved by defining a new procedure that applies a series of existing procedures to its arguments in a specific order.

Consider the general form of function composition:

```
(define (compose f g)
  (lambda (x)
    (f (g x))))
```

Here, compose is a procedure that takes two procedures, f and g, and returns a new procedure. This new procedure first applies g to its argument and then applies f to the result of g. The resulting procedure can be used like any other procedure in Scheme.

For example, assume we have two procedures: square and increment.

```
(define (square x) (* x x))
(define (increment x) (+ x 1))
```

Using compose, we can create a new function that increments a number and then squares the result.

```
(define increment-then-square (compose square increment))
```

Calling increment-then-square with an argument will execute as follows:

```
(increment-then-square 3)
```

```
16
```

In this case, the value 3 is first passed to the increment procedure, resulting in 4. Then, square is applied to 4, yielding 16.

Function composition streamlines combining multiple operations without the need to write intermediate code explicitly. It also makes the intention of data transformations clear. By leveraging the composability of functions, we can build complex behavior from simpler, well-defined parts.

The compose procedure defined above is basic and composes only two functions. Incorporating more advanced techniques, we can create a compose procedure that handles an arbitrary number of functions:

```
(define (compose* . funcs)
  (if (null? funcs)
      (lambda (x) x)
      (let loop ((fs (cdr funcs))
                 (result (car funcs)))
        (if (null? fs)
            result
            (loop (cdr fs)
                  (let ((f (car fs)))
                    (lambda (x) (result (f x)))))))))
```

This procedure makes use of Scheme's list processing capabilities and variadic procedures (procedures that take a variable number of arguments). The compose* procedure uses . to collect all its arguments into a list, processes each function in reverse order, and creates a chain of composed functions. The base case is the identity function, lambda (x) x, returning the input unchanged if no functions are provided.

To illustrate the use of compose*, consider three procedures: double, increment, and square.

```
(define (double x) (* x 2))
(define (increment x) (+ x 1))
(define (square x) (* x x))
```

Using compose*, we can combine these into a single function:

```
(define double-increment-square (compose* square increment double))
```

Evaluating double-increment-square with an argument proceeds as follows:

```
(double-increment-square 2)
```

25

In this example, the number 2 is first doubled to 4, then incremented to 5, and finally squared to 25.

Function composition is intrinsic to many higher-order functions like map, filter, and fold. It provides an essential abstraction mechanism in functional programming, allowing for the concise expression of complex transformations. By composing simpler functions, we can build more nuanced operations while maintaining code integrity and readability.

5.10 Closures and Lexical Scoping

The concepts of closures and lexical scoping are fundamental in understanding the behavior and capabilities of functions in Scheme. Both play a critical role in functional programming by enhancing flexibility and control over variable bindings and lifetimes.

Closures are functions that capture and enclose their lexical environment at the time they are defined. This means they carry with them all the variables that were in scope when the function was created. This is possible in Scheme because functions are first-class citizens; they can be passed around and manipulated just like any other data type.

Lexical scoping, also known as static scoping, refers to the way variable bindings are resolved in terms of where the variables were defined, not where they are called. This means that a function's scope is determined by its physical placement in the code, and the function will retain access to the variables in the scope where it was defined, even if it is called from a different scope.

To illustrate these concepts, let's examine a piece of Scheme code that demonstrates closures and lexical scoping:

```
(define (make-counter)
  (let ((count 0))
    (lambda ()
      (set! count (+ count 1))
      count)))

(define counter1 (make-counter))
(define counter2 (make-counter))
```

In this code, the make-counter procedure returns a lambda expression, which is an anonymous function. This lambda expression increments the count variable and returns its value.

When make-counter is called, it creates a new lexical scope where count is initialized to 0. The lambda expression returned by make-counter captures this scope, including the count variable. Each call to make-counter creates a new, independent closure that includes its own version of the count variable.

The closures created and assigned to counter1 and counter2 are independent of each other, each maintaining its own count variable. To see this in action, consider the following interactive session:

```
(counter1)
(counter1)
(counter2)
(counter2)
(counter1)
```

This will produce the following output:

```
1
2
1
2
3
```

counter1 and counter2 each maintain a separate count, demonstrating the encapsulation provided by closures. This encapsulation is achieved through lexical scoping, allowing each closure to reference its own environment independent of others.

Understanding the distinction between lexical and dynamic scoping is crucial. In dynamic scoping, used by some languages, the call chain at runtime is used to resolve variable bindings, rather than the lexical structure of the code. Scheme, however, employs lexical scoping, where bindings are determined by the program text. This provides more predictable and maintainable behavior, as the scope of each variable is evident from the code itself.

Examining another example helps solidify these concepts:

```
(define x 10)

(define (enclose)
  (let ((x 5))
    (lambda () x)))

(define enclosed-counter (enclose))
(enclosed-counter)
```

In this code, there is a global x defined with a value of 10. The enclose function defines a local x with a value of 5 within its let scope, and returns a lambda expression that references this local x.

When enclosed-counter is called, it accesses the x defined in the lexical scope of enclose, not the global x. Thus, the output will be:

```
5
```

Even though enclosed-counter is executed in the global scope, it retains the let binding of x from when it was defined. This is a direct consequence of lexical scoping, ensuring that the variable bindings are maintained based on the code's structure, not the execution context.

Closures enable powerful abstraction techniques, like creating private state within a function that cannot be accessed or modified directly from outside the function. This encapsulation mechanism is a cornerstone of many advanced functional programming techniques and design patterns.

Lexical scoping also aids in reasoning about code, as the scope and lifetime of variables are more predictable and easier to follow. When combined, closures and lexical scoping empower Scheme programmers to write more modular, maintainable, and robust programs.

These concepts pave the way for more advanced topics such as higher-order functions, continuations, and more sophisticated forms of state management in functional programming, establishing a strong foundation for further exploration and mastery of Scheme.

5.11 Recursive and Iterative Procedures

In Scheme, procedures can be broadly categorized into recursive and iterative, each with distinct characteristics and use cases. Understanding the differences between these two types of procedures is essential for writing efficient and effective programs.

Recursion is a technique where a procedure calls itself in order to solve a problem. This technique is particularly useful for problems that can be broken down into smaller, simpler subproblems. A classic example of recursion is the calculation of the factorial of a number.

```
(define (factorial n)
  (if (= n 0)
      1
      (* n (factorial (- n 1)))))
```

When factorial is called with a positive integer, it checks if n is zero. If it is, the procedure returns 1. Otherwise, it multiplies n by the factorial of $n - 1$, thereby reducing the problem's size with each call until the base case is reached.

Iteration, on the other hand, involves using looping constructs to repeatedly execute a block of code until a condition is met. Scheme provides looping constructs, but idiomatic Scheme often employs tail recursion as a form of iteration. Tail recursion is a special case of recursion where the recursive call is the last operation in the procedure, allowing the Scheme interpreter or compiler to optimize the recursive call to avoid growing the call stack. This is known as tail-call optimization.

Consider the iterative version of the factorial procedure using tail recursion:

```
(define (factorial-iter n)
  (define (iter product counter)
    (if (> counter n)
        product
        (iter (* product counter) (+ counter 1))))
  (iter 1 1))
```

In this example, factorial-iter defines an inner helper procedure iter with two parameters: product to accumulate the result and counter to keep track of the current number. The helper procedure iteratively multiplies the product by the counter until the counter exceeds n, at which point it returns the product. This tail-recursive approach can be optimized to run in constant space, making it as efficient as an iterative loop.

To compare the two formulations, let's examine their execution:

```
> (factorial 5)
120

> (factorial-iter 5)
120
```

Both factorial and factorial-iter produce the same result, but the latter is more efficient due to tail-call optimization.

Another common example that illustrates the difference between recursion and iteration is the Fibonacci sequence. The naive recursive implementation directly translates the mathematical definition into code:

```
(define (fib n)
  (if (< n 2)
      n
      (+ (fib (- n 1)) (fib (- n 2)))))
```

This implementation, while intuitive, is highly inefficient due to repeated calculations of the same values. For large n, it exhibits exponential time complexity.

An iterative approach using tail recursion significantly improves the performance:

```
(define (fib-iter n)
  (define (iter a b count)
    (if (= count 0)
        a
        (iter b (+ a b) (- count 1))))
  (iter 0 1 n))
```

Here, fib-iter utilizes a helper procedure iter to maintain two accumulators, a and b, corresponding to consecutive Fibonacci numbers. The procedure continues updating these accumulators until the count reaches zero.

The performance improvements are evident upon execution:

```
> (fib 10)
55

> (fib-iter 10)
55
```

The recursive and iterative versions of fib both yield the same result, but the iterative solution is far more efficient.

Understanding when to use recursion versus iteration is crucial. Recursive procedures are well-suited for problems with a natural recursive structure, such as tree traversal or divide-and-conquer algorithms. Iterative approaches or tail-recursive formulations are preferable for problems that require large data manipulation to avoid excessive memory usage.

Additionally, comprehending these distinctions lays the groundwork for advanced topics such as memoization and dynamic programming. Memoization leverages recursion while optimizing repeated subproblem solutions, which will be examined further in the context of performance enhancement techniques.

5.12 Memoization and Its Applications

Memoization is an optimization technique primarily used to speed up function execution by storing the results of expensive function calls and reusing those results when the same inputs occur again. This is particularly useful in the context of recursive functions where the same subproblems may be solved multiple times. In Scheme, memoization can significantly enhance performance, especially in the context of algorithmically intensive computations.

The central idea of memoization is maintaining a data structure, commonly an associative array (or dictionary), to cache previously computed values. Let's consider the basic implementation of memoization in Scheme.

Here's how we could implement a basic memoization scheme for a Fibonacci function. First, let's define the Fibonacci function without memoization:

```
(define (fib n)
  (if (< n 2)
      n
      (+ (fib (- n 1)) (fib (- n 2)))))
```

When n increases, the function fib is called exponentially, which results in unnecessary computations and inefficiency. By applying memoization, redundant function calls can be avoided. Below is a memoized version of the fib function:

```
(define memo-fib
  (let ((cache (make-hash-table)))
    (lambda (n)
      (if (hash-table-exists? cache n)
          (hash-table-ref cache n)
          (let ((result (if (< n 2)
                            n
                            (+ (memo-fib (- n 1)) (memo-fib (- n 2))))))
            (hash-table-set! cache n result)
            result)))))
```

In this memoized version:

- cache is a hash table used to store precomputed Fibonacci numbers.
- memo-fib checks if the result for the given n is already in the cache using hash-table-exists?.
- If the result exists in the cache, it retrieves the value with hash-table-ref.
- If the result does not exist, it computes the value, stores it in the cache with hash-table-set!, and then returns the result.

This approach dramatically reduces the number of computations, optimizing the algorithm from exponential to linear time complexity.

Beyond simple numerical computations like Fibonacci numbers, memoization can be applied to a broader range of problems, including dynamic programming and optimization problems. Here's an example where memoization is used for a dynamic programming problem, specifically solving the Knapsack problem:

```
(define (knapsack items capacity)
  (let ((cache (make-hash-table)))
    (define (ks n c)
      (let ((key (cons n c)))
        (if (hash-table-exists? cache key)
            (hash-table-ref cache key)
            (let ((result (if (= n 0)
                              0
                              (let* ((item (list-ref items (- n 1)))
                                     (weight (car item))
                                     (value (cadr item)))
                                (if (> weight c)
                                    (ks (- n 1) c)
                                    (max (ks (- n 1) c)
                                         (+ value (ks (- n 1) (- c weight)))))))))
              (hash-table-set! cache key result)
              result))))
    (ks (length items) capacity)))
```

In this example:

- ks is a nested procedure defined within the knapsack function. It utilizes memoization to store results of subproblems.
- Each subproblem is represented by a key, which is a pair (cons n c), where n is the number of items and c is the remaining capacity of the knapsack.
- The result of each subproblem is stored in cache to avoid redundant computations.
- The function computes the maximum value that can be achieved with the given constraints, using the cached values for previously computed subproblems.

Memoization can also be extended to higher-order functions. Consider a function that takes another function as an argument and returns a memoized version of it:

```
(define (memoize f)
  (let ((cache (make-hash-table)))
    (lambda args
      (let ((key (list args)))
        (if (hash-table-exists? cache key)
            (hash-table-ref cache key)
            (let ((result (apply f args)))
              (hash-table-set! cache key result)
              result))))))
```

In this higher-order memoization function:

- $\mathrm{memoize}$ takes a function f as its argument and returns a new function.
- The new function checks if the result for the given arguments args is already cached.
- If the result exists, it retrieves the value from the cache; otherwise, it computes the function, stores the result in the cache, and returns it.

Memoization not only improves the efficiency of recursive and dynamic programming problems but also serves as an illustrative example of functional programming principles like closures and higher-order functions. It reveals the power of combining procedural abstraction with mutable state to achieve significant performance improvements. As such, memoization is a crucial optimization technique in both academic and practical software development.

Chapter 6

Working with Lists and Pairs

This chapter focuses on the essential operations for working with lists and pairs in Scheme. It covers constructing lists with 'cons', accessing elements using 'car' and 'cdr', and performing basic list operations such as 'length', 'append', and 'reverse'. The chapter discusses nested lists and deep recursion, the use of the 'list' function, and the creation and manipulation of pairs. It includes common list processing functions, mapping and filtering techniques, as well as the use of association lists and advanced list manipulation methods.

6.1 Introduction to Lists and Pairs

In Scheme, lists and pairs constitute foundational data structures crucial for effective programming. Understanding their construction, manipulation, and the functions that operate on them is essential for achieving proficiency in Scheme.

A pair in Scheme is an ordered group of two values, generated using the cons function. The cons function takes two arguments and returns a new pair. The syntax is as follows:

```
(cons <car> <cdr>)
```

Here, <car> is the first element of the pair, and <cdr> is the second element. The terms car and cdr are historically derived from the LISP programming language, which Scheme is based on.

When both car and cdr themselves are either pairs or lists, the cons function can be used recursively to construct more complex structures. Lists are simply a recursive collection of pairs wherein the cdr of each pair is either another pair (representing the list continuation) or the empty list, denoted as '().

For instance, to construct a list of three elements, say A, B, and C, one can utilize cons in the following manner:

```
(cons 'A (cons 'B (cons 'C '())))
```

This results in the list (A B C). To access elements of a pair, Scheme provides the car and cdr functions:

```
(car (cons 'A 'B)) ; returns 'A
(cdr (cons 'A 'B)) ; returns 'B
```

Applying these functions to nested pairs allows extraction of individual list elements:

```
(car (cdr (cons 'A (cons 'B (cons 'C '()))))) ; returns 'B
(car (cdr (cdr (cons 'A (cons 'B (cons 'C '())))))) ; returns 'C
```

An empty list, represented as '(), is a significant construct in Scheme. It signifies the end of a list structure. Consequently, lists can be perceived as pairs where the cdr eventually points to '().

Scheme's list function provides a convenient mechanism for list creation without explicitly employing cons. It constructs a list out of its arguments:

```
(list 'A 'B 'C) ; identical to (cons 'A (cons 'B (cons 'C '())))
```

Scheme lists possess several fundamental properties:

- Lists are *heterogeneous*, meaning they can store elements of different types, such as numbers, symbols, and even other lists.
- Lists are inherently *immutable*, as modifications generate new lists rather than altering the existing ones.
- Lists facilitate significant operations, including traversals, searching, filtering, and transformations.

The intrinsic connection between pairs and lists is paramount in understanding Scheme's list operations. Lists are merely a convention to represent sequences using pairs.

List operations such as length and append depend on recursive processing of these structures. The function length, for example, computes the number of elements in a list:

```
(length (list 'A 'B 'C)) ; returns 3
```

Implementing length involves recursively traversing the list until encountering the end represented by '(). Similarly, list concatenation using append merges elements of two or more lists:

```
(append (list 'A 'B) (list 'C 'D)) ; yields (A B C D)
```

The internal implementation of append iterates through each element, copying pairs while establishing a new consolidated list.

Understanding lists and pairs in Scheme streamlines the complexity of common programming tasks. It lays the groundwork for advanced concepts, such as deep recursion, nested lists, and sophisticated list processing functions that build upon the foundational knowledge of lists and pairs.

Mastering these basics facilitates the comprehension of advanced topics later discussed in this book.

6.2 Constructing Lists with 'cons'

In Scheme, the construction of lists is foundational to numerous functional programming patterns. The cons function is integral to list construction, combining two elements to form a pair, more commonly referred to in Lisp terminology as a cons cell. To facilitate clarity, we will delve into the syntactic and semantic components of cons, additionally exploring its interaction with lists and other data structures.

The cons function creates a pair from two arguments. Its general form is:

```
(cons element1 element2)
```

Here, element1 can be any Scheme object, as can element2. When element2 is a list, cons constructs a new list with element1 at the front. This fundamental operation underpins most list manipulations in Scheme.

Consider the following example where element1 is a single number and element2 is a list:

```
(cons 1 '(2 3 4))
```

The result of this operation is a new list:

```
(1 2 3 4)
```

cons does not modify the original list but returns a new list with element1 prepended. Understanding this insertion's efficient, constant-time performance is essential for designing algorithms in functional programming.

When cons is applied to non-list second arguments, it produces a pair where the second element is not a proper list. This is distinguishable by the notation .(dot):

```
(cons 1 2)
```

The resulting pair is:

```
(1 . 2)
```

This pair is not a list but rather a two-element structure, emphasizing another usage of cons in constructing general-purpose pairs.

Nested list construction using cons illustrates the function's recursive nature. For example:

```
(cons 1 (cons 2 (cons 3 '())))
```

The equivalent expression using standard list notation is:

```
(1 2 3)
```

Here, the empty list '() serves as the base case, terminating the recursion and forming the full list. This pattern is vital for deep recursion and complex data structures, such as trees and graphs.

In a more advanced context, constructing lists of pairs or nested lists involves repeated applications of cons:

```
(cons (cons 'a 1) (cons (cons 'b 2) '()))
```

This code constructs the association list:

```
((a . 1) (b . 2))
```

Evaluating and constructing such lists efficiently allows us to manage key-value data, simulate associative arrays, and support various data abstractions.

When constructing lists programmatically, it is common to use loops or recursion. The iterative construction of a list of numbers from n down to 1 is illustrated here:

```
(define (countdown n)
  (if (<= n 0)
      '()
      (cons n (countdown (- n 1)))))
```

Calling (countdown 5) produces:

```
(5 4 3 2 1)
```

This function demonstrates recursion—the backbone of list processing in Scheme. Each cons appends the counter to the accumulating list until the base case of zero or a negative number is met.

Moreover, when using Scheme's macro system or higher-order functions, cons can dynamically generate code or data structures. For example, the map function sequentially applies cons to build transformed lists:

```
(map (lambda (x) (cons x (* x x))) '(1 2 3 4))
```

Resulting in:

```
((1 . 1) (2 . 4) (3 . 9) (4 . 16))
```

Here, each number is paired with its square, showcasing how cons facilitates mapping operations and data transformations.

Thorough familiarity with the cons operation underpins effective Scheme programming, enabling sophisticated list manipulations and data structure design. By mastering cons, one builds a robust foundation for advanced functional programming concepts.

6.3 Accessing List Elements: 'car' and 'cdr'

In Scheme, two fundamental procedures, car and cdr, are pivotal for accessing elements within lists. These functions derive their names from the original Lisp programming language and offer powerful ways to manipulate and traverse list structures.

The car function retrieves the first element of a pair or list, while the cdr function returns the remainder of the list, excluding the first element. To illustrate these operations, consider the following Scheme expression:

```
(define my-list (cons 1 (cons 2 (cons 3 '()))))
```

The variable my-list now holds a list with the elements 1, 2, and 3. Applying the car and cdr functions to this list yields the following results:

```
(car my-list) ; This returns 1

(cdr my-list) ; This returns (2 3)
```

In Scheme, lists are inherently recursive structures. The car operation isolates the first element, whereas cdr recursively applies to yield the sublist excluding the first element. The recursive nature of lists can be better understood through the application of car and cdr to deeper nested lists.

Consider another example:

```
(define nested-list (cons (cons 1 2) (cons 3 (cons 4 '()))))
```

For this nested list, car and cdr operations can be demonstrated as follows:

```
(car nested-list) ; This returns (1 . 2)

(cdr nested-list) ; This returns (3 4)

(car (cdr nested-list)) ; This returns 3
```

These examples underscore the principal capabilities of car and cdr. However, these functions extend beyond merely accessing elements; they are instrumental in constructing complex list processing routines.

To deepen our understanding, it is essential to recognize how car and cdr operations can be compounded to traverse and manipulate lists extensively. Consider the following recursive function that calculates the length of a list:

```
(define (list-length lst)
  (if (null? lst)
      0
      (+ 1 (list-length (cdr lst)))))
```

In the list-length function, the base case checks if the list is null, returning zero in such a case. If the list is non-empty, the function recursively calls itself with the cdr of the list, incrementing the count by one at each recursive step. This progression iterates through each list element from the head to the end, effectively calculating the list's total length.

The same principles apply to constructing new structures by appending elements. Consider an example where the car and cdr function are employed within an algorithm to reverse a list:

```
(define (reverse-list lst)
  (define (reverse-iter lst acc)
    (if (null? lst)
        acc
        (reverse-iter (cdr lst) (cons (car lst) acc))))
  (reverse-iter lst '()))
```

The reverse-list function employs an auxiliary function, reverse-iter, which follows the idiom of tail-recursion. The core mechanism involves constructing the reversed list by iteratively moving the head element of lst to the acc accumulator until lst becomes empty.

Utilizing car and cdr, complex nested structures can be processed and manipulated with exceptional granularity. For instance, extracting specific elements from a deeply nested list structure necessitates compounded applications of these operations, as shown below:

```
(define complex-list '(1 (2 (3 4) 5) 6))

(car (cdr (car (cdr complex-list)))) ; This returns 3
```

Here, the list complex-list encloses another list within its second element. The compounded operations progressively navigate through the nested structure to access the desired element.

The car and cdr functions are integral to list element access and manipulation in Scheme. Their combined use allows for the traversal and reconstruction of list-based data structures efficiently. Leveraging these functions within recursive and iterative paradigms enables the implementation of a broad spectrum of list processing algorithms, further illustrating their robustness in functional programming.

6.4 Basic List Operations: length, append, reverse

Understanding fundamental operations on lists is crucial for proficient Scheme programming. This section explores three primary list operations: length, append, and reverse. Each function provides essential capabilities for handling lists, enabling more complex data manipulations and algorithm implementations.

length

The length function calculates the number of elements in a list. It traverses the entire list and counts each element.

```
(length '(1 2 3 4 5))
```

In this example, the function returns:

```
5
```

The length function's complexity is $O(n)$, where n is the number of elements in the list. This linear time complexity is due to the necessity of visiting each element once.

append

The append function concatenates two or more lists. Its primary role is to build larger lists from smaller segments.

```
(append '(1 2 3) '(4 5 6))
```

The output of this function call is:

```
(1 2 3 4 5 6)
```

Appending multiple lists also follows a similar syntax:

```
(append '(1 2) '(3 4) '(5 6))
```

This returns:

```
(1 2 3 4 5 6)
```

The append function requires traversing each list except the last, making its complexity $O(n+m)$ for two lists where n and m are the lengths of the respective lists.

reverse

The reverse function produces a new list with the elements in the opposite order.

```
(reverse '(1 2 3 4 5))
```

The returned list is:

```
(5 4 3 2 1)
```

```
Function reverse(lst):
    if lst is empty then
        return ();
    else
        return concatenate reverse(cdr lst) and car lst;
```

A common application of reverse is when a list needs to be processed in the reverse order or generating data structures like stacks.

This recursive algorithm demonstrates the operation of reverse. The complexity is $O(n^2)$ due to repeatedly appending to lists.

In practical applications, understanding these functions' behavior and complexity is vital. They form the basis for more complex operations, such as list mapping, filtering, and folding, discussed in subsequent sections. Ensure your list manipulation strategies are optimized for the given constraints and performance requirements.

6.5 Nested Lists and Deep Recursion

Nested lists are lists that contain other lists as their elements. These structures are frequently used in Scheme programming to represent more complex hierarchical data. Understanding nested lists is crucial because they appear in many practical applications, such as tree traversal, parsing expressions, and representing nested data structures.

Nested lists are constructed using the same operators as flat lists, namely cons, list, and their variants. Consider the following example, which constructs a nested list:

```
(define nested-list (list 1 2 (list 3 4) 5 (list 6 (list 7 8))))
```

The above expression creates a nested list where the elements are 1, 2, another list (3 4), 5, and one more list (6 (7 8)). To visualize this structure, it helps to mentally or graphically represent the nesting levels.

Accessing elements within nested lists requires careful use of car and cdr. To extract the element 4 from our nested-list:

```
(car (cdr (car (cdr (cdr nested-list)))))
```

Nested lists often necessitate recursive functions to process their elements. Recursion allows functions to handle each sublist individually, applying the same logic regardless of the tree depth. Let us explore a common recursive problem: calculating the total number of elements in a nested list, known as the deep-length.

```
(define (deep-length lst)
  (cond
    ((null? lst) 0)
    ((list? (car lst)) (+ (deep-length (car lst)) (deep-length (cdr lst))))
    (else (+ 1 (deep-length (cdr lst))))))
```

The deep-length function uses three cases:

- If the list is empty (null?), the length is 0.
- If the first element (car lst) is a list, it recursively calculates the deep-length of the first element and the rest of the list (cdr lst).
- Otherwise, it adds 1 for the first element and recursively processes the rest of the list.

Another common operation on nested lists is to flatten them into a single list of individual elements. Consider the function flatten:

```
(define (flatten lst)
  (cond
    ((null? lst) '())
    ((list? (car lst)) (append (flatten (car lst)) (flatten (cdr lst))))
    (else (cons (car lst) (flatten (cdr lst))))))
```

The flatten function works as follows:

- If the list is empty, it returns an empty list.
- If the first element is a list, it flattens both the first element and the rest of the list, then appends the results.
- Otherwise, it places the first element at the beginning of the flattened rest of the list.

These two functions, deep-length and flatten, illustrate the power of recursion in dealing with nested lists. Complex operations on nested data can often be reduced to these two core patterns: processing elements directly or recursively diving into sublists.

Deep recursion refers to recursive calls that occur at multiple levels of a nested structure. Handling deep recursion efficiently in Scheme is critical because the depth of recursion can influence both performance and memory usage. Scheme implementations typically support tail recursion optimization, where tail-recursive functions reuse stack frames, mitigating the risk of stack overflow for deeply nested recursive calls.

Consider a tail-recursive version of the deep-length function, which accumulates the count as it traverses the nested structure:

```
(define (deep-length-tail lst)
  (define (helper lst acc)
    (cond
      ((null? lst) acc)
      ((list? (car lst)) (helper (cdr lst) (+ acc (deep-length-tail (car lst)))))
      (else (helper (cdr lst) (+ acc 1)))))
  (helper lst 0))
```

By implementing an inner helper function, we carry an accumulator (acc) through the recursive calls, ensuring the function remains tail-recursive. This form captures the accumulated length up to the current recursion point, achieved by adding either the count of nested elements or simply 1 for non-list elements.

Understanding and utilizing deep recursion empowers Scheme programmers to handle intricate data structures and perform complex transformations. Mastery of techniques such as tail recursion guarantees optimal resource usage, which is essential in developing robust and efficient Scheme applications.

6.6 Using 'list' to Create Lists

The list function in Scheme provides a convenient way to create lists without explicitly using the cons function for every element. Unlike cons, which constructs pairs, list directly constructs a list out of its arguments. This is particularly useful when one needs to create a list with more than a few elements as it is more readable and succinct.

For example, consider the task of creating a list of numbers from 1 to 5. Using cons, this would look like:

```
(cons 1 (cons 2 (cons 3 (cons 4 (cons 5 '())))))
```

While this is an accurate way to construct the list, it becomes cumbersome as the list grows in length. Instead, we can utilize the list function to achieve the same result more elegantly:

```
(list 1 2 3 4 5)
```

The above line of code outputs:

```
(1 2 3 4 5)
```

Given its straightforward syntax, list becomes indispensable for dynamically constructing lists during execution. Its arguments can be literals, variables, or even expressions that evaluate to list elements. Let's explore a few practical examples to deepen our understanding of list's versatility.

```
(define x 10)
(define y 20)
(list (+ x y) (- y x) (* x y))
```

The execution of the code above will generate the following output:

```
(30 10 200)
```

In the example, (+ x y), (- y x), and (* x y) are expressions that evaluate to numerical results. These results are then aggregated by the list function into a single list.

Additionally, list can create nested lists seamlessly. Nested lists are lists within lists, and the list function syntax remains consistent while handling multiple levels of nesting.

```
(list 1 (list 2 3) (list 4 (list 5 6)))
```

The above line of code outputs:

```
(1 (2 3) (4 (5 6)))
```

This example demonstrates how the list function can be employed to construct complex structures. Here, the inner calls to list form sublists that are then included in the outer list.

When using the list function, it is important to note that the created list is properly nested and adheres to the correct list structure. Contrast this with improper lists which can result from incorrect use of cons.

To dynamically create lists from sequences or ranges, one might use the list function in conjunction with recursion or higher-order functions.

Consider the task of generating a list of the first n natural numbers:

```
(define (generate-list n)
  (if (= n 0)
      '()
      (cons n (generate-list (- n 1)))))
```

Using this function:

```
(generate-list 5)
```

This will produce:

(5 4 3 2 1)

If the order needs to be reversed, one could modify the function or refine the approach using reverse:

```
(reverse (generate-list 5))
```

Which results in:

(1 2 3 4 5)

Integrating list with list processing functions like map, filter, or foldl can further exploit the power of lists in functional programming. Here is an example of creating a list of squared numbers using map and list:

```
(map (lambda (x) (* x x)) (list 1 2 3 4 5))
```

This returns:

(1 4 9 16 25)

The list function in conjunction with map applies the squaring operation to each element in the list, efficiently producing the desired result.

The list function is a fundamental tool in Scheme, promoting concise and readable code for list creation tasks that range from simple to complex. Its integration with other list processing paradigms in Scheme continually reinforces its utility and significance in functional programming.

6.7 Constructing Pairs with 'cons'

In Scheme, a pair is a fundamental data structure that is built using the cons procedure. A pair is a compound data object that contains two components, which are typically referred to as the car and cdr of the pair. To construct a pair, the cons procedure is used, which stands for "construct". The cons procedure takes two arguments and creates a new pair out of them.

Unlike lists, which have an inherent linear sequence, pairs are essentially just two elements bundled together. This leads to a vast range of applications, including the construction of more complex data structures like trees and association lists.

```
(define my-pair (cons 1 2))
```

In the example above, my-pair is defined as a pair consisting of the elements 1 and 2. These elements are the car and the cdr of my-pair, respectively.

```
> (car my-pair)
1
> (cdr my-pair)
2
```

Here, (car my-pair) returns 1, and (cdr my-pair) returns 2. These operations retrieve the first and second elements of the pair, respectively.

The cons procedure is highly versatile. It can take any Scheme object as its arguments, allowing for pairing various types of data, including lists and other pairs. This capability enables the construction of complex nested structures.

```
(define nested-pair (cons (cons 1 2) (cons 3 4)))
```

The nested-pair here is a pair where both the car and cdr are themselves pairs. Here's how you can retrieve elements from such nested structures:

```
> (car nested-ppair)
(1 . 2)
> (cdr nested-pair)
(3 . 4)
```

As demonstrated, (car nested-pair) returns the pair (1 . 2), and (cdr nested-pair) returns (3 . 4). To dig deeper, we can further apply car and cdr on the results:

```
> (car (car nested-pair))
1
> (cdr (car nested-pair))
2
> (car (cdr nested-pair))
3
> (cdr (cdr nested-pair))
4
```

This retrieval technique allows comprehensive access to elements within a nested structure.

Another important aspect of using cons is its ability to pair compound data structures, like lists, to create hierarchical data. For instance:

```
(define pair-of-lists (cons '(1 2 3) '(4 5 6)))
```

In this case, pair-of-lists is a pair where both the car and cdr are lists.

Accessing the elements of this structure works similarly:

```
> (car pair-of-lists)
(1 2 3)
> (cdr pair-of-lists)
(4 5 6)
```

Therefore, the cons procedure empowers us to bundle combinations of simple and complex data efficiently.

When constructing more complex structures, the cons procedure's flexibility shines through. You can use it to link multiple elements dynamically, forming extensive data structures such as binary trees. Each tree node might be represented as a pair where the car holds the node's value and the cdr references another pair, representing the left and right subtrees.

Here's an illustrative example of a simple binary tree:

```
(define binary-tree
  (cons 10
        (cons (cons 5 '()) (cons (cons 15 '()) '()))))
```

This forms a binary tree with the root node valued at 10. The left subtree has a root node of 5, and the right subtree has a root node of 15. The empty lists at the leaves indicate the absence of further branches.

```
> (car binary-tree)
10
> (car (cdr binary-tree))
(5)
> (car (cdr (cdr binary-tree)))
(15)
```

In these queries, (car binary-tree) returns 10, the root value. (car (cdr binary-tree)) retrieves the left subtree, and (car (cdr (cdr binary-tree))) retrieves the right subtree.

Pairs constructed with cons provide an efficient way to handle diverse data structures, allowing precise data access and manipulation. They form the bedrock of various complex data handling paradigms in Scheme, showcasing the elegance and power of the language's simplistic, yet flexible, constructs.

6.8 Decomposing Pairs with 'car' and 'cdr'

In Scheme, pairs are a fundamental concept, and understanding how to decompose them is crucial for effective list manipulation. The functions 'car' and 'cdr' are the primary tools used to decompose pairs. A pair in

Scheme is created using the 'cons' function. For example, '(cons 1 2)' creates the pair '(1 . 2)'.

When 'cons' is used to construct lists, pairs form the building blocks. To decompose or access elements of these pairs, we use 'car' and 'cdr':

```
(define example-pair (cons 1 2))
(car example-pair) ; returns 1
(cdr example-pair) ; returns 2
```

The 'car' function returns the first element of the pair, while the 'cdr' function returns the second element. When dealing with lists, which are chains of pairs, 'car' yields the head of the list, and 'cdr' yields the rest of the list, excluding the head.

Consider the list '(1 2 3)' constructed as nested pairs:

```
(define example-list (cons 1 (cons 2 (cons 3 '()))))
```

Using 'car' and 'cdr' successively allows accessing elements within the nested pair structure:

```
(car example-list) ; returns 1
(car (cdr example-list)) ; returns 2
(car (cdr (cdr example-list))) ; returns 3
```

Scheme enables both flat and nested pair structures. In flat structures, 'car' and 'cdr' can easily access the elements, whereas in nested, deeper access requires multiple applications of 'car' and 'cdr'.

Nested pairs can be visualized as tree structures where each node has a left (car) and right (cdr) child. Here's a more complex example for clarity:

```
(define nested-pairs (cons (cons 1 2) (cons 3 4)))
(car (car nested-pairs)) ; returns 1
(cdr (car nested-pairs)) ; returns 2
(car (cdr nested-pairs)) ; returns 3
(cdr (cdr nested-pairs)) ; returns 4
```

Through 'car' and 'cdr', one can navigate this tree to retrieve specific data. This navigation is particularly important when working with recursive algorithms. For instance, suppose a need arises to recursively process each element of a list to produce a new list one could use:

```
(define (process-pairs pair-list)
  (if (null? pair-list)
      '()
      (cons (process-element (car pair-list))
            (process-pairs (cdr pair-list)))))

(define (process-element elem)
```

```
  (* elem 2)) ; an example function that doubles the element

(process-pairs '(1 2 3 4)) ; returns (2 4 6 8)
```

Here, ‘process-pairs‘ recursively processes each element of the list using ‘car‘ and ‘cdr‘, applying ‘process-element‘ to double each element.

Working with pairs and lists efficiently also involves understanding the aliasing that occurs with 'car' and 'cdr'. Consider a list:

```
(define my-list (list 1 2 3))
(define first-part (car my-list))
(define rest-part (cdr my-list))
```

Changing ‘first-part‘ or ‘rest-part‘ does not change ‘my-list‘, illustrating immutability within the pairs:

```
(set! first-part 100)
(set-cdr! my-list '(100))
my-list ; returns (1 100)
```

These modifications lead to practical applications. When managing larger data structures, understanding the interplay between 'car' and 'cdr' is vital, especially for efficient algorithm implementation and data manipulation.

In summary, 'car' and 'cdr' are instrumental for decomposing pairs, allowing precise control over list structures. This foundational knowledge in Scheme programming enables rigorous and effective list and pair manipulations essential for advanced data handling and algorithm design.

6.9 Common List Processing Functions

Scheme provides a diverse set of built-in functions to manipulate lists effectively. Understanding and utilizing these functions properly is crucial for proficient list processing.

map: The map function applies a given procedure to each element of one or more lists, returning a list of the results. The procedure must accept the same number of arguments as there are lists.

```
(map (lambda (x) (* x 2)) '(1 2 3 4 5))
```

```
(2 4 6 8 10)
```

In this example, each element of the list '(1 2 3 4 5) is multiplied by 2. map can also handle multiple lists:

```
(map + '(1 2 3) '(4 5 6))
```

(5 7 9)

Here, the + procedure is applied to corresponding elements of '(1 2 3) and '(4 5 6).

filter: The filter function creates a list of elements for which a given predicate returns true. This is useful for extracting subsequences based on specific criteria.

```
(filter (lambda (x) (> x 3)) '(1 2 3 4 5))
```

(4 5)

In this case, filter selects elements greater than 3.

fold (foldl and foldr): Folding functions traverse a list while accumulating a result. foldl (fold left) starts from the left, while foldr (fold right) starts from the right.

```
(foldl + 0 '(1 2 3 4 5))
```

15

```
(foldr cons '() '(1 2 3 4 5))
```

(1 2 3 4 5)

foldl sums the list elements, initializing the accumulation with 0. foldr reconstructs the list by consing elements to an empty list.

assoc and **assq**: These functions search for a pair in an association list where the car (key) matches a given key. assoc performs the search using equal? while assq uses eq?.

```
(define alist '((a . 1) (b . 2) (c . 3)))
(assoc 'b alist)
```

(b . 2)

assoc returns the pair (b . 2) from the association list alist.

member and **memq**: These functions check membership in a list. member uses equal? while memq uses eq?.

```
(member 'b '(a b c d))
```

(b c d)

member returns the sublist starting with the found element 'b.

length: This function returns the number of elements in a list.

```
(length '(1 2 3 4 5))
```

5

length straightforwardly counts the elements of the list '(1 2 3 4 5).

append: This function concatenates lists, forming a single list containing the elements of each argument list.

```
(append '(1 2) '(3 4) '(5 6))
```

(1 2 3 4 5 6)

In this example, append creates a single list including all elements from the input lists.

reverse: This function returns a list with elements in reverse order.

```
(reverse '(a b c d))
```

(d c b a)

Here, reverse inverts the order of the list '(a b c d).

The diverse functions provided by Scheme for list processing are fundamental tools for any programmer. Grasping their usage enables more effective and efficient solutions in numerous scenarios.

6.10 Mapping and Filtering Lists

In Scheme, the map and filter functions are crucial for processing lists. These higher-order functions allow for applying a procedure to each element of a list (map) or selectively including elements based on a predicate (filter). Utilizing these functions effectively enables concise and expressive operations on lists.

map applies a given procedure to each element of a list, returning a new list containing the results. The procedure must accept a number of arguments equal to the number of lists provided. The result is a list constructed by applying the procedure to the corresponding elements of the input lists.

```
(map (lambda (x) (* x 2)) '(1 2 3 4))
```

(2 4 6 8)

In the above example, each element of the list '(1 2 3 4) is doubled, resulting in a new list (2 4 6 8). The lambda expression defines an anonymous function that multiplies its input by two.

map can also operate on multiple lists simultaneously. When used in this fashion, the procedure must take as many parameters as there are lists, and it processes corresponding elements in parallel.

```
(map + '(1 2 3) '(4 5 6))
```

(5 7 9)

Here, map applies the addition (+) procedure to the corresponding elements of the input lists, producing a new list (5 7 9).

The filter function constructs a new list containing only those elements of a source list that satisfy a specified predicate. The predicate is a procedure that returns a boolean value.

```
(filter odd? '(1 2 3 4 5 6))
```

(1 3 5)

In this example, filter returns a list of all the odd numbers from the input list '(1 2 3 4 5 6). The predicate odd? is applied to each element, and only those for which the predicate returns true are included in the result.

We can define even?, a predicate for filtering even numbers:

```
(filter (lambda (x) (= (modulo x 2) 0)) '(1 2 3 4 5 6))
```

(2 4 6)

In this example, the list (1 2 3 4 5 6) is filtered to include only even numbers, using a lambda expression that defines a predicate for checking evenness.

Combining map and filter can yield powerful list transformations. For instance, to double the elements of a list and then filter out the even numbers from the resultant list:

```
(filter odd? (map (lambda (x) (* x 2)) '(1 2 3 4 5)))
```

(2 6 10)

In this example, the list '(1 2 3 4 5) is first transformed by map to produce (2 4 6 8 10), and then filter narrows it down to the even numbers.

Applying these principles ensures efficient and readable list processing.

Users can leverage the flexibility and minimalism of map and filter to perform various complex transformations succinctly.

6.11 Association Lists

Association lists, or a-lists, are a fundamental data structure in Scheme used to represent mappings from keys to values. They are essentially lists of pairs, where each pair consists of a key and its associated value. This structure is particularly useful for implementing dictionaries, symbol tables, and lookup tables in Scheme.

An association list is constructed using the cons function applied to pairs, where each pair is itself constructed using cons. For clarity, consider the following example of an association list that maps strings to integers:

```
(define alist (list (cons "one" 1) (cons "two" 2) (cons "three" 3)))
```

This defines alist as

```
(("one" . 1) ("two" . 2) ("three" . 3))
```

Accessing the value associated with a key in an association list is typically performed using the assoc function. The assoc function traverses the list and returns the first pair whose car matches the given key. If no such pair exists, assoc returns #f.

```
(assoc "two" alist)
```

This evaluates to

```
("two" . 2)
```

If the key is not present in the association list:

```
(assoc "four" alist)
```

This evaluates to

```
#f
```

To retrieve the value associated with a key, the cdr of the pair returned by assoc is taken:

```
(cdr (assoc "two" alist))
```

This evaluates to

```
2
```

Adding a new key-value pair to an association list usually involves using the cons function to add the pair to the front of the list:

```
(define alist (cons (cons "four" 4) alist))
```

This redefines alist as

(("four" . 4) ("one" . 1) ("two" . 2) ("three" . 3))

If you want to update the value associated with an existing key, you need to filter out the old pair and add the new one:

```
(define (update-alist key value alist)
  (cons (cons key value) (filter (lambda (pair) (not (equal? (car pair) key))) alist)))
```

Using this function:

```
(define alist (update-alist "two" 22 alist))
```

This results in alist being

(("two" . 22) ("four" . 4) ("one" . 1) ("three" . 3))

The filter function used in update-alist can be defined as follows:

```
(define (filter pred lst)
  (if (null? lst)
      '()
      (let ((first (car lst))
            (rest (cdr lst)))
        (if (pred first)
            (cons first (filter pred rest))
            (filter pred rest)))))
```

Deleting a key-value pair from an association list is achieved by filtering out the pair with the given key:

```
(define (delete-key key alist)
  (filter (lambda (pair) (not (equal? (car pair) key))) alist))
```

Applying delete-key:

```
(define alist (delete-key "two" alist))
```

This results in alist being

(("four" . 4) ("one" . 1) ("three" . 3))

Association lists provide a simple yet powerful way to handle mappings in Scheme. Their simplicity comes from the inherent list operations and absence of complex data structures. However, for large datasets, more efficient data structures such as hash tables or balanced trees might be preferred due to their faster lookups.

6.12 Advanced List Manipulation Techniques

Advanced list manipulation in Scheme involves a deeper understanding of recursive patterns, higher-order functions, and the efficient processing of complex data structures. This section delves into sophisticated techniques beyond basic operations, enabling the development of more efficient and elegant code.

1. Exploiting Higher-Order Functions

Higher-order functions extend the expressiveness of Scheme by allowing functions to operate on other functions. Two primary higher-order functions in list manipulation are map and filter.

map applies a given function to each element of a list and returns a new list of the results. For instance, consider a function square that squares a number:

```
(define (square x) (* x x))
(map square '(1 2 3 4)) ; Output: (1 4 9 16)
```

filter creates a new list containing only the elements that satisfy a specified predicate. For example, using a predicate even?:

```
(filter even? '(1 2 3 4 5 6)) ; Output: (2 4 6)
```

2. Folding: Reducing Lists to Values

fold (also known as reduce) is a powerful higher-order function that processes a list to produce a single value. There are two common types: foldl and foldr, denoting left fold and right fold.

```
(define (sum a b) (+ a b))
(foldl sum 0 '(1 2 3 4)) ; Output: 10
(foldr sum 0 '(1 2 3 4)) ; Output: 10
```

The difference between foldl and foldr becomes apparent with non-commutative operations. Consider a subtraction operation:

```
(define (subtract a b) (- a b))
(foldl subtract 0 '(1 2 3 4)) ; Output: -10
(foldr subtract 0 '(1 2 3 4)) ; Output: 2
```

3. Zip and Unzip Functions

Zipping is the process of combining two lists element-wise into a single list of pairs, while unzipping separates pairs back into two lists.

A simple zip function can be illustrated as follows:

```
(define (zip lst1 lst2)
  (if (or (null? lst1) (null? lst2))
      '()
      (cons (cons (car lst1) (car lst2))
            (zip (cdr lst1) (cdr lst2)))))
(zip '(1 2 3) '(4 5 6)) ; Output: ((1 . 4) (2 . 5) (3 . 6))
```

The corresponding unzip function can be implemented as:

```
(define (unzip lst)
  (if (null? lst)
      (cons '() '())
      (let ((unzipped (unzip (cdr lst))))
        (cons (cons (caar lst) (car unzipped))
              (cons (cdar lst) (cdr unzipped))))))
(unzip '((1 . 4) (2 . 5) (3 . 6))) ; Output: ((1 2 3) (4 5 6))
```

4. List Comprehensions and Generators

Although Scheme does not support list comprehensions natively as some other languages do, similar behavior can be achieved using existing constructs. For generating a list of numbers that fit certain criteria, we can define:

```
(define (range start end)
  (if (> start end)
      '()
      (cons start (range (+ start 1) end))))

(define (comprehend pred range-fn start end)
  (filter pred (range-fn start end)))

; Example: List of even numbers from 1 to 10
(comprehend even? range 1 10) ; Output: (2 4 6 8 10)
```

5. Efficient List Reversal

While the built-in reverse function in Scheme provides a straightforward way to reverse a list, crafting a more efficient version using tail recursion can be educational.

```
(define (reverse-tail-helper lst acc)
  (if (null? lst)
      acc
      (reverse-tail-helper (cdr lst) (cons (car lst) acc))))

(define (reverse-tail lst)
  (reverse-tail-helper lst '()))
(reverse-tail '(1 2 3 4)) ; Output: (4 3 2 1)
```

6. Flattening Nested Lists

Flattening, or converting a nested list into a single list of elements, can be complex due to varying depths of nested structures. A recursive approach is typically used:

```
(define (flatten lst)
  (cond
    ((null? lst) '())
    ((list? (car lst)) (append (flatten (car lst)) (flatten (cdr lst))))
    (else (cons (car lst) (flatten (cdr lst))))))
(flatten '(1 (2 (3 4) 5) 6)) ; Output: (1 2 3 4 5 6)
```

7. Association List Manipulations

Association lists (alists) are lists of pairs used to store key-value mappings. Common operations include searching for a key, adding a new pair, and updating an existing value.

To search for a key:

```
(define (assoc key alist)
  (cond
    ((null? alist) #f)
    ((equal? (caar alist) key) (car alist))
    (else (assoc key (cdr alist)))))
(assoc 'b '((a . 1) (b . 2) (c . 3))) ; Output: (b . 2)
```

To add or update a key-value pair:

```
(define (assoc-update key value alist)
  (cond
    ((null? alist) (cons (cons key value) '()))
    ((equal? (caar alist) key) (cons (cons key value) (cdr alist)))
    (else (cons (car alist) (assoc-update key value (cdr alist))))))
(assoc-update 'b 4 '((a . 1) (b . 2))) ; Output: ((a . 1) (b . 4))
```

Advanced list manipulation techniques significantly enhance the functionality and efficiency of Scheme programs. Proficiency in these methods facilitates the creation of complex data processing algorithms while maintaining readability and performance.

Chapter 7

Input and Output in Scheme

This chapter provides a comprehensive guide to input and output operations in Scheme. It covers basic I/O functions such as 'display', 'newline', and 'read', as well as reading and writing characters and strings. The chapter details file handling, including opening, closing, reading, and writing files using 'read-line' and 'write-line'. Advanced topics like binary I/O, formatted I/O with 'format', and error handling during I/O operations are also discussed. Additionally, the chapter introduces the concept of ports and explores advanced techniques for efficient I/O management.

7.1 Introduction to Input and Output in Scheme

Input and Output (I/O) operations are fundamental components of any programming language, allowing programs to interact with the external world by receiving data from the user or other sources and providing feedback or results. In Scheme, I/O operations are managed through a well-defined set of functions and procedures that leverage its minimalist yet powerful syntactic framework.

To begin understanding Scheme I/O, it is essential to recognize two primary types of data communication: input, where the program receives information, and output, where the program sends out information. Scheme provides a variety of built-in procedures and constructs to handle these operations efficiently.

The basic input and output functions in Scheme, such as display, newline, and read, form the foundation of more complex I/O operations. These functions allow Scheme programs to handle basic interactions, including printing text to the console, reading user input, and controlling the format of output.

- display: Outputs a representation of a value to the current output port.
- newline: Outputs a newline character to the current output port.
- read: Reads and returns a Scheme expression from the current input port.

The display function is utilized to output a value to the current output port, usually the console. Its usage is straightforward:

```
(display "Hello, World!")
```

The above line of code prints the string "Hello, World!" to the console. It is also possible to display other types of data, such as numbers and lists, using the same function:

```
(display 42)
(display '(1 2 3))
```

This would output:

```
42
(1 2 3)
```

The newline function plays a crucial role in formatting text output by inserting a newline character into the output stream. For example:

```
(display "First line.")
(newline)
(display "Second line.")
```

would produce:

```
First line.
Second line.
```

Scheme's read function reads data from the input port and returns it as a Scheme expression. The following example demonstrates reading input from the user:

```
(define user-input (read))
(display "You entered: ")
(display user-input)
(newline)
```

When this code is executed, the program waits for user input. Suppose the user enters the number 123; the output will be:

```
You entered: 123
```

Additionally, I/O operations in Scheme extend beyond these basic functions. Understanding that I/O operations often involve handling characters and strings is imperative for creating more sophisticated programs.

read-char and write-char functions are used to handle character-level input and output operations. For example:

```
(define c (read-char)) ; Read a character
(write-char c) ; Write a character
```

If the user inputs the character 'A', the output will be the same character 'A'. These functions read and write single characters, providing finer control over the I/O process.

File handling in Scheme is another important aspect discussed further in this chapter. It involves opening files for reading or writing, processing file contents, and closing files once operations are complete. Scheme provides a suite of file I/O functions, such as open-input-file, open-output-file, and close-input-port, which will be detailed in subsequent sections.

Ports, which represent an abstract interface to input and output devices, are central to Scheme's I/O system. Understanding ports and their operations is crucial for efficiently managing input and output, especially when dealing with multiple data streams.

Advanced I/O techniques and error handling strategies in Scheme help achieve robust and fault-tolerant programs. These strategies include formatted output using format, managing various data types, and handling exceptional conditions during I/O operations.

By integrating the fundamental principles laid out in this section, and progressing through the more advanced techniques detailed in the subsequent sections, a comprehensive understanding of Scheme's I/O capabilities can be achieved. This foundation supports the development of robust applications that interact with users and other systems effectively.

7.2 Basic I/O Functions: 'display', 'newline', and 'read'

Scheme provides fundamental I/O functions that are integral to any programming task involving interaction with the user or with files. Key among these functions are display, newline, and read. Understanding how these functions operate is essential for efficient input and output handling in Scheme.

display is one of the simplest ways to output data to the console. It takes one argument, which is the value to be displayed. This function converts the argument to a string and prints it to the standard output port. The following example demonstrates the use of display to output a string and a number.

```
(display "Hello, world!")
(display 42)
```

The output of this code will be:

```
Hello, world!42
```

It is crucial to note that display does not automatically insert a newline character; consecutive calls to display will result in concatenated output. To format the output more clearly, the newline function can be used.

The newline function, as its name suggests, prints a newline to the standard output port. This function does not require any arguments. Here is an example that utilizes newline to separate output:

```
(display "Hello, world!")
(newline)
(display 42)
(newline)
```

The output for this example will be:

```
Hello, world!
42
```

newline is particularly useful in ensuring that subsequent outputs appear on new lines, improving readability.

When it comes to input, Scheme's read function is fundamental. This function reads a Scheme expression from the standard input port. The read expression can be of any Scheme data type, including numbers, strings, symbols, and lists. Here is a sample usage:

```
(define input (read))
```

```
(display "You entered: ")
(display input)
(newline)
```

If the user inputs (4 5 6), the output will be:

```
You entered: (4 5 6)
```

read reads a complete expression, making it highly versatile for various data types. However, it also means that read will not return until a valid expression is completely entered, which is something to keep in mind for interactive programs.

Consider a scenario where more structured input/output is required. Using display and read together facilitates basic formatted I/O. For instance, to prompt the user for specific data and then read it, you might write:

```
(display "Enter your name: ")
(define name (read))
(display "Hello, ")
(display name)
(display "!")
(newline)
```

If the user inputs "Alice", the execution would result in:

```
Enter your name: "Alice"
Hello, "Alice"!
```

In Scheme, while the display function outputs textual data without format consideration, combining it with newline and read enables the creation of interactive programs. Let us explore some practical applications to solidify understanding.

Suppose there's a need to read and display a list of numbers. The following code demonstrates this process:

```
(display "Enter a list of numbers: ")
(define numbers (read))
(display "You entered: ")
(display numbers)
(newline)
```

If the input is (1 2 3 4 5), the resulting output is:

```
Enter a list of numbers: (1 2 3 4 5)
You entered: (1 2 3 4 5)
```

In more advanced I/O operations, handling different data types effectively and ensuring that input and output are correctly formatted are essential skills. Programs must manage various cases and handle potential user errors gracefully, which will be explored in subsequent sections.

Applying these fundamental functions in more complex scenarios sets the stage for efficient and effective program development. Understanding the detailed mechanisms behind display, newline, and read provides a solid foundation for mastering Scheme's input and output capabilities.

7.3 Reading and Writing Characters

In Scheme programming, the ability to read and write individual characters is essential for manipulating text at a granular level. This functionality is crucial when dealing with operations where byte-level precision or the need to process data character-by-character arises. The procedure for reading and writing characters in Scheme is straightforward and can be achieved through a few key functions.

Reading Characters

Scheme provides the read-char function to read the next character from an input port, returning the character read. Typically, it reads from the current input port unless another input port is specified.

```
(define ch (read-char))
```

In the code snippet above, read-char reads the next character from the default input port and binds the read character to the variable ch. If no input port is specified, it uses the default input port, which is usually the keyboard.

read-char can also take an optional argument specifying an input port:

```
(define ch (read-char input-port))
```

Suppose that reading characters reaches the end of the input. In that case, read-char will return the end-of-file object. It is crucial to handle this scenario to prevent unexpected behaviors. The end-of-file object is typically checked using the eof-object? predicate:

```
(let loop ()
  (let ((ch (read-char)))
    (if (eof-object? ch)
        (display "End of input.")
        (begin
          (display ch)
```

```
        (loop)))))
```

This recursive function continues reading characters until the end of the input is reached, at which point it displays a message and terminates.

Writing Characters

Writing characters to an output stream is just as important and is accomplished using the write-char function. This function writes a specified character to the given output port or the default output port if no port is specified.

```
(write-char #\A)
```

In this example, the character #\A is written to the default output port. The write-char function can also take an optional output port argument:

```
(write-char #\A output-port)
```

This capability allows for greater flexibility when directing output to various destinations, such as files or network ports.

To handle a sequence of characters, a loop can be used to write each character individually:

```
(define (write-string str)
  (let loop ((index 0))
    (when (< index (string-length str))
      (write-char (string-ref str index))
      (loop (+ index 1)))))
```

In this function, write-string takes a string str as input. It writes each character of the string to the default output port using write-char and the string-ref function to access each character by index.

Practical Example: File Handling

Often, one needs to read from or write to files instead of just the standard input and output ports. Scheme provides mechanisms to open files and then perform character-based I/O operations.

```
(define input-port (open-input-file "example.txt"))
(let loop ((ch (read-char input-port)))
  (unless (eof-object? ch)
    (display ch)
    (loop (read-char input-port))))
(close-input-port input-port)
```

In this example, open-input-file is used to open the file named "example.txt" for reading. The read-char function reads characters from the file until the end-of-file object is encountered. Each character is displayed, and finally, the input port is closed using close-input-port.

Similarly, writing characters to a file is accomplished by opening an output file port:

```
(define output-port (open-output-file "output.txt"))
(write-char #\A output-port)
(close-output-port output-port)
```

Here, open-output-file opens or creates the file "output.txt" for writing. The character #\A is then written to this file. After writing, it is crucial to close the output port using close-output-port to ensure data is properly flushed and resource leaks are prevented.

By integrating these functions effectively, one can achieve robust character-level input and output operations in Scheme, paving the way for more sophisticated text processing tasks. Readers should practice using these functions to gain proficiency in handling low-level text data efficiently.

7.4 Working with Strings in I/O

When working with strings in Scheme for input and output operations, it is crucial to understand the available functions and their correct usage. Scheme provides a variety of procedures to facilitate effective manipulation of strings, allowing both reading from and writing to standard input and output, as well as handling strings within files.

display and newline are foundational I/O functions, introduced earlier, that simplify writing strings to the console. The display function outputs the string without any additional formatting, and the newline function advances the cursor to the next line.

```
(display "Hello, World!")
(newline)
```

The above code will display the string "Hello, World!" followed by moving the cursor to the next line.

Reading Strings

Reading strings from input can be performed using the read, read-line, and read-string functions. Each function caters to different needs, from reading complete s-expressions to capturing specific lines or portions of text.

read

The read function reads the next s-expression from the input. When the input is a string, one must utilize a string port to handle the string correctly.

```
(define input-string "This is a test string.")
(define input-port (open-input-string input-string))
(display (read input-port))
(close-input-port input-port)
```

This code snippet opens an input port from a string, reads from it, and displays the read content.

read-line

The read-line function reads the entire line from the input until a newline character is encountered.

```
(define input-string "First line\nSecond line")
(define input-port (open-input-string input-string))
(display (read-line input-port)) ; Output: First line
(newline)
(display (read-line input-port)) ; Output: Second line
(close-input-port input-port)
```

Here, read-line is used to read multiple lines from the input-string.

read-string

For scenarios requiring fixed-length string reading, read-string is utilized.

```
(define input-string "Read this part only.")
(define input-port (open-input-string input-string))
(display (read-string 4 input-port)) ; Output: Read
(close-input-port input-port)
```

In this example, read-string reads the first four characters from the provided input port.

Writing Strings

Writing strings to an output destination can be straightforward with functions tailored for this purpose, like write, write-string, and display.

write

The write function outputs a readable representation of the data to the given port.

```
(define output-port (open-output-string))
(write "Hello, Scheme!" output-port)
(define result (get-output-string output-port))
(display result) ; Output: "Hello, Scheme!"
(close-output-port output-port)
```

This snippet demonstrates writing a string in a readable format and retrieving it from the output port.

write-string

The write-string function allows writing a string without creating a readable representation, making it suitable for direct string outputs.

```
(define output-port (open-output-string))
(write-string "Direct text output." output-port)
(define result (get-output-string output-port))
(display result) ; Output: Direct text output.
(close-output-port output-port)
```

Combining Reading and Writing

In practical applications, efficient data handling often involves combining reading and writing operations. Consider an example involving reading from an input string, processing the data, and writing the output to a separate string.

```
(define input-string "123 456 789")
(define output-port (open-output-string))
(define input-port (open-input-string input-string))

(let loop ((input (read input-port)))
  (unless (eof-object? input)
    (write-string (number->string (* input 2)) output-port)
    (write-string " " output-port)
    (loop (read input-port))))

(define result (get-output-string output-port))
(display result) ; Output: 246 912 1578
(close-input-port input-port)
(close-output-port output-port)
```

In this code, the input string of numbers is doubled and the results are written to an output string.

Understanding these functions equips you with the necessary tools to manage strings effectively in Scheme I/O operations. Their versatility ensures you can handle a variety of input and output tasks efficiently.

7.5 File Handling: Opening and Closing Files

In Scheme, handling files is an essential aspect of managing persistent data storage. Below, we delve into the requisite procedures for opening and closing files, ensuring data security and integrity. Scheme provides robust mechanisms to handle different file operations—commonly through ports—which serve as the conduit for data flows between the program and the file system.

The primary procedure for opening a file in Scheme is open-input-file for reading and open-output-file for writing. These functions return a port that can be subsequently used to read from or write to the file.

Opening a File for Input

To open a file for reading, use the open-input-file procedure:

```
(define input-port (open-input-file "example.txt"))
```

In this example, input-port is bound to a port associated with the file example.txt. If the file does not exist, an error is raised.

Opening a File for Output

For writing purposes, the open-output-file procedure is utilized:

```
(define output-port (open-output-file "example.txt"))
```

This example binds output-port to a port for writing to example.txt. If the file does not exist, it will be created. If it does exist, its contents will be erased unless explicitly managed—this is an aspect we will explore further when discussing file modes.

Closing Files

It is a good practice to close files when their operations are complete. This releases system resources and prevents data corruption or loss. Scheme provides the close-input-port and close-output-port procedures for this purpose.

To close an input port:

```
(close-input-port input-port)
```

To close an output port:

```
(close-output-port output-port)
```

Example of Opening and Closing Files

Below is a complete example that demonstrates opening a file for output, writing a string to it, and then closing the file:

```
(define output-port (open-output-file "example-output.txt"))
(display "Hello, Scheme!" output-port)
(close-output-port output-port)
```

Similarly, the following example opens a file for input, reads its contents, and then closes the file:

```
(define input-port (open-input-file "example-output.txt"))
(define file-contents (read input-port))
(close-input-port input-port)
file-contents
```

If example-output.txt contains the string "Hello, Scheme!", the variable file-contents will be bound to this string.

Handling File Opening Errors

When opening a file, especially for input, there is the possibility of encountering errors such as the file not being found. Scheme provides the with-input-from-file and with-output-to-file procedures to handle such situations more gracefully, using a form of exception handling.

For example, using with-input-from-file ensures the file is correctly handled:

```
(with-input-from-file "example-output.txt"
  (lambda ()
    (let ((contents (read)))
      contents)))
```

This snippet reads the contents of example-output.txt within the scope of the lambda and ensures the file is properly managed.

Equally, with-output-to-file facilitates writing to a file within a controlled scope:

```
(with-output-to-file "example-output.txt"
  (lambda ()
    (display "Hello, Scheme!")))
```

These higher-order procedures take care of opening the file, performing the necessary operations, and closing the file, significantly reducing the likelihood of inadvertent errors.

File Modes and Append Mode

For more advanced file operations, such as appending to an existing file without overwriting its contents, Scheme allows additional file modes. Using open-output-file, we can specify the mode to ensure data integrity:

```
(define output-port (open-output-file "example-output.txt" :append))
(display "Appending this text." output-port)
(close-output-port output-port)
```

Here, the :append mode ensures the string "Appending this text." is added to the end of example-output.txt without erasing its original content.

Through meticulous applications of these procedures and modes, Scheme programmers can perform file operations efficiently and safely, adhering to best practices for resource management and error handling. This robust approach to file handling serves as a foundation for performing more complex I/O tasks effectively within Scheme programs.

7.6 Reading from Files: 'read' and 'read-line'

Understanding how to read data from files is fundamental for developing robust Scheme programs. In this section, we will delve into the intricacies of using the read and read-line functions in Scheme. These functions are pivotal for efficiently handling file input operations.

The read function is designed to read Scheme expressions from an input port. This function will read until it encounters an end-of-file marker or a syntax error. The read-line function, on the other hand, reads an entire line of data from the input port, returning it as a string, excluding the newline character.

```
; Example: Reading a list from a file using 'read'
(let ((port (open-input-file "data.scm"))) ; Open the file 'data.scm'
  (let ((data (read port))) ; Read the first expression from the file
    (close-input-port port) ; Close the input port
    data)) ; Return the read data
```

This block of code demonstrates how to open a file for reading and read a Scheme expression from it. The open-input-file function is used to obtain an input port for the file "data.scm". This port is then passed to the read function to read the next Scheme expression from the file. After reading, it is crucial to close the input port using the close-input-port function to release system resources.

The read function can read various types of Scheme data, including lists, symbols, numbers, strings, and more. When the end of the file is reached, read returns a special end-of-file object, which can be checked using the eof-object? predicate.

```
; Complete example: Reading multiple expressions from a file
(let ((port (open-input-file "data.scm")))
  (let loop ((expr (read port)) (result '()))
    (if (eof-object? expr)
        (begin
          (close-input-port port)
          (reverse result)) ; Return the list in the correct order
        (loop (read port) (cons expr result)))))
```

This example employs a loop to read multiple expressions from a file until the end-of-file object is encountered. The loop function accumulates the read expressions into a list, reversing the list at the end to maintain the proper order since the cons operation adds to the front of the list.

In contrast, the read-line function is used for line-based input operations. The following example illustrates how to read lines from a file one at a time:

```
; Example: Reading lines from a file using 'read-line'
(let ((port (open-input-file "data.txt")))
  (let loop ((line (read-line port)) (result '()))
    (if (eof-object? line)
        (begin
          (close-input-port port)
          (reverse result)) ; Return the list of lines in the correct order
        (loop (read-line port) (cons line result)))))
```

In the example above, the loop function reads each line using read-line and accumulates them in a list. As with read, the end-of-file object is used to signal the termination of input, ensuring that all lines are read and stored correctly.

Considerations must be given to the encoding of the file's contents and how the Scheme interpreter handles different types of data. For instance, if the file contains complex data structures, additional parsing might be required after reading.

Checking for possible I/O errors is integral to robust file handling. Scheme does not always handle I/O errors explicitly within the functions discussed, so embedding error checks or using exception handling mechanisms is advised for production-level code.

Programs often have to handle different types of data within the same file. Suppose a file contains not just lines of text but also numeric or symbolic data. In such cases, you might find a combination of read and read-line to be beneficial. Here is an example demonstrating this:

```
; Example: Reading mixed data from a file
(let ((port (open-input-file "mixed-data.txt")))
  (let loop ((line (read-line port)) (result '()))
    (if (eof-object? line)
        (begin
          (close-input-port port)
          (reverse result)) ; Return the list of read data
        (let ((datum (with-input-from-string line read)))
          (loop (read-line port) (cons datum result))))))
```

In this scenario, read-line reads a line, and with-input-from-string along with read interprets each line as a Scheme expression. This approach is highly flexible, as it allows for reading and interpreting varied types of data embedded within the same file.

By thoroughly understanding the functionalities of read and read-line, you can achieve an efficient and reliable mechanism for file input operations in Scheme. It is essential to handle file resources carefully by closing files properly and anticipating potential errors, thereby ensuring the stability and reliability of your Scheme programs.

7.7 Writing to Files: 'write' and 'write-line'

Writing data to files is a fundamental operation in Scheme, enabling persistent storage of output that can be utilized for various applications, ranging from simple logs to comprehensive data records. This section delves into the functions write and write-line, explaining their syntax, usage, and common practices to ensure effective file writing operations.

The write function in Scheme converts expressions into a textual representation and writes them to an output port, typically a file. To utilize write, one must first open a file and obtain a port, which serves as the medium for I/O operations.

```
; Opening a file for writing
(define output-port (open-output-file "output.txt"))
```

Once the file is open, data can be written to it using write. It is crucial to ensure the port is properly managed and closed after the writing operations are complete to prevent resource leaks.

```
; Writing data to the file
(write 'Hello, World! output-port)
```

The output will similarly appear in the file as:

```
Hello, World!
```

Unlike display, the write function includes additional quotation marks and other Scheme expression details in the output, making it suitable for writing data that needs to be accurately read back into Scheme.

write-line provides a convenient way to write a line of text to a file, automatically appending a newline character at the end, thus allowing each invocation of write-line to start on a new line.

```
; Writing a line of text to the file
(write-line "This is the first line." output-port)
(write-line "This is another line." output-port)
```

The content of the file after the operations will be:

```
This is the first line.
This is another line.
```

It is equally important to handle string data accurately when writing to files. The following example demonstrates writing string data:

```
; Writing string data to the file
(write "Hello, Scheme!" output-port)
```

After completing the writing operations, close the file using:

```
; Closing the file
(close-output-port output-port)
```

Proper error handling is a best practice during file operations to handle situations wherein the file operations might fail, e.g., due to permissions or non-existent directories. Ensuring the code gracefully handles such exceptions involves checking conditions and using error-handling mechanisms available in Scheme.

Another aspect is efficient use of resources, particularly through buffered I/O which can significantly improve performance. Scheme implementations often manage this efficiently, but understanding the buffer sizes and flushing mechanisms can be beneficial for advanced tasks.

Finally, for more complex data structures, converting them to a format suitable for write or write-line might involve serialization techniques. Libraries offering JSON or XML serialization can be interfaced with write operations to store structured data.

While write and write-line are fundamental functions for writing data to files, considering file handling best practices, efficient resource usage, and error management ensures robust and reliable operations.

7.8 Binary I/O and Handling Byte Streams

Binary I/O operations in Scheme are essential for applications requiring efficient and precise data manipulation, particularly when dealing with non-textual data like images, multimedia files, or serialized objects. This section delves into the specifics of handling binary I/O and byte streams, illustrating how these operations are implemented in Scheme.

The core functions for performing binary I/O in Scheme revolve around ports. Ports are abstract layers that facilitate the communication between Scheme programs and the external world, such as files or network sockets. Unlike text ports, binary ports handle raw byte data directly, ensuring that no interpretation or conversion of data occurs.

To effectively manage binary I/O, one must comprehend the standard procedures for opening, reading from, and writing to binary ports.

```
(define input-port (open-binary-input-file "example.bin"))
(define output-port (open-binary-output-file "example.bin"))
```

The open-binary-input-file and open-binary-output-file functions create input and output binary ports respectively. These ports serve as channels through which bytes are read or written. It is crucial to ensure that files are properly closed after operations to release resources and maintain data integrity. This is achieved through the close-input-port and close-output-port functions.

```
(close-input-port input-port)
(close-output-port output-port)
```

Reading from a binary port typically involves functions such as read-u8, read-byte, or read-bytes. These functions read unsigned 8-bit integers or blocks of bytes from the input port, respectively.

```
(define byte (read-u8 input-port))
(define byte-vector (read-bytes 10 input-port))
```

The read-u8 function reads a single byte from the input port, returning an integer between 0 and 255. The read-bytes function reads a specified number of bytes and returns them as a byte vector.

Similarly, writing to binary ports involves functions like write-u8 and write-bytes. These allow for writing single bytes or arrays of bytes to the output port.

```
(write-u8 255 output-port)
(write-bytes #{0 1 2 3 4 5 6 7 8 9} output-port)
```

The write-u8 function writes a single byte with a value between 0 and 255 to the output port. The write-bytes function writes a byte vector to the output port.

Handling binary I/O correctly often requires careful management of ports and proper error handling. Scheme provides the try-catch mechanism to catch and manage I/O exceptions.

```
(define (safe-read-byte port)
  (catch 'end-of-file
    (lambda () (read-u8 port))
    (lambda () #f))) ; returns #f on end-of-file
```

In the above example, catch is utilized to handle the 'end-of-file' exception, which is raised when attempting to read beyond the file's end. Here, the function returns #f to indicate the end of the file.

Binary I/O operations are further enhanced by supporting advanced techniques such as buffering. Buffering improves efficiency by reducing the number of system calls. Byte buffers can be manually managed to read from or write to ports in larger chunks, improving I/O performance.

```
(define buffer (make-bytevector 1024))
(let loop ((n (read-bytes! buffer input-port)))
  (when (> n 0)
    ;; Process the buffer here
    (loop (read-bytes! buffer input-port))))
```

The example above demonstrates the use of a byte vector as a buffer. The read-bytes! function fills the buffer with up to 1024 bytes from the input port. The loop reads multiple chunks until the end of the file is reached.

Handling byte streams in Scheme requires the proficient use of these functions to achieve efficient and correct data reading and writing operations. By leveraging ports and buffers, the performance and reliability of Scheme programs dealing with binary data are significantly enhanced.

7.9 Formatted I/O with format

The format procedure is an essential tool in Scheme for producing formatted strings and directing them to various output locations. This capability is especially useful when clear and well-organized output is required, particularly for human-readable formats. The format procedure is highly versatile and operates similarly to formatted I/O functions in other programming languages, such as printf in C.

format follows the general structure:

```
(format destination control-string arg1 arg2 ...)
```

- destination determines where the output will be sent.
- control-string is a string specifying how the arguments should be formatted.
- The arg1, arg2, etc., are the variables or expressions to be formatted.

The destination parameter can be:

- #t: Output is directed to the current output port.
- #f: The formatted output string is returned.
- A port object: The formatted output is sent to the specified port.

The control-string contains literal text interspersed with format directives, each beginning with a tilde (~) character. These directives specify how the corresponding arguments should be formatted.

Common format directives include:

- ~a: Display an argument with display.
- ~s: Display an argument with write.
- ~d: Display an integer in decimal format.
- ~f: Display a floating-point number.

To illustrate, consider the following example:

```
(let ((age 30)
      (name "Alice"))
  (format #t "Name: ~a, Age: ~d~%" name age))
```

Here, the format procedure outputs:

Name: Alice, Age: 30

Typically, the control-string can be composed of literal text, which is copied directly to the output, and format directives, each of which is replaced by the formatted representation of the corresponding argument.

Advanced Formatting Options

The format procedure includes options enabling alignment, padding, and precision. Consider the following directives:

- ~%: Emits a newline character.
- ~N%: Emits N newline characters.
- ~t: Inserts a tab character.
- ~N,a: Adjusts the width for an argument (useful for alignment).
- ~Max,Min,X,X: Specifies maximum and minimum padding and alignment for numbers.

Applying these advanced directives, we can achieve various outputs. For example:

```
(let ((price 23.456))
  (format #t "~10,2f" price))
```

This specifies a width of 10 and 2 decimal places, resulting in:

```
23.46
```

Custom Formatting Functions

Scheme allows the definition of custom formatting functions to handle complex formatting needs. This is achieved by extending the basic format capabilities with user-defined procedures.

```
(define (format-currency amount)
  (format #f "$~{~,.2f}" amount))

(let ((amount 12345.678))
  (display (format-currency amount)))
```

The custom format-currency function in this example formats a numeric amount into a string representing monetary value, with two decimal places and a dollar sign. The amount provided to it results in:

$12,345.68

Error Handling in format

Proper error handling is crucial for robust I/O operations. When implementing format, ensure that all arguments match the expected types and quantity specified by the format directives. Scheme typically raises an error if mismatched. Utilize guard to capture and manage such exceptions gracefully.

```
(guard (e
        ((exn:fail? e)
         (format #t "Error in format: ~a~%" (exn:message e))))
  (let ((invalid_input "abc"))
    (format #t "Integer: ~d" invalid_input)))
```

This code snippet ensures that any formatting error is captured and an appropriate message is displayed.

Employing format allows precise control over output layouts and readability, greatly enhancing user interfaces and debugging processes in Scheme applications. The flexibility to direct output, align, pad, and format strings to specific requirements makes it an indispensable tool for developers.

7.10 Error Handling during I/O Operations

Error handling is a critical aspect of performing input and output (I/O) operations in Scheme. Proper error handling ensures that your programs can gracefully deal with unexpected issues, such as file not found errors, read/write permission issues, or corrupted input. Scheme, like many programming languages, provides mechanisms to handle such errors using exceptions and condition handling constructs.

Scheme's error handling mechanisms involve the use of with-exception-handler, raise, and condition-case. These constructs allow you to define how your program should respond to different types of errors that occur during I/O operations.

with-exception-handler installs a new exception handler, which is a function that is called with the raised exception. raise is used to trigger exceptions, and condition-case allows you to specify how to handle specific types of conditions.

Consider the following example, which demonstrates a basic use of with-exception-handler and raise for handling errors during file opening:

```
(define (safe-open-file filename mode)
  (with-exception-handler
    (lambda (exn)
      (display "An error occurred: ")
      (display (condition-message exn))
      (newline)
      #f)
    (lambda ()
      (open-input-file filename))))
```

In this example, the function safe-open-file attempts to open a file in the specified mode. If an exception occurs (e.g., the file does not exist or the permissions do not allow opening it), the exception handler displays an error message and returns #f to indicate failure.

Let's extend this concept further by handling multiple types of I/O errors using condition-case. Assume we have a function that reads a line from a file and handles errors like file not found or permission denied.

```
(define (read-line-safe port)
  (condition-case
    (read-line port)
    ((file-not-found-condition)
     (lambda (exn)
       (display "File not found: ")
       (display (condition-message exn))
       (newline)
       #f))
    ((permission-denied-condition)
     (lambda (exn)
       (display "Permission denied: ")
       (display (condition-message exn))
       (newline)
       #f))
    ((read-error-condition)
     (lambda (exn)
       (display "Error reading file: ")
       (display (condition-message exn))
       (newline)
       #f))))
```

In the read-line-safe function, condition-case is used to handle different exceptions separately. Each condition is associated with an error-handling lambda function that performs specific actions and logs error messages. This approach allows for more granular control over error handling.

When dealing with file I/O, it is crucial to manage resources efficiently and ensure that files are properly closed even when errors occur. Scheme provides dynamic-wind to manage such scenarios.

```
(define (process-file filename)
  (let ((port #f))
```

```
(with-exception-handler
  (lambda (exn)
    (when port (close-input-port port))
    (display "An error occurred: ")
    (display (condition-message exn))
    (newline)
    #f)
  (lambda ()
    (dynamic-wind
      (lambda () (set! port (open-input-file filename)))
      (lambda () (let ((line (read-line port)))
                   (display line) (newline)))
      (lambda () (when port (close-input-port port))))))))
```

Here, dynamic-wind is used to ensure that the input port is properly opened before the main operation and closed afterward, regardless of whether an error occurs during the read operation. The dynamic-wind construct accepts three arguments: a pre-thunk to execute before the primary operation, a primary thunk to execute during the main operation, and a post-thunk to execute after the main operation.

By employing the above techniques, you can ensure that your Scheme programs are robust and capable of handling a wide variety of I/O-related errors effectively. This enhances the overall reliability and user experience, mitigating the risk of unexpected program crashes or data corruption.

7.11 Using Ports in Scheme

Ports provide a flexible and abstract way to handle input and output operations in Scheme. Instead of dealing directly with files, strings, or other data sources, Scheme programs use ports to mediate the flow of data. This section explores the creation, utilization, and management of ports to achieve efficient and effective data handling.

At its core, a port represents a source or sink of data. There are several types of ports in Scheme, including input ports, output ports, and bidirectional ports, which can handle both input and output.

To open an input port to read data from a file, the open-input-file procedure is used:

```
(define input-port (open-input-file "example.txt"))
```

This code snippet creates a new input port linked to example.txt. With this port, we can perform various read operations, such as reading characters, lines, or the entire file content.

To read a single character from the input port, the read-char procedure is employed:

```
(define char (read-char input-port))
```

For reading a line of text, the read-line procedure is utilized:

```
(define line (read-line input-port))
```

Closing the port after operations is crucial to free resources:

```
(close-input-port input-port)
```

Output ports operate similarly. To open an output port for writing to a file, the open-output-file procedure is employed:

```
(define output-port (open-output-file "output.txt"))
```

This snippet creates an output port associated with output.txt. To write a character or string to the file, the write-char and write procedures can be used:

```
(write-char #\A output-port)
(write "This is a test." output-port)
```

Line-based writing is also straightforward:

```
(display "This is a line of text." output-port)
(newline output-port)
```

Again, it is essential to close the output port once writing is complete:

```
(close-output-port output-port)
```

Ports are not limited to file operations. Scheme provides functionalities for creating ports from strings and other data sources. The open-input-string and open-output-string procedures allow manipulation of string data through ports. Here is an example using a string as an input port:

```
(define input-port (open-input-string "This is a test string."))
(define str (read-line input-port))
(close-input-port input-port)
```

An interesting feature of ports in Scheme is the ability to handle custom ports. By creating custom implementations of ports, it is possible to streamline data flows between different parts of an application or encompass special data sources and sinks. Custom ports use the make-custom-textual-input-port and make-custom-textual-output-port procedures.

Consider a custom input port example:

```
(define (dummy-reader buffer start count)
  (let loop ((i 0))
    (if (< i count)
        (begin
          (vector-set! buffer (+ start i) #\*)
          (loop (+ i 1)))
        count)))

(define custom-input-port
  (make-custom-textual-input-port 'custom-port
                                  dummy-reader
                                  (lambda () #t)
                                  (lambda () '())))
```

This code demonstrates a custom input port that always provides the '*' character when read. The dummy-reader function writes '*' into the buffer, and make-custom-textual-input-port creates the port.

Utilizing custom output ports follows a similar approach. Custom ports can be especially useful for testing or intercepting I/O operations for logging or debugging purposes.

In Scheme, ports serve as the backbone for performing I/O operations flexibly and efficiently. They abstract the underlying source or sink, be it a file, string, or custom data stream, allowing Scheme programs to handle input and output uniformly. Understanding and utilizing ports, both built-in and custom, is essential for mastering I/O operations in Scheme, providing a robust mechanism to manage data flow.

Overall, mastering ports in Scheme integrates seamlessly into building advanced I/O management techniques and expands the capabilities of Scheme programs to more efficiently handle varied data sources and sinks.

7.12 Advanced I/O Techniques

Advanced input and output (I/O) techniques in Scheme allow for more efficient and controlled operations when dealing with data streams. These techniques involve sophisticated handling of ports, buffered I/O, non-blocking I/O operations, and I/O multiplexing. This section delves into each of these areas to provide a deep understanding of how to implement advanced I/O in Scheme programs.

Buffered I/O: Buffered I/O improves performance by reducing the number of system calls made during read and write operations. Instead of performing I/O operations directly on the file descriptor, data is first accumulated in a buffer. When the buffer reaches a certain size, a bulk read or write operation takes place. Scheme provides mechanisms to utilize buffered I/O efficiently.

To illustrate buffered I/O, let's examine a typical buffered read and write operation. The following example demonstrates how to use a buffer to read and write a file in Scheme:

```
(define BUFFER-SIZE 1024)

(define (buffered-read file)
  (let ((in-port (open-input-file file))
        (buffer (make-string BUFFER-SIZE))
        (contents '()))
    (let loop ()
      (let ((n (read-string! buffer in-port)))
        (if (positive? n)
            (begin
              (set! contents (cons (substring buffer 0 n) contents))
              (loop)))))
    (close-input-port in-port)
    (apply string-append (reverse contents))))

(define (buffered-write file data)
  (let ((out-port (open-output-file file)))
    (let loop ((remaining-data data))
      (if (not (string-null? remaining-data))
          (let ((to-write (substring remaining-data 0 (min BUFFER-SIZE (string-length
                remaining-data)))))
            (write-string to-write out-port)
            (loop (substring remaining-data (string-length to-write))))))
    (close-output-port out-port)))
```

In the code snippet above, buffered-read and buffered-write functions demonstrate how buffering can be employed for reading from and writing to files.

Non-blocking I/O: Non-blocking I/O allows a program to initiate an I/O operation and then proceed without waiting for the operation to complete. This is particularly useful in interactive and networked applications where blocking I/O operations can lead to inefficiencies and unresponsiveness.

In Scheme, non-blocking I/O can be achieved using the set-port-non-blocking! procedure provided by some implementations. The following example illustrates non-blocking input from a file:

```
(define in-port (open-input-file "example.txt"))

(set-port-non-blocking! in-port)

(let read-loop ((results '()))
  (let ((char (read-char in-port)))
    (if (eof-object? char)
```

```
    (begin
      (close-input-port in-port)
      (display "End of file reached.\n")
      (reverse results))
    (if (char-ready? in-port)
        (read-loop (cons char results))
        (begin
          (display "No data available, doing other work...\n")
          (sleep 1)
          (read-loop results))))))
```

Here, the read-loop function continues to read characters if they are available, otherwise it performs other tasks (simulated with sleep 1) until data becomes available again.

I/O Multiplexing: I/O multiplexing is used when a program needs to manage multiple I/O streams simultaneously. It enables the program to monitor multiple ports and determine which ones are ready for reading or writing without blocking. This is commonly implemented using the select system call or equivalent mechanisms.

In Scheme, the select function may not be part of the standard library, but can typically be accessed through FFI (Foreign Function Interface). Below is a hypothetical example illustrating the concept of I/O multiplexing by monitoring multiple input ports:

```
(define input-ports (list (open-input-file "file1.txt")
                          (open-input-file "file2.txt")))

(define (select-ports ports)
  ; Hypothetical function
  ; Returns a list of ports ready for reading
  (ffi-select-read-ports ports))

(let multiplexed-read ()
  (let ((ready-ports (select-ports input-ports)))
    (for-each (lambda (port)
                (let ((data (read-string 1024 port)))
                  (display data)))
              ready-ports)
    (multiplexed-read)))
```

In this pseudocode, ffi-select-read-ports is a hypothetical FFI function that returns a list of ports ready for reading. The multiplexed-read function reads from the available ports and continues to monitor them in a loop.

When implementing advanced I/O techniques, careful consideration must be given to error handling and resource management. Ensuring that all ports are properly closed after usage and handling exceptions can prevent resource leaks and undefined behavior in a program. Efficient I/O management often requires understanding the underlying system details and leveraging the features provided by Scheme in combination with system-level calls.

Chapter 8

Macros and Metaprogramming

This chapter delves into the creation and use of macros for metaprogramming in Scheme. It begins with the basics of macro definitions using 'define-syntax' and 'syntax-rules', followed by the implementation of hygienic macros. Advanced macro patterns, recursive macros, and macro expansion and transformation are discussed in detail. The chapter also covers debugging macros and differentiates between the use cases for macros and functions. Practical applications and case studies are provided to illustrate the power and flexibility of macros in Scheme programming.

8.1 Introduction to Macros and Metaprogramming

Macros in Scheme provide the programmer with a powerful tool for extending the language's syntax, introducing new syntactic forms, and enabling metaprogramming. Metaprogramming refers to the practice of writing programs that can generate or manipulate other programs, or even modify themselves. This section aims to familiarize you with these concepts and underscore their significance in Scheme programming.

Macros differ from functions in that they operate on the syntactic structure of expressions rather than their evaluated values. This distinction enables macros to produce more complex transformations and to introduce new syntactic constructs that are not directly expressible using functions alone.

```
(define-syntax my-macro
  (syntax-rules ()
    ((my-macro args)
     (display "Hello, world!"))))
```

In this example, my-macro is a simple macro that matches any list starting with my-macro followed by its arguments and always produces a display expression. When my-macro is invoked, it will display the string "Hello, world!" regardless of the provided arguments.

Unlike typical function calls, which the Scheme interpreter evaluates based on the rules of lambda calculus, macros undergo a different process:

- **Syntax Analysis**: Macros receive their arguments in unevaluated form. This property allows them to analyze, decompose, and restructure the input expressions.
- **Transformation**: Macros transform the given syntax into another syntax expression following user-defined rules.
- **Expansion**: The transformed syntax is inserted back into the program, where it is then subjected to the standard evaluation rules of Scheme.

Macros make it possible to implement syntactic abstractions efficiently. Consider a scenario where certain repetitive code patterns can be abstracted. Using macros, you can encapsulate these patterns and reuse them with ease.

```
(define-syntax when
  (syntax-rules ()
    ((when test body)
     (if test body '()))))

(when (> 3 2)
  (display "3 is greater than 2"))
```

In this when macro example, the macro rewrites when expressions into if expressions, simplifying the program's syntax. When the condition (> 3 2) is true, "3 is greater than 2" is displayed.

When designing macros, it is crucial to ensure they do not inadvertently capture variables in unintended ways, leading to bugs or inconsistencies. This problem is mitigated using hygienic macros, which maintain the lexical scope of variables and prevent accidental captures. Scheme provides constructs such as syntax-rules to create such hygienic macros.

```
(define-syntax let*
  (syntax-rules ()
    ((let* ()
       body)
     (begin body))
    ((let* ((name1 value1) more ...)
       body)
     (let ((name1 value1))
       (let* (more ...)
         body)))))
```

Here, the let* macro implements a series of nested let expressions, generating code that maintains the variable scopes. Using syntax-rules, we ensure that let* behaves predictably without unintended variable capture.

Metaprogramming with macros also encompasses more advanced techniques such as macro-expansion time computation, recursive macros, and context-sensitive transformations. These capabilities allow detailed control over the generated code, making macros suitable for tasks ranging from simple syntactic sugar to sophisticated compile-time code optimizations.

While macros empower Scheme programmers to transcend beyond the boundaries of built-in syntax, they should be used judiciously. Overuse or misuse of macros can lead to convoluted code, making maintenance and debugging challenging. Thus, a deep understanding of macro mechanics and their appropriate applications is essential for leveraging their full potential effectively.

The process and concepts introduced here lay the groundwork for more advanced discussions in subsequent sections, where we will delve into defining macros, ensuring hygienic transformations, and employing complex macro patterns to solve non-trivial problems in Scheme programming.

8.2 The Basics of Macro Definitions

Scheme macros provide a powerful mechanism for code generation and transformation. At their core, macros enable programmers to define new syntactic constructs in a manner similar to function definitions. This section explores the fundamental concepts involved in macro definitions, focusing on the define-syntax and syntax-rules forms.

Macros in Scheme are defined using the define-syntax form. This form associates an identifier with a transformation rule expressed by syntax-rules. A macro takes input in the form of code and produces code as output. This is done at compile time, allowing for optimizations and transformations that functions cannot achieve.

Let us begin with a simple example of a macro definition:

```
(define-syntax my-macro
  (syntax-rules ()
    ((_ x) (+ x x))))
```

In this example, my-macro is defined using define-syntax. The syntax-rules form specifies the transformation rules for the macro. Within syntax-rules, the first pair of parentheses represents the list of syntax keywords (which is empty in this case), and the subsequent expressions define the transformation patterns. The pattern (_ x) matches any input where the macro is called with a single argument. When the macro is invoked, it produces code that doubles its argument by adding it to itself.

Consider the invocation of my-macro:

```
(my-macro 5)
```

The macro my-macro takes the argument 5 and transforms it into (+ 5 5). The resulting expression is evaluated to yield the value 10.

Macros can accommodate more sophisticated patterns and complex transformations. The primary advantage of macros over functions is their ability to manipulate code structure. For instance, macros can introduce new variables, control flow constructs, or modify existing structures within their expansion.

```
(define-syntax when
  (syntax-rules ()
    ((_ test body ...) (if test (begin body ...)))))
```

In this example, the when macro performs code transformation to provide a syntactic convenience. The when macro takes a condition test and a sequence of expressions body. If the test evaluates to true, the expressions in body are executed in sequence. Otherwise, nothing happens. The transformation effectively translates the when macro into an if expression combined with begin to sequence the body expressions.

Another compelling application of macros is the ability to enable domain-specific languages (DSLs) within Scheme. For example, let us define a simple DSL for arithmetic operations:

```
(define-syntax arithmetic
  (syntax-rules ()
    ((_ (+ a b)) (list '+ a b))
    ((_ (- a b)) (list '- a b))
    ((_ (* a b)) (list '* a b))
    ((_ (/ a b)) (list '/ a b))))
```

This macro named arithmetic enables a specific notation for arithmetic operations. When invoked with arguments matching its patterns, it produces a list representing the corresponding arithmetic operation:

```
(arithmetic (+ 4 2)) ; Produces (list '+ 4 2)
(arithmetic (* 3 5)) ; Produces (list '* 3 5)
```

The expansion of the macro provides structured data that can be further processed or evaluated in various contexts.

While defining macros, ensuring the correct and hygienic handling of variables is crucial. Macros must avoid variable capture and unintended interactions with the enclosing lexical scope. Scheme provides constructs such as gensym and the implicit hygiene of syntax-rules to address these concerns. However, these concepts will be explored in greater detail in subsequent sections.

By manipulating code at the syntactic level, macros offer unparalleled flexibility in Scheme programming. They empower programmers to introduce new syntactic constructs, streamline repetitive patterns, and create embedded DSLs. Mastering the basics of macro definitions lays the foundation for more advanced macro techniques and metaprogramming concepts, transforming the way we approach Scheme programming.

8.3 Using 'define-syntax' and 'syntax-rules'

In Scheme, define-syntax and syntax-rules are foundational constructs for defining macros. A macro in Scheme is a rule or pattern that specifies how input expressions should be transformed into output expressions. This allows programmers to introduce new syntactic constructs in a seamless and consistent manner.

define-syntax is used to associate a macro name with a macro transformer. The transformation rules are defined using syntax-rules. The general form of a macro definition is as follows:

```
(define-syntax macro-name
  (syntax-rules ()
    [pattern1 template1]
    [pattern2 template2]
    ...
    [patternN templateN]))
```

Here, each pattern-template pair defines how an input expression matching the pattern should be converted into a corresponding output expression.

Example: A Simple Macro

Consider a simple macro inc that increments its argument by 1. The definition of inc using define-syntax and syntax-rules can be written as follows:

```
(define-syntax inc
  (syntax-rules ()
    [(inc x) (+ x 1)]))
```

With this definition, any occurrence of (inc x) in the code will be transformed into (+ x 1). For example:

```
(inc 5)
```

is transformed into:

```
(+ 5 1)
```

This example demonstrates the simplicity and power of macros in expanding the language's syntax.

Multiple Patterns

Macros can have multiple patterns to handle different forms of input expressions. These patterns are specified sequentially, and the first matching pattern is applied. Consider a macro unless that evaluates an expression only if a condition is false. We can define it as follows:

```
(define-syntax unless
  (syntax-rules ()
    [(unless condition body)
     (if (not condition) body)]))
```

This macro can be used to execute body only if condition evaluates to #f. For instance:

```
(unless #f (display "This will print."))
(unless #t (display "This will not print."))
```

Recursive Macros

Macros can also invoke themselves recursively. Recursive macros are useful for creating syntactic constructs that involve repetition. Consider a macro repeat that repeats an expression a specified number of times:

```
(define-syntax repeat
  (syntax-rules ()
    [(repeat 0 body)]
    [(repeat n body)
     (begin body (repeat (- n 1) body))]))
```

In this example, (repeat 0 body) is the base case and does nothing. The recursive case (repeat n body) expands to executing body once and then recursively calling repeat with n-1. Usage example:

```
(repeat 3 (display "Hello\n"))
```

The code above will print:

```
Hello
Hello
Hello
```

Macro Hygiene

It is important to note that Scheme macros are hygienic, meaning they avoid unintended variable capture. Hygienic macro systems ensure that the variables introduced by the macro do not accidentally interfere with variables in the context where the macro is used. This is achieved by renaming variables in a consistent manner. Thus, the interactions between macros and the surrounding code are controlled and predictable.

Practical Example

To illustrate a more practical usage, consider a macro when that evaluates a sequence of expressions only if a condition is true:

```
(define-syntax when
```

```
  (syntax-rules ()
    [(when condition body1 body2 ...)
     (if condition
         (begin body1 body2 ...))]))
```

With this definition, when can be used to conditionally execute multiple expressions. For example:

```
(when (> 5 3)
  (display "5 is greater than 3\n")
  (display "Condition is true\n"))
```

If the condition (> 5 3) evaluates to true, it will execute the sequence of expressions in the body.

```
5 is greater than 3
Condition is true
```

Utilizing define-syntax and syntax-rules, Scheme programmers can define powerful and reusable syntactic constructs, enhancing both the expressiveness and readability of their code. Through careful definition and use of macros, it is possible to achieve significant abstraction and code reuse, essential qualities in advanced programming practices.

8.4 Hygienic Macros in Scheme

Hygienic macros are a crucial aspect of Scheme metaprogramming, designed to avoid common pitfalls associated with macro expansion, particularly name capture. By ensuring that macros do not inadvertently capture identifiers, hygienic macros maintain the integrity of the code and reduce the likelihood of subtle, hard-to-detect bugs. In Scheme, hygienic macros are typically created using syntax-rules or syntax-case.

The primary concern that hygienic macros address is *name capture*. This scenario occurs when a macro inadvertently uses an identifier that is already in use in the expanded code's context, potentially changing the meaning of the program. For instance, consider the following non-hygienic macro example:

```
(define-syntax non-hygienic-increment
  (syntax-rules ()
    ((non-hygienic-increment x)
     (let ((y 1))
       (+ x y)))))
```

When this macro is used in conjunction with a binding for y in the surrounding code, it may lead to unexpected behavior:

```
(let ((y 5))
  (non-hygienic-increment 10))
```

The expansion would result in:

```
(let ((y 5))
  (let ((y 1))
    (+ 10 y)))
```

In this example, the outer binding of y is shadowed by the inner binding introduced by the macro, leading to (+ 10 1) instead of the expected (+ 10 5). This is a classic instance of name capture.

Hygienic macros avoid this problem by ensuring the identifiers introduced by the macro are distinct and do not interfere with the surrounding code. Scheme's syntax-rules offers a way to define such macros conveniently. Here is a hygienic version of the increment macro:

```
(define-syntax hygienic-increment
  (syntax-rules ()
    ((hygienic-increment x)
     (let ((y 1))
       (+ x y)))))
```

When expanded, the macro reliably uses its own scope for y, preventing any unintended shadowing:

```
(let ((y 5))
  (hygienic-increment 10))
```

The expansion results in:

```
(let ((y 5))
  (let ((y 1))
    (+ 10 y)))
```

Here, Scheme ensures that the y introduced by the macro is distinct from y from the macro invocation context.

Hygiene Through syntax-rules

The syntax-rules system in Scheme provides a high-level pattern matching syntax for macro definitions, preserving hygiene by default. This means that it intrinsically avoids name capture issues. Consider the following macro that swaps the values of two variables:

```
(define-syntax swap!
  (syntax-rules ()
    ((swap! x y)
     (let ((tmp x))
```

```
        (set! x y)
        (set! y tmp)))))
```

Using swap! in any context will not affect the local environment adversely:

```
(let ((a 3) (b 5))
  (swap! a b)
  (list a b))
```

This code correctly expands and executes as expected:

```
(let ((a 3) (b 5))
  (let ((tmp a))
    (set! a b)
    (set! b tmp))
  (list a b))
```

The identifier tmp introduced within the macro is unique to the instance of expansion, ensuring it does not conflict with any tmp variables in the code that surround the macro use.

Handling Hygiene with syntax-case

For more complex macros, Scheme provides syntax-case, which affords greater flexibility while also maintaining hygienic guarantees. It allows more control over the transformation process, enabling the construction of macros that can manipulate syntactic structures with precision.

Consider a macro that creates a function to add a specific number to its input:

```
(define-syntax add-n
  (lambda (stx)
    (syntax-case stx ()
      ((_ n)
       (let ((n-identifier (syntax-e #'n)))
         #'(lambda (x) (+ x n-identifier)))))))
```

In this example, syntax-case is used to pattern match on the input syntax and generate a new lambda expression. The identifier n-identifier ensures that the number to add is correctly captured and used within the generated function without interfering with any external bindings.

```
(define add-five (add-n 5))
(add-five 10)
```

Here, the macro expands into:

```
(define add-five (lambda (x) (+ x 5)))
(add-five 10)
```

The syntax-e function extracts the value of n from the syntax object and ensures the produced lambda function correctly encapsulates the number to add.

Hygienic macros in Scheme, whether defined using syntax-rules or syntax-case, provide a robust mechanism to extend the language safely and concisely. They uphold the modularity and readability of code by preventing the subtle and often tricky issues of name capture, enabling programmers to write macros that integrate seamlessly with existing codebases.

8.5 Creating Syntactic Sugar with Macros

Syntactic sugar refers to syntax within a programming language that is designed to make things easier to read or to express, but does not alter the functionality of the language itself. In Scheme, macros provide an excellent mechanism for creating syntactic sugar, allowing developers to introduce new syntactic constructs without modifying the underlying language compiler or interpreter.

To begin creating syntactic sugar using macros in Scheme, it is essential to understand the use of define-syntax and syntax-rules. These constructs allow us to define pattern-based macros in a way that ensures the resulting code is hygienic. Let us consider a basic example that introduces a more readable form for a cond expression.

```
(define-syntax when
  (syntax-rules ()
    ((when test body ...)
     (cond (test body ...)))))
```

In the above example, the when macro simplifies conditional execution. Instead of using cond which can be verbose for simple conditions, when provides a more concise syntax. Here is how it can be utilized:

```
(when (> x 5)
  (display "x is greater than 5")
  (newline))
```

The expanded code will be transformed into:

```
(cond ((> x 5)
  (display "x is greater than 5")
  (newline)))
```

```
Output:
x is greater than 5
```

This macro provides an essential insight into the mechanism of creating syntactic sugar: the original Scheme constructs remain unchanged while the readability is enhanced.

Moving further, consider another scenario where the regular use of list operations can be simplified. Commonly used list operations, such as car, cdr, and cons, can be integrated into a more intuitive macro expression.

```
(define-syntax list-heads
  (syntax-rules ()
    ((list-heads first second rest)
     (let ((list '()))
       (set! first (car rest))
       (set! second (cadr rest))
       (set! rest (cddr rest))
       (list first second rest)))))
```

This list-heads macro ensures that working with the first and second elements of a list, along with the rest of the list, is simplified. Usage is demonstrated below:

```
(define first '')
(define second '')
(define rest '(1 2 3 4 5))

(list-heads first second rest)
```

After the macro expansion, the values of first, second, and rest are as follows:

```
first: 1
second: 2
rest: (3 4 5)
```

Macros such as these highlight the flexibility and power of syntactic sugar in making code both concise and readable.

Another facet of syntactic sugar in Scheme through macros is the introduction of looping constructs. Scheme does not have a built-in looping syntax similar to languages with for or while loops; instead, recursive functions are used. However, macros can be employed to create loop constructs for user-friendliness:

```
(define-syntax for-loop
  (syntax-rules (:)
    ((for-loop (var start end)
       body ...)
     (let loop ((var start))
       (if (<= var end)
           (begin
             body ...
             (loop (+ var 1))))))))

(for-loop (i 1 5)
```

```
  (display i)
  (newline))
```

This for-loop macro introduces a syntax familiar to users of other languages. The above code translates into an iterative process from 1 to 5, with the output being:

```
1
2
3
4
5
```

Through this construct, we have effectively reduced the cognitive overhead associated with understanding and implementing recursion, providing a more straightforward and elegant looping mechanism.

In summary, creating syntactic sugar with macros leverages the metaprogramming capabilities of Scheme to enhance code readability and usability. Such practices enable defining new syntactic constructs that align closely with the developers' intent without compromising the language's underlying structure. By focusing on simplicity and clarity, macros serve as an essential tool for Scheme programmers to write more expressive and maintainable code.

8.6 Advanced Macro Patterns and Techniques

In this section, we explore advanced macro patterns and techniques in Scheme. These advanced techniques build on the fundamental concepts discussed earlier—particularly those related to define-syntax and syntax-rules. These patterns enhance the flexibility and power of macros, enabling efficient metaprogramming.

One advanced pattern is the use of pattern variables with ellipses. Ellipses (...) indicate that a pattern variable can match within a repeating pattern. This mechanism is particularly useful for macros that handle variable-length argument lists. Consider the following example:

```
(define-syntax sum
  (syntax-rules ()
    ((_ x ...) (+ x ...))))
```

This macro, sum, takes a variable number of arguments and produces their sum. When expanded with arguments, the macro will create a nested call to +. For instance:

```
> (sum 1 2 3 4)
10
```

Here, individual elements from 1 to 4 are matched to x ... and expanded into a sum expression.

Another powerful technique involves using recursive macros to generate complex syntactic structures. These allow for constructs such as loops or traversals within the macro expansion process. For example, consider a macro to generate a sequence of variable definitions:

```
(define-syntax define-sequence
  (syntax-rules ()
    ((_ (name val) ...)
     (begin (define name val) ...))))
```

This define-sequence macro allows for batch defining of variables:

```
> (define-sequence (a 1) (b 2) (c 3))
> (list a b c)
(1 2 3)
```

Incorporating conditionals into macros to decide how the expansion should proceed based on input patterns is also a critical technique. For instance, we can create a conditional macro that provides different expansions based on the presence or absence of a certain sub-pattern:

```
(define-syntax max
  (syntax-rules ()
    ((_ x) x)
    ((_ x y) (if (> x y) x y))
    ((_ x y z ...) (max (max x y) z ...))))
```

This max macro finds the maximum value of a sequence of numbers. It uses pattern matching to handle different numbers of arguments and employs recursion to manage more than two arguments:

```
> (max 1 5 3 9 2)
9
```

Next, macros can be written to manipulate code structures deeply, such as capturing and renaming variables to avoid name clashes. Consider the advanced case of creating a macro to generate let expressions where variable names should be unique to avoid clashes:

```
(define-syntax unique-let
  (syntax-rules ()
    ((_ ((name val) ...) body)
     ((lambda (name ...)
        body)
      val ...))))
```

The unique-let macro generates a lambda expression that ensures each name is unique within the body:

```
> (unique-let ((x 1) (y 2))
    (+ x y))
3
```

Moreover, advanced macros often utilize auxiliary rules to handle intermediate steps in expansion. Consider a macro to transform a list of expressions into a series of and expressions:

```
(define-syntax and-series
  (syntax-rules ()
    ((_ x) x)
    ((_ x y ...) (and x (and-series y ...)))))
```

This and-series macro expands its arguments into a nested series of and expressions, ensuring short-circuit evaluation:

```
> (and-series #t #t #f #t)
#f
```

In scenarios where the syntactic context needs transforming, a rewrite computation macro might be employed. These scenarios often require the syntax-case system, which offers greater control over pattern matching and transformation, but it is beyond our current focus.

To summarize, advanced macro patterns such as using ellipses, defining sequence macros, incorporating conditionals, and ensuring unique variable names provide extensive customization and control in Scheme programming. Mastery of these techniques allows developers to create more intricate and efficient metaprogramming tools.

8.7 Macro Expansion and Transformation

Understanding the intricacies of macro expansion and transformation is essential for mastering macros in Scheme. This involves parsing the input expressions, transforming them according to the macro's rules, and substituting the results back into the original program. Macro expansion occurs during the compilation phase, allowing the programmer to introduce new syntactic constructs or alter existing ones dynamically.

Macro expansion is initiated when the Scheme evaluator encounters a macro invocation. Using the define-syntax keyword, one defines the macro transformation rules typically with the syntax-rules keyword. These rules determine how the input code should be transformed. Consider the following example:

```
(define-syntax increment
  (syntax-rules ()
    ((_ x) `(set! ,x (+ ,x 1)))))
```

In this snippet, the increment macro takes a variable x and generates a form that increments its value by one. The transformation rule ((_ x) (set! ,x (+ ,x 1))) defines this behavior.

To observe macro expansion in action, consider:

```
(let ((a 5))
  (increment a)
  a)
```

When the increment macro is invoked, the Scheme compiler expands it into the corresponding set! expression:

```
(let ((a 5))
  (set! a (+ a 1))
  a)
```

In more complex scenarios, macro transformations can involve multiple patterns and nested transformations. Macros can be designed to match different input structures and transform them accordingly. An advanced example is a conditional macro that behaves similarly to an if statement but supports multiple branches using cond-like syntax:

```
(define-syntax my-cond
  (syntax-rules (else)
    ((_ (else expr ...))
     (begin expr ...))
    ((_ (test expr ...) clause ...)
     (if test
         (begin expr ...)
         (my-cond clause ...)))))
```

The my-cond macro recursively processes each clause until it encounters the keyword else, at which point it executes the associated expressions. Each branch's condition is evaluated in sequence, and the corresponding expressions are executed if the condition is true. If all conditions are false, the else clause is executed.

To illustrate the transformation of my-cond, consider the following:

```
(my-cond
  ((> 5 2) 'greater)
  ((< 5 2) 'less)
  (else 'equal))
```

During macro expansion, my-cond transforms into nested if expressions:

```
(if (> 5 2)
    'greater
    (if (< 5 2)
```

```
'less
(begin 'equal)))
```

This process exemplifies how macros can simplify complex decision-making constructs into more readable and maintainable code.

In practice, macro transformations often employ hygienic techniques to prevent variable capture and ensure that the expanded code does not unintentionally interfere with other parts of the program. Scheme's macros are designed to manage hygiene implicitly. However, more control can be achieved using the syntax-case system, which provides explicit manipulation of syntax objects while preserving hygiene.

Consider the following use of syntax-case to create a swapping macro:

```
(define-syntax swap!
  (lambda (stx)
    (syntax-case stx ()
      ((_ x y)
       (with-syntax ((temp (datum->syntax stx 'temp)))
         #'(let ((temp x))
             (set! x y)
             (set! y temp)))))))
```

Here, the swap! macro swaps the values of two variables. The with-syntax clause introduces a temporary variable to facilitate the swap while preserving hygiene. The datum->syntax function ensures that temp is treated as a unique identifier within the macro's scope, avoiding conflicts with existing variables named temp outside the macro.

By mastering macro expansion and transformation, one can create powerful and flexible abstractions in Scheme. These techniques enable the development of domain-specific languages, custom control structures, and syntactic extensions that can streamline code and improve expressiveness.

8.8 Writing and Using Recursive Macros

Recursive macros in Scheme allow for powerful metaprogramming capabilities by enabling macros to invoke themselves during expansion. This section focuses on defining and utilizing these recursive macros effectively in Scheme, ensuring an understanding of their syntax, application, and common use cases. The emphasis will be on practical comprehension through code examples and thorough explanations.

```
(define-syntax my-loop
  (syntax-rules ()
```

```
((my-loop n body ...)
 (if (> n 0)
     (begin
       body ...
       (my-loop (- n 1) body ...))))))
```

In the above example, my-loop is a recursive macro that executes a given body of expressions n times. The definition utilizes syntax-rules to pattern-match on the input syntax. When invoked, it checks if n is greater than 0, and if so, it executes body and recursively calls itself with n-1.

To dissect this macro: - The syntax-rules form specifies the pattern and the template for the macro definition. - The pattern matches the structure (my-loop n body ...), where n is the number of iterations and body ... represents one or more expressions to be executed. - In the template, the macro checks if n is greater than 0 using the if expression. - If true, it evaluates body ... using the begin form and then recursively calls my-loop with n-1.

This recursive approach is beneficial, allowing for repeated execution of code without explicit looping constructs. Let's observe its application by invoking my-loop:

```
(my-loop 3
  (display "Hello, world!")
  (newline))
```

The output of this macro invocation is:

```
Hello, world!
Hello, world!
Hello, world!
```

Each display followed by newline prints "Hello, world!" three times, demonstrating the recursive expansion of my-loop.

In developing more complex recursive macros, it is essential to understand how these macros can manipulate their input syntax and leverage recursion for powerful custom syntactic transformations. Consider the following example, where a recursive macro generates a tree structure:

```
(define-syntax gen-tree
  (syntax-rules ()
    ((gen-tree depth leaf node)
     (if (= depth 0)
         leaf
         (node (gen-tree (- depth 1) leaf node)
               (gen-tree (- depth 1) leaf node))))))
```

Here, gen-tree recursively generates a binary tree of a specified depth with leaf at the nodes, using node to combine branches. The pattern matched is (gen-tree depth leaf node), and the template recursively constructs the tree until the specified depth reaches 0.

Using this macro to generate a simple binary tree might look like this:

```
(gen-tree 2 'leaf 'cons)
```

Evaluating this macro results in the following tree structure represented in Scheme's list form:

```
(cons (cons 'leaf 'leaf) (cons 'leaf 'leaf))
```

The resulting tree structure clearly represents a binary tree of depth 2, with 'leaf' as the leaf nodes and 'cons' used to combine nodes.

When developing recursive macros, it is critical to ensure freshness of identifiers to maintain hygiene and prevent unintentional variable capture. Scheme's hygienic macro system helps manage this automatically by ensuring that each macro expansion generates unique identifiers where necessary.

Finally, utilizing debugging techniques, such as trace and explicit macro-step expansion, can simplify the process of developing and refining recursive macros. Ensuring that each recursive step and expansion meets the intended syntactic and semantic transformation is vital in creating robust and reliable macros.

Recursive macros expand the boundaries of metaprogramming in Scheme, offering potent tools for syntactic abstraction while keeping the underlying structures semantically coherent and efficiently managed. Ensuring attention to detail in their definition and expansion helps leverage their full potential in complex Scheme programs.

8.9 Debugging Macros

When working with macros in Scheme, ensuring correctness and reliability is paramount. Debugging macros can be more challenging than debugging functions due to the extra layer of abstraction introduced by macro expansion. This section provides strategies and tools to effectively debug macros, aiming to identify and resolve issues that may arise during macro development.

Scheme provides several facilities to help with debugging macros. These include examining macro expansions, using tracing, and validating the syntactic structure of macros. Understanding these tools and techniques is crucial for identifying logical errors, unexpected expansions, and unintended behavior.

Examining Macro Expansions The first step in debugging macros involves examining their expansions to understand how code is transformed. Scheme implementations typically offer built-in mechanisms to view macro expansions.

For example, in Racket (a popular Scheme dialect), you can use the expand function to see how a macro call is expanded:

```
(syntax->datum (expand '(your-macro-call)))
```

This command outputs the expanded form of the your-macro-call macro expression, making it easier to inspect and verify. Consider the following macro definition and its expansion:

```
(define-syntax my-if
  (syntax-rules ()
    ((_ test then else)
     (if test then else))))

(syntax->datum (expand '(my-if #t 'true 'false)))
```

The output of the above command would be:

```
(if #t 'true 'false)
```

This expansion reveals that the my-if macro correctly transforms into an if expression, affirming its intended behavior.

Using Tracing Another effective technique for debugging macros involves tracing their execution. Tracing allows you to follow the execution flow and understand how macros are processed during compilation.

In Racket, you can use the syntax-parse library's debugging facilities. By adding debugging annotations, you can monitor the behavior of macros at various stages. Here is an example:

```
(require syntax/parse)
(require syntax/parse/define)
(require syntax/location)

(define-syntax (my-macro stx)
  (syntax-parse stx
    [(_ a b)
     #:do [(printf "Expanding with ~a and ~a\n" #'a #'b)]
     #'(list a b)]))
```

When my-macro is invoked, the debug message will be printed, providing real-time feedback on the macro's expansion process.

Validating Syntactic Structure Ensuring that macros produce syntactically correct code is another critical aspect of debugging. Errors in the generated code can lead to unexpected behavior or compilation failures. One way to validate the syntactic structure is by employing syntax-case to enforce rules and constraints within macro definitions.

Consider the following example, where we check that the arguments passed to a macro are symbols:

```
(define-syntax validate-symbols
  (lambda (stx)
    (syntax-case stx ()
      [(_ symbol1 symbol2)
       (and (symbol? (syntax-e #'symbol1))
            (symbol? (syntax-e #'symbol2))
            #'(list 'symbols-are-valid))
       [else #'(error "Arguments must be symbols")]])))
```

Invoking validate-symbols with non-symbol arguments will trigger an error, thus ensuring the syntactic correctness of the macro's inputs:

```
(validate-symbols 'foo 'bar) ; Valid: returns (symbols-are-valid)
(validate-symbols 1 'bar) ; Error: Arguments must be symbols
```

Common Pitfalls and Solutions There are several common pitfalls to be aware of when debugging macros. These include name clashes, incorrect pattern matching, and unexpected captures in non-hygienic macros. Understanding these issues and their solutions is critical for effective macro debugging.

- **Name Clashes**: Ensure that macro-generated names do not clash with existing variable names. This can be mitigated using hygienic macros or by generating unique identifiers using syntax-id-rules.

- **Pattern Matching Errors**: Verify that the syntax patterns in syntax-rules or syntax-case correctly match the intended macro usage. Use diagnostics and error messages to provide feedback when patterns don't match.

- **Unexpected Captures**: Non-hygienic macros can inadvertently capture variables, leading to unexpected behavior. Safeguard against this by using hygienic macro techniques or carefully scoping variables to avoid clashes.

Debugging macros requires a thorough understanding of macro expansion, careful examination of generated code, and the use of tools and techniques to trace and validate the macro's behavior. By employing these strategies, one can effectively identify and resolve issues in macro definitions, ensuring robust and reliable Scheme programs.

8.10 The Role of Macros in Metaprogramming

Macros play a crucial role in the realm of metaprogramming by providing powerful tools for code transformation and generation. Unlike functions, which operate on values and return results, macros operate directly on the syntactic structure of the code itself, allowing profound modifications before actual code execution. This capability is central to metaprogramming, which is the practice of writing programs that can manipulate other programs (or themselves) as data.

In Scheme, the metaprogramming capabilities of macros are utilized through constructs such as define-syntax and syntax-rules. These constructs empower developers to create new syntactic forms and abstraction layers that can dramatically reduce code complexity and enhance readability. By encapsulating common patterns and boilerplate code, macros not only simplify code maintenance but also enable custom language constructs tailored to specific problem domains.

Consider the concept of Domain-Specific Languages (DSLs). A DSL is a mini-language optimized for a particular category of problems, offering specialized syntax and semantics. Using Scheme macros, one can embed a DSL within a Scheme program, thereby optimizing and clarifying domain-specific code without sacrificing the general-purpose nature of Scheme. This is achieved by defining macros that translate high-level domain-specific syntax into lower-level Scheme expressions.

To illustrate, let us define a simple DSL for describing HTML content. Instead of manually writing nested HTML tags, we can create macros to express HTML structure more intuitively. Here is an example:

```
(define-syntax html
  (syntax-rules ()
    ((html content ...)
     `(println "<!DOCTYPE html>"
               "<html>"
               ,@content
               "</html>"))))

(define-syntax body
  (syntax-rules ()
    ((body content ...)
     `(println "<body>"
               ,@content
               "</body>"))))

(define-syntax p
  (syntax-rules ()
    ((p text)
     `(println "<p>" ,text "</p>"))))
```

Utilizing these macros, an HTML document can be represented as follows:

```
(html
  (body
    (p "Hello, world!")
    (p "This is a paragraph.")))
```

When executed, the above code generates the corresponding HTML output:

```
<!DOCTYPE html>
<html>
  <body>
    <p>Hello, world!</p>
    <p>This is a paragraph.</p>
  </body>
</html>
```

Beyond DSLs, macros are instrumental in implementing language features that are cumbersome or inefficient to express through standard functions. An example is the concept of lazy evaluation, where expressions are evaluated only when their values are needed. Scheme macros can be used to transform expressions into lazily evaluated forms without altering the underlying evaluation strategy of Scheme.

Consider the following macro for lazy evaluation:

```
(define-syntax lazy
  (syntax-rules ()
    ((lazy expr)
     `(lambda () ,expr))))

(define (force promise)
  (promise))
```

Using the lazy macro, expressions can be deferred, and force can be used to evaluate them:

```
(let ((x (lazy (+ 2 3))))
  (println (force x))) ; Output: 5
```

Here, the expression (+ 2 3) is wrapped in a lambda, effectively deferring its evaluation until force is called. This lazy evaluation technique is particularly useful in the context of infinite data structures or computationally expensive operations that may not need to be executed immediately.

Macros also facilitate metaprogramming by enabling code generation and transformation at compile-time, which can lead to significant performance optimizations. For instance, consider a scenario where specific computations need to be performed at compile-time rather than runtime. By utilizing macros, developers can precompute values and embed the results directly into the code, thereby reducing runtime overhead.

An example of a macro performing compile-time computation is as follows:

```
(define-syntax square
  (syntax-rules ()
    ((square x)
     `(* ,x ,x))))

(define value 5)
(square value) ; Equivalent to (* 5 5) at compile-time
```

In this example, the square macro replaces the use of (square value) with the multiplication expression (* 5 5), which can be computed during compilation, leading to potentially improved runtime efficiency.

Moreover, macros offer a platform for creating more readable and maintainable code by abstracting repetitive or verbose patterns. By encapsulating common idioms into macros, we reduce boilerplate and enhance the conceptual clarity of the codebase. The resulting programs become easier to understand and extend, which is particularly valuable in large-scale software development.

For instance, consider a logging mechanism that requires repeated boilerplate code to check if logging is enabled:

```
(define logging-enabled true)

(define-syntax log
  (syntax-rules ()
    ((log message)
     `(when logging-enabled
        (println ,message)))))
```

```
; Usage
(log "This is a log message.")
```

In this example, the log macro encapsulates the conditional check, simplifying the logging process and making the intention of the code more explicit.

Through these examples and principles, it is clear that macros extend the expressive power of Scheme, enabling sophisticated metaprogramming paradigms. They bridge the gap between general-purpose programming and problem-specific solutions, offering a unique blend of flexibility and efficiency.

8.11 Macros vs. Functions: When to Use Each

There is often a debate over when to utilize macros versus functions in Scheme programming. Both constructs are powerful tools in a programmer's arsenal, but each serves different purposes and comes with its own set of benefits and limitations. Understanding the key differences between macros and functions, as well as their appropriate use cases, is essential for effective Scheme programming.

Macros operate at the syntactic level, allowing programmers to create new syntactic forms and extend the language. Functions, on the other hand, operate at the semantic level, encapsulating computations and behaviors. The distinction is crucial when deciding which to use for a given task.

1. Compilation vs. Runtime:

Macros are expanded at compile-time, transforming the code before it is evaluated. This means macros can modify the structure of the code, introduce new variables, or even generate entirely new forms of expressions. They provide a way to perform operations that are impossible at runtime.

In contrast, functions are evaluated at runtime. A function call results in the execution of a block of code with the given arguments, and it cannot alter the surrounding code structure.

```
;; Example of a macro
(define-syntax when
  (syntax-rules ()
```

```
    ((when condition body ...)
     (if condition
         (begin body ...)))))
;; Macro usage
(when (> x 10)
  (display "x is greater than 10")
  (newline))

;; Example of a function
(define (square x)
  (* x x))
;; Function usage
(square 5) ; Output: 25
```

2. Code Generation:

Because macros manipulate the code itself, they are ideal for code generation tasks. They can reduce code duplication by generating repetitive structures, enabling more concise and maintainable code.

Functions, while capable of reducing redundancy by abstracting common operations, cannot generate new syntactic constructs. They are better suited for encapsulating behavior rather than structure.

```
;; Macro to generate repetitive code
(define-syntax define-addition
  (syntax-rules ()
    ((define-addition name a b)
     (define name (+ a b)))))

(define-addition add-five-and-ten 5 10)
(add-five-and-ten) ; Output: 15
```

3. Performance Considerations:

Macros, due to their compile-time expansion, introduce no run-time overhead. This can lead to more efficient code, especially when dealing with complex or repetitive patterns. However, this efficiency gain must be weighed against the potential for more complex debugging and maintenance.

Functions, because they execute at runtime, carry the typical overhead associated with function calls. This overhead is generally not significant but can become a factor in performance-critical code sections.

4. Scope and Hygiene:

Hygienic macros in Scheme ensure that macros do not inadvertently capture or clash with variables outside their scope. This careful handling helps avoid subtle bugs related to variable binding and scope rules.

Functions naturally respect lexical scope, making them less prone to such issues. They provide clear and predictable scoping rules, which can simplify debugging and reasoning about the code.

```
;; Hygienic macro example
(define-syntax swap
  (syntax-rules ()
    ((swap a b)
     (let ((tmp a))
       (set! a b)
       (set! b tmp)))))

(let ((x 1) (y 2))
  (swap x y)
  (display x) ; Output: 2
  (display y)) ; Output: 1
```

5. Error Handling and Debugging:

Debugging macro-related errors can be challenging because the code transformation occurs at compile-time. An error in the expanded code may not directly indicate an issue with the macro definition itself. This requires a deeper understanding of the macro expansion process and potentially more sophisticated debugging tools.

Functions typically produce more straightforward error messages related to their execution. Debugging functions is generally more intuitive, as errors occur within the scope of the function call and are usually tied to specific input values or operational logic.

Use Case Scenarios:

- **Use Macros When:**
  - You need to create new syntactic constructs or extend the language syntax.
  - You want to perform code generation tasks that reduce redundancy.
  - Compile-time code transformations can lead to performance optimizations.
- **Use Functions When:**
  - You need to encapsulate behavior and computation that does not require syntactic transformation.
  - Simplicity, readability, and ease of debugging are crucial.
  - You want to ensure clear scoping rules and avoid complexity introduced by macro expansion.

Understanding these distinctions ensures that you can leverage the power of both macros and functions, applying each appropriately to create efficient, maintainable, and effective Scheme programs.

8.12 Case Studies: Practical Applications of Macros

In this section, we will explore practical implementations of macros through several case studies. These examples illustrate the versatility of macros in Scheme programming, emphasizing their capability to simplify code, create domain-specific languages, and enforce coding standards.

1. Simplifying Repetitive Code Patterns

Consider a scenario in which we frequently need to check and set the value of a variable if it is not already set. Without macros, each instance of this pattern must be explicitly written, potentially leading to verbosity and increased risk of errors. We can create a macro to streamline this process.

```
(define-syntax check-and-set
  (syntax-rules ()
    ((_ var value)
     (if (not (bound? var))
         (set! var value)))))
```

With this macro, the expression (check-and-set my-var 10) expands to:

```
(if (not (bound? my-var))
    (set! my-var 10))
```

This reduces redundancy and ensures consistency in our codebase.

2. Creating Domain-Specific Languages (DSLs)

Macros can be used to design mini-languages within Scheme, tailored to specific problem domains. For instance, we can create a DSL for expressing finite state machines (FSMs).

```
(define-syntax define-fsm
  (syntax-rules ()
    ((_ name (state . transitions) . states)
     (define name (lambda (current-state event)
                    (cond ((eq? current-state 'state)
                           (case event . transitions))
                          . states))))))
```

To define an FSM for a simple traffic light system, one would write:

```
(define-fsm traffic-light
  (red (stop -> green)
       (timeout -> green))
  (green (go -> yellow)
         (timeout -> yellow))
  (yellow (slow -> red)
          (timeout -> red)))
```

This approach isolates FSM logic from the rest of the system, enhancing readability and maintainability.

3. Enforcing Coding Standards

Macros can enforce coding standards or design patterns within a codebase. For example, ensuring that every function follows a specific logging mechanism can be achieved using macros.

```
(define-syntax define-logged-function
  (syntax-rules ()
    ((_ name args . body)
     (define name
       (lambda args
         (begin
           (log "Entering function" 'name)
           (let ((result (begin . body)))
             (log "Exiting function" 'name)
             result))))))
```

A defined function using this macro will conform to a standardized structure:

```
(define-logged-function example-func (x y)
  (+ x y))
```

This expands to:

```
(define example-func
  (lambda (x y)
    (begin
      (log "Entering function" 'example-func)
      (let ((result (+ x y)))
        (log "Exiting function" 'example-func)
        result))))
```

The macro ensures consistent logging behavior across all functions, facilitating easier debugging and monitoring.

4. Code Transformation and Optimization

Macros can also be employed for code transformation and optimization. Suppose we need to optimize a mathematical expression by converting it into a more computationally efficient form.

```
(define-syntax optimize-expression
  (syntax-rules ()
```

```
((_ (* x x))
 (square x))
((_ (* x 2))
 (shiftLeft x 1))
((_ x)
 x)))
```

When used:

```
(optimize-expression (* x x))
(optimize-expression (* y 2))
```

This expands to:

```
(square x)
(shiftLeft y 1)
```

This macro transforms specific patterns into optimized forms, thereby improving the efficiency of mathematical operations.

Each case study presented underscores the power and flexibility of macros in Scheme programming. Through practical examples, we have demonstrated the capability of macros to simplify repetitive code patterns, create specialized mini-languages, enforce coding standards consistently, and optimize code performance. The application of macros as shown in these case studies can lead to more readable, maintainable, and efficient code. This methodological use of macros truly exemplifies their significance in metaprogramming within the Scheme language.

Chapter 9

Error Handling and Debugging

This chapter addresses error handling and debugging in Scheme, outlining the different types of errors such as syntax, runtime, and logical errors. It covers signaling errors using 'error' and 'raise', as well as handling them with 'guard' and 'with-exception-handler'. The chapter introduces common debugging techniques, utilizing the Scheme debugger, and inspecting stack traces and error messages. It includes specific strategies for debugging recursive functions and testing Scheme code, providing insights into preventing common errors and presenting real-world debugging case studies.

9.1 Introduction to Error Handling and Debugging in Scheme

Error handling and debugging are critical aspects of software development that aim to ensure programs behave correctly under a variety of conditions. In Scheme, a dialect of Lisp, these concepts are paramount due to its functional nature and reliance on recursive structures. Understanding how to properly handle and debug errors allows developers to write more robust and maintainable code. This section provides an overview of error handling and debugging mechanisms in Scheme, setting the foundation for more detailed discussions that follow.

Errors in Scheme can arise from various sources, including syntax errors, runtime errors, and logical errors. Syntax errors occur when the code violates the grammatical rules of the language, such as an incorrect parenthesis structure or use of undefined syntax. Runtime errors happen during the execution of a program, often due to invalid operations like division by zero or accessing a non-existent list element. Logical errors, while syntactically correct, lead to incorrect results due to flaws in the program's logic.

Scheme provides built-in functions like error and raise to signal errors explicitly. The error function generates an error condition along with a message, halting the program's execution unless caught and handled. The raise function, on the other hand, allows throwing exceptions to be caught by an appropriate handler, giving more control over error management. Here's a basic usage of error in Scheme:

```
(define (safe-divide a b)
  (if (= b 0)
      (error "Division by zero")
      (/ a b)))
```

When safe-divide is called with a divisor of zero, it will immediately signal an error with the message "Division by zero".

To handle errors, Scheme offers constructs like guard and with-exception-handler. The guard construct provides a way to catch and manage exceptions in a concise manner. Here is an illustration:

```
(define (safe-open-file filename)
  (guard (exn (else #f))
    (call-with-input-file filename read)))
```

In this example, guard is used to catch any exceptions that might occur when attempting to open a file. If an error occurs, the handler returns #f, indicating failure, instead of propagating the error.

Additionally, the with-exception-handler function allows for more granular control over error handling. It binds an exception handler to a given expression, ensuring that any errors occurring within the expression are managed by the specified handler:

```
(define (custom-handler exn)
  (display "An error occurred: ")
  (display (exn-message exn))
  (newline))

(with-exception-handler custom-handler
  (lambda ()
```

```
  (error "This is a test error")))
```

In this piece of code, custom-handler is defined to display an error message. The with-exception-handler then binds this handler to the expression that intentionally raises an error.

Debugging involves not just handling errors but also identifying and fixing the causes of unexpected behavior. Scheme's debugging facilities enable the inspection of stack traces, evaluation of expressions in specific contexts, and step-through execution. Modern Scheme implementations include debuggers that allow setting breakpoints, stepping through code, and examining variable states.

The practice of debugging in Scheme benefits greatly from understanding recursive functions, which are prevalent in functional programming. Thorough testing of code ensures that edge cases are considered and potential errors are identified early. This chapter elaborates on various techniques and tools available for debugging Scheme programs, reinforcing the importance of methodical and systematic approaches to error handling and debugging.

Understanding and leveraging these error handling and debugging tools in Scheme can significantly improve the reliability and correctness of your programs.

9.2 Types of Errors in Scheme: Syntax, Runtime, and Logical

Errors in Scheme programming can be categorized into three primary types: syntax errors, runtime errors, and logical errors. Understanding these distinctions is crucial for effective debugging and error handling.

Syntax Errors

Syntax errors occur when the code written does not conform to the grammatical rules of the Scheme language. Such errors are usually detected by the compiler or interpreter during the parsing phase before the program runs. Common syntax errors include missing parentheses, incorrect keyword usage, and other deviations from the language's formal syntax.

Consider the following code snippet which has a syntax error:

```
(define (add x y)
```

```
    (+ x y)
)
```

If we accidentally omit a closing parenthesis, the code would generate a syntax error:

```
(define (add x y)
    (+ x y)
```

Attempting to run this code results in a message akin to the following, indicative of a syntax error:

```
Error: unexpected end of file while reading
```

Correcting the syntax requires ensuring all parentheses are properly balanced, and that all Scheme constructs follow the correct grammatical rules.

Runtime Errors

Runtime errors occur during the execution of a program, even if the code is syntactically correct. These errors typically arise from operations that are undefined or invalid in the current context, such as division by zero, accessing out-of-bound elements in a list, or calling functions with inappropriate argument types.

Consider the following example that will cause a runtime error:

```
(define (divide x y)
    (/ x y)
)

(divide 10 0)
```

This code defines a function divide that performs division, and then attempts to divide 10 by 0. Executing this code would result in a runtime error:

```
Error: division by zero
```

Runtime errors can often be caught using error handling constructs such as guard and with-exception-handler, which will be discussed in subsequent sections.

Logical Errors

Logical errors cannot be identified by the interpreter or compiler; they are mistakes in the program's logic that produce incorrect or unintended behavior. These errors are particularly insidious because the program runs to completion without crashing, but delivers incorrect results.

Consider the following function intended to calculate the factorial of a non-negative integer:

```
(define (factorial n)
  (if (= n 0)
      1
      (* n (factorial (- n 1)))))
```

Suppose we mistakenly alter the function to the following:

```
(define (factorial n)
  (if (= n 1)
      1
      (* n (factorial (- n 1)))))
```

This change introduces a logical error, as the base case for the factorial of 0 is now missing. Calculating the factorial of 0 using this modified function:

```
(factorial 0)
```

Would result in an infinite recursion, ultimately causing a stack overflow:

```
Error: maximum recursion depth exceeded
```

Detecting logical errors involves thorough testing and validation of the code's logic against expected behavior. Effective strategies include unit testing, peer code reviews, and formally specifying the program's requirements.

Each type of error necessitates different detection and correction strategies. Establishing a robust error handling and debugging discipline is imperative for writing reliable Scheme programs.

9.3 Using 'error' and 'raise' to Signal Errors

In Scheme, error handling is a crucial part of maintaining robust and reliable programs. Scheme provides built-in mechanisms to signal errors, allowing developers to indicate when an exceptional situation has arisen. Two primary procedures for signaling errors are error and raise. Understanding the usage and differences between these procedures is essential for effective error handling.

The error procedure is used to signal an error and typically includes an error message and, optionally, additional details about the error. This procedure will stop the execution of the current program, output the specified error message, and return control to the program's error handler, if one is present. The basic form of error is:

```
(error message arg ...)
```

The message is a string describing the error, and the optional arg parameters provide additional context. For example:

```
(error "Division by zero" 1 0)
```

Using this example, the program execution will halt, and the error handler will display the message "Division by zero" along with the arguments 1 and 0. This approach is useful for providing clear, descriptive error messages that can aid debugging.

The raise procedure, on the other hand, is more flexible and general. It is used to propagate an exception object, which can be any Scheme object, including an error object. Unlike error, raise does not format the message but simply passes the exception object to the active exception handler. The basic form of raise is:

```
(raise object)
```

Here, object is the exception to be propagated. The raise procedure is typically used in conjunction with exception handling mechanisms to create and propagate custom exceptions, as shown in the following example:

```
(define (safe-divide a b)
  (if (zero? b)
      (raise 'division-by-zero)
      (/ a b)))
```

In this example, the safe-divide function will raise the symbol 'division-by-zero if the second argument b is zero. This approach allows the calling context to handle the specific exception as needed.

To further illustrate the usage of error and raise, consider the following more detailed example:

```
(define (sqrt-safe x)
  (if (< x 0)
      (error "Square root of negative number" x)
      (sqrt x)))

(let ((result (with-exception-handler
                (lambda (exn)
                  (display "Error encountered: ")
                  (display exn)
                  (newline)
                  #f) ; Return a default value
                (lambda ()
                  (sqrt-safe -4)))))
```

```
  (display "Result: ")
  (display result)
  (newline))
```

This code snippet defines a function sqrt-safe that computes the square root of a number. If the input number is negative, it signals an error using the error procedure. The with-exception-handler is used to handle the error by displaying a message and returning a default value of #f. When the function is called with -4, the error message "Square root of negative number" will be displayed along with the value -4.

Another example demonstrating the use of raise to propagate a custom exception is as follows:

```
(define (sqrt-robust x)
  (if (< x 0)
      (raise (cons 'sqrt-error (list "Negative input" x)))
      (sqrt x)))

(let ((result (with-exception-handler
                (lambda (exn)
                  (display "Exception encountered: ")
                  (display (cdr exn))
                  (newline)
                  #f) ; Return a default value
                (lambda ()
                  (sqrt-robust -4)))))
  (display "Result: ")
  (display result)
  (newline))
```

In this example, the sqrt-robust function raises a custom exception using a cons cell. The exception handler checks the exception object and extracts the relevant information to display a specific message.

Choosing between error and raise depends on the requirements of the program. When a simple error message is sufficient, error is often the most straightforward choice. However, when more complex exception handling is needed, raise provides the necessary flexibility to create and propagate custom exceptions.

It is essential to appropriately signal errors and raise exceptions in order to write robust and maintainable Scheme programs. Proper use of error and raise ensures that exceptional conditions are clearly communicated and can be handled effectively by the calling code or exception handlers. By adhering to these practices, developers can create resilient applications that gracefully handle errors and exceptional situations.

9.4 Catching and Handling Errors with 'guard'

In Scheme, handling errors effectively is crucial for building robust programs. The guard construct provides a powerful mechanism to catch and manage exceptions. It allows the programmer to specify a protective barrier around a block of code that automatically handles any errors arising within that block. This section delves into the syntax and functionality of guard, illustrating how to use it through practical examples.

The guard expression in Scheme wraps a potentially failing operation with an error-handling clause. It has the following general form:

```
(guard (condition-handler)
   protected-expression)
```

- condition-handler: A lambda expression that specifies how to handle the error condition.
- protected-expression: The expression or series of expressions that are being guarded.

When an error occurs within the protected-expression, the condition-handler is invoked with the error condition, allowing the program to recover or handle the error gracefully.

Consider the following example, where a division by zero might occur:

```
(define (safe-divide x y)
  (guard (c (lambda () (display "Error: Division by zero\n") 0))
    (/ x y)))
```

In this example, if the denominator y is zero, an error would normally be raised. However, using guard, the division operation is protected, and instead of propagating the error, the condition-handler displays an error message and returns 0.

To further illustrate the usage, consider a more complex scenario involving multiple guarded operations:

```
(define (process-data lst)
  (guard (c (lambda () (display "Error: Invalid data\n")))
    (map (lambda (x) (/ 10 x)) lst)))
```

Here, process-data attempts to map a division operation over a list. If any element in the list is zero, thus causing a division by zero error, the condition-handler captures the error and outputs an error message.

The guard mechanism also supports more intricate error handling by allowing pattern matching on error conditions. This is useful when dealing with multiple types of errors within the same protected-expression. The following example demonstrates handling different types of errors:

```
(define (complex-operation x y)
  (guard (c (lambda (ex)
              (cond ((eq? ex 'division-by-zero)
                     (display "Caught Division by Zero Error\n"))
                    ((eq? ex 'other-error)
                     (display "Caught Other Error\n")))))
    (if (= y 0)
        (raise 'division-by-zero)
        (/ x y))))
```

In this instance, the complex-operation function raises specific error conditions using raise. The guard is set to catch these conditions and select the appropriate error message to display based on the type of error encountered.

Using guard greatly simplifies the task of error management by encapsulating error-handling logic within a well-defined construct. This not only makes the code cleaner and more readable but also ensures that all potential errors within the guarded expression are consistently handled. Through careful application of guard, we can build more reliable and user-friendly Scheme applications.

Error handling with guard enhances the robustness of Scheme programs, enabling the graceful handling of unexpected conditions and recovering from errors without compromising the program's stability.

9.5 Writing Robust Code with 'with-exception-handler'

The with-exception-handler construct in Scheme is crucial for creating robust programs capable of gracefully handling errors. By capturing exceptions effectively, you can ensure that your program can respond to unexpected situations without crashing, providing more user-friendly error messages and potentially recovering from errors.

The with-exception-handler procedure allows you to specify an error handler function that will be invoked whenever an exception occurs within a dynamic extent. This handler can inspect the exception, perform logging, clean up resources, and decide whether to propagate the exception or to recover and continue execution. The general form of with-exception-handler is:

```
(with-exception-handler handler-thunk protected-thunk)
```

In this construct, handler-thunk is a procedure that takes a single argument (the raised exception) and is called when an error occurs. The protected-thunk is a procedure that encapsulates the code to be executed under the scope of the handler.

Consider the following example, where an attempt to divide by zero is safeguarded:

```
(define (safe-divide x y)
  (let ((handler (lambda (exn)
                   (display "Error: Division by zero detected.\n")
                   0))) ;; Return 0 as a default value
    (with-exception-handler handler
      (lambda ()
        (/ x y)))))
```

The safe-divide function attempts to divide x by y. If y is zero, an exception is raised, triggering the handler. The handler outputs an error message and returns 0 to prevent the program from crashing.

For a deeper understanding, consider a case where you want to handle multiple types of exceptions differently. You can write more sophisticated handlers to inspect the nature of the exception and take appropriate actions.

```
(define (complex-operation)
  (let ((handler (lambda (exn)
                   (cond ((eq? (exn-type exn) 'zero-division)
                          (display "Cannot divide by zero.\n")
                          -1)
                         ((eq? (exn-type exn) 'file-not-found)
                          (display "File not found.\n")
                          'file-error)
                         (else
                          (display "Unknown error occurred.\n")
                          'unknown-error)))))
    (with-exception-handler handler
      (lambda ()
        ;; hypothetical operations that might cause exceptions
        (let ((result (/ 10 0))) ;; zero division error
          (display result)
          result)))))
```

In this example, complex-operation performs hypothetical operations that might raise exceptions. The handler checks the type of exception using the fictitious exn-type function and responds accordingly. For a division by zero, it displays an error message and returns -1. For a file-not-found error, it displays another specific message and returns 'file-error. For any other unknown errors, it logs them and returns 'unknown-error.

It is often beneficial to combine with-exception-handler with other error handling constructs, such as guard or dynamic-wind, to manage resources like file handles or network connections correctly.

Consider an example where resource cleanup is necessary:

```
(define (process-file filename)
  (let* ((port (open-input-file filename))
         (handler (lambda (exn)
                    (close-input-port port)
                    (display "An error occurred while processing the file.\n")
                    'file-error)))
    (with-exception-handler handler
      (lambda ()
        (let ((content (read-port port)))
          (close-input-port port)
          content)))))
```

Here, process-file function opens a file and attempts to read its content. If any exception occurs during the file processing, the handler ensures that the file port is closed before logging the error and returning 'file-error. This guarantees that even if an error interrupts the normal flow, resources are not left open or in an inconsistent state.

Additionally, for debugging and development purposes, it may be useful to have an exception handler that logs the exceptions for later analysis. Combining with-exception-handler with logging mechanisms can be particularly beneficial for maintaining and improving large codebases:

```
(define (log-exception exn)
  (with-output-to-file "error-log.txt"
    (lambda ()
      (display "Exception logged:\n")
      (write exn)
      (newline))))

(define (robust-operation)
  (let ((handler (lambda (exn)
                   (log-exception exn)
                   (display "An error occurred. Check error-log.txt for details.\n")
                   'operation-error)))
    (with-exception-handler handler
      (lambda ()
        ;; hypothetical operation that might cause an exception
        (/ 10 0)))))
```

In this scenario, robust-operation divides 10 by 0, triggering an exception. The handler logs the exception details to a file, provides a user-friendly message, and returns 'operation-error.

Writing robust code in Scheme using with-exception-handler involves designing appropriate handler functions that ensure error cases are managed effectively. This approach enhances the resilience and maintainability of your Scheme programs by preventing unexpected crashes and providing mechanisms for error recovery and resource management. Ensuring that handlers are comprehensive and contextually appropriate for the types of exceptions they manage is fundamental for robust Scheme programming.

9.6 Common Debugging Techniques

Debugging Scheme code requires a systematic approach to identify and rectify errors. Effective debugging techniques can save significant time and effort, ensuring that programs function correctly. This section elaborates on several crucial debugging techniques that programmers can utilize to troubleshoot and correct issues in their Scheme programs.

One essential technique is **inserting print statements** to understand the flow of the program and the values of variables at specific stages. This method is simple yet powerful, especially for tracking how data changes over time. Scheme provides the display and newline functions for outputting text to the console. For instance:

```
(define (factorial n)
  (if (= n 1)
      1
      (begin
        (display "Current value of n: ") (display n) (newline)
        (* n (factorial (- n 1))))))
```

In this example, the output will show the value of n at each recursive step, facilitating the identification of unexpected behavior.

Another fundamental technique is **using assertions**. Assertions allow programmers to assert that certain conditions must hold true at specific points in the code. In Scheme, this can be done using the assert procedure. An assertion failure indicates a logical error in the program:

```
(define (safe-divide a b)
  (assert (not (= b 0)) "Division by zero error")
  (/ a b))
```

Here, an assertion ensures that the divisor b is not zero, preventing a runtime error and providing a clear error message.

Utilizing **step-by-step execution** is another invaluable technique. Scheme debuggers typically allow programs to be run in a step-by-step fashion, executing one expression at a time. This method helps programmers observe the evaluation process in detail. For example:

```
$ chez --debug program.scm
```

Step-by-step execution can be initiated, and breakpoints can be set to pause execution at critical points, allowing detailed inspection of the environment and variable states.

Examining stack traces is pivotal when an error occurs. Stack traces provide a snapshot of the call stack at the moment of error, showing the sequence of function calls that led to the fault. This information can help trace back the source of the problem. For instance:

```
Error: Division by zero
  [0] (safe-divide 10 0)
  [1] (main)
```

The stack trace reveals that the error originated in the safe-divide function, called from main, which helps narrow down the location of the error.

Refactoring code is another crucial technique. Simplifying code can uncover hidden bugs and enhance readability. Functions should be decomposed into smaller, manageable pieces, each handling a distinct task, which makes it easier to isolate and debug errant behavior. Consider the following refactoring exercise:

Original code:

```
(define (process-data data)
  (let ((step1 (expensive-computation1 data))
        (step2 (expensive-computation2 step1)))
    (expensive-computation3 step2)))
```

Refactored code:

```
(define (process-data data)
  (let ((result1 (expensive-computation1 data)))
    (let ((result2 (expensive-computation2 result1)))
      (expensive-computation3 result2))))
```

By refactoring, we gain clarity on each computation step, increasing the ease of debugging each part of the process.

Employing **unit tests** is a proactive debugging method, catching errors early in the development cycle. Unit tests verify that individual units of code work as intended. Scheme's testing frameworks, such as SRFI-64 or Racket's rackunit, facilitate writing and running tests. An example test case might look as follows:

```
(require (only (srfi 64) test-begin test-end test-equal?))

(test-begin "safe-divide tests")

(test-equal? "Divide by non-zero" 5 (safe-divide 10 2))
(test-assert "Division by zero should error"
             (let/ec return
               (with-exception-handler (lambda (e) (return #t))
                 (lambda () (safe-divide 10 0)))
               #f))

(test-end)
```

Here, two tests are defined to validate the behavior of the safe-divide function, with one ensuring that a division by a non-zero number works correctly and another verifying that a division by zero triggers an error.

Utilizing logging frameworks also aids debugging by providing runtime information over extended periods, especially for complex and large-scale systems. Scheme logging utilities help record messages, warnings, and errors systematically. An example of such usage could be:

```
(require 'log)
(define my-logger (make-logger))
(log my-logger 'info "Application started.")
(define (safe-divide a b)
  (assert (not (= b 0)) "Division by zero error")
  (log my-logger 'debug "Performing division.")
  (/ a b))
(log my-logger 'info "Application finished.")
```

In this sample, logs provide insights into application execution flow, facilitating the identification of unexpected behavior or performance bottlenecks.

Finally, engaging in **pair programming** can also be beneficial. Collaborating with another programmer allows for real-time code review and brainstorming, which can significantly enhance the debugging process. Different perspectives can lead to quicker identification of errors and more robust solutions.

Each of these techniques brings unique advantages to the debugging process in Scheme programming, enabling developers to produce reliable and maintainable code.

9.7 Using the Scheme Debugger

The Scheme debugger is an essential tool for identifying and resolving errors in Scheme programs. It facilitates the examination of program execution, stack traces, and variable states, which aids in pinpointing the source of errors. Proper use of the debugger can greatly enhance your ability to fix bugs efficiently.

To activate the Scheme debugger, you typically need to start the REPL (Read-Eval-Print Loop) in debugging mode. The specific command can vary between different Scheme implementations, but for most versions, you can start the REPL with the debug flag. For instance, in Racket, you could start the REPL with the following command:

```
racket -l errortrace -t your_program.scm -m
```

Once the REPL is in debugging mode, you can execute your code as usual. When an error occurs, the debugger will allow you to inspect the current state of the program.

Breakpoints

Breakpoints are a common debugging feature that allows you to pause the execution of your program at specified points. This can be especially useful for examining the values of variables and the control flow. In many Scheme implementations, you can set a breakpoint directly in the source code using a special form or a command. For example, in MIT Scheme, you can set a breakpoint using the break function:

```
(break)
```

Placing (break) at the desired location in your code will cause the debugger to pause execution when it reaches that point.

Step-by-step Execution

The debugger allows you to execute your program line by line, a process known as stepping. This technique provides granular control over program execution, letting you observe the effects of each expression. After pausing at a breakpoint, you can use commands such as step or next to proceed through your code incrementally. In some Scheme implementations, stepping commands might look like this:

```
(step) ;; Executes the next expression
(next) ;; Moves to the next line of code
```

Inspecting Variables

While the program is paused, examining the current state of variables is crucial. Most Scheme debuggers provide commands to print the values of variables. For instance, in a paused state, you might use:

```
(print var\-name)
```

This command displays the current value of varname, allowing you to verify if the variable holds the expected data.

Stack Traces

When an error occurs, the debugger provides a stack trace, which is a report showing the active stack frames at a given point in time. This trace is instrumental in identifying the function calls that led to the error. Here's an example of what a stack trace might look like:

```
ERROR: unbound variable: x
  1. foo() - file: "test.scm", line: 12
  2. bar() - file: "test.scm", line: 8
  3. <top level> - file: "test.scm", line: 20
```

Each line represents a function call, showing the function name, file, and line number. This hierarchical display helps trace the origin of an error through the call stack.

Example Debugging Session

Consider the following Scheme program that contains an error:

```
(define (factorial n)
  (if (<= n 0)
      1
      (* n (factorial (- n 1)))))

(define (main)
  (let ((result (factorial 5)))
    (print result)))

(main)
```

Suppose you start the REPL in debug mode and run the program, encountering an unexpected behavior. By setting breakpoints and stepping through the code, you might find the location and cause of the error.

1. Set a breakpoint at the beginning of the factorial function:

```
(define (factorial n)
  (break)
  (if (<= n 0)
      1
      (* n (factorial (- n 1)))))
```

2. Run the program and inspect the value of n each time the breakpoint is hit:

```
(debug)> (main)
```

```
(debug)> (print n)
5
(debug)> (step)
(debug)> (print n)
4
```

Continuing this process reveals the flow of recursive calls and confirms that factorial calculates correctly for the given input.

Advanced debugging techniques include modifying variable values during a paused execution, rerunning specific stack frames, and utilizing conditional breakpoints that activate only when certain conditions are met, further empowering the debugging process. Each of these methods can provide further insight and control over diagnosing and correcting errors in Scheme programs.

9.8 Inspecting Stack Traces and Error Messages

In Scheme programming, understanding and interpreting stack traces and error messages is crucial for efficient debugging and error resolution. Errors provide insights into the source code's deficiencies, and stack traces offer a snapshot of the function call history leading up to the error. This section delves into methods for inspecting stack traces and deciphering error messages.

When a runtime error occurs, Scheme typically generates an error message accompanied by a stack trace. The error message describes the issue, while the stack trace lists the sequence of function calls that were active at the time of the error. This information is invaluable for pinpointing the exact location and cause of the issue.

Consider the following Scheme code that induces a runtime error:

```
(define (divide x y)
  (if (= y 0)
      (error "Division by zero")
      (/ x y)))

(divide 4 0)
```

The above code defines a function divide that divides x by y, but raises an error if y is zero. When this function is called with divide 4 0, Scheme will output an error message and a stack trace. An example of such an output might look like this:

```
Error: Division by zero
Stack Trace:
  1. [divide 4 0]
```

The error message, "Division by zero," describes what went wrong, while the stack trace provides the context, showing the function divide was called with arguments 4 and 0.

Detailed Interpretation of Stack Traces

A stack trace is typically a linear sequence of frames, each representing a function call. The frame contains details such as the function name, its arguments, and sometimes the exact line number in the source code. This information helps in tracing back the sequence of events that led to the error.

In Scheme, stack traces are represented in a straightforward manner. Each frame in the stack trace usually consists of the function name and the arguments it was called with. For larger programs, the stack trace can be more elaborate:

```
Error: Invalid operation
Stack Trace:
  1. [calculate 5 'a']
  2. [process "input.txt"]
  3. [main]
```

In this example: - main function was called. - main called process with the argument "input.txt". - process called calculate with the arguments 5 and 'a', leading to an invalid operation error.

Tools for Inspecting Stack Traces

Modern Scheme implementations provide debugging tools to inspect stack traces more effectively. These tools not only display stack traces but also allow interactive exploration of the program's state at each frame.

The following is a simple example of using a debugger in Scheme to handle errors interactively. Suppose we have the same erroneous divide function as before. We can use a Scheme debugger to stop execution when the error occurs and inspect the stack trace:

```
(define (divide x y)
  (if (= y 0)
      (begin
        (display "Error: Division by zero\n")
        (debug))
      (/ x y)))

(divide 4 0)
```

When the error occurs, the 'debug' function is invoked, and the debugger provides an interactive environment to explore the stack trace and variables.

Best Practices for Error Messages and Stack Traces

Clear and informative error messages are crucial for effective debugging. Always include enough information to understand the nature of the error without overwhelming the user. For example, instead of a generic message like "Error occurred," specify the error: "Division by zero."

For stack traces, ensure they are accessible and human-readable. When developing with Scheme, enable all debugging flags and optimizations that allow detailed stack traces to be generated.

Integrating proper logging alongside error signaling can also be beneficial. Use logging to record stack traces and error messages systematically. This aids in offline analysis and helps in environments where interactive debugging isn't feasible.

Mastering the inspection of stack traces and error messages significantly enhances the debugging process in Scheme programming. By understanding the function call history and interpreting error messages accurately, developers can swiftly locate and rectify issues, leading to more robust and reliable code.

9.9 Debugging Recursive Functions

Debugging recursive functions in Scheme requires a deep understanding of how recursion works and a systematic approach to identifying and resolving issues. Recursive functions are often used to solve complex problems by breaking them down into simpler subproblems. However, this same power also introduces complexities that can lead to challenging debugging scenarios.

When debugging recursive functions, there are several key aspects we need to focus on:

- **Base Case Correctness:** Ensuring that the base case(s) are correctly defined and will eventually be reached.
- **Recursive Case Correctness:** Ensuring that the recursive calls are made with the correct arguments and that they progress towards the base case.

- **Termination and Performance:** Checking that the recursion terminates correctly and efficiently, without redundant or infinite calls.
- **Intermediary State Inspection:** Examining the intermediary states and variables at each step of the recursion to understand the flow of execution.

Base Case Correctness

The base case is a critical component of any recursive function. It defines the simplest instance of the problem, which terminates the recursion. Incorrectly defined base cases can lead to infinite recursion or incorrect results. Consider the following example of a factorial function:

```
(define (factorial n)
  (if (= n 0)
      1
      (* n (factorial (- n 1)))))
```

In this example, the base case is (= n 0). If we mistakenly change it to (= n 1), the function will produce incorrect results for input values greater than 1. To debug base cases, verify the correctness of the condition and the return value.

Recursive Case Correctness

The recursive case should reduce the problem size progressively toward the base case. Issues in the recursive case may cause incorrect arguments to be passed along, leading to incorrect results or infinite loops. For example:

```
(define (sum-numbers n)
  (if (= n 0)
      0
      (+ n (sum-numbers (+ n 1)))))
```

In this faulty implementation, the argument for the recursive call is (+ n 1), which increases rather than decreases the problem size. This results in infinite recursion.

```
> (sum-numbers 5)
ERROR: maximum recursion depth exceeded
```

Correcting the problem:

```
(define (sum-numbers n)
```

```
  (if (= n 0)
      0
      (+ n (sum-numbers (- n 1)))))
```

Termination and Performance

Even if a recursive function terminates, performance considerations are essential, especially for large input sizes. Recursive functions can build up large call stacks, leading to stack overflow or excessive computation time. Consider optimizing recursion using techniques such as tail recursion.

Non-tail recursive example:

```
(define (non-tail-fibonacci n)
  (if (< n 2)
      n
      (+ (non-tail-fibonacci (- n 1))
         (non-tail-fibonacci (- n 2)))))
```

Tail-recursive optimization:

```
(define (tail-fibonacci n)
  (define (fib-helper a b count)
    (if (= count 0)
        a
        (fib-helper b (+ a b) (- count 1))))
  (fib-helper 0 1 n))
```

Inspect the stack trace when dealing with performance issues or unexpected termination:

```
> (non-tail-fibonacci 5)
Stack Trace:
(some stack trace details here)
ERROR: stack overflow
```

Intermediary State Inspection

To fully understand and debug recursive functions, inspect the state of important variables at each recursion level. Use print statements or debugging tools to track the values. For example, in the previously defined factorial function, adding a print statement helps:

```
(define (factorial n)
  (begin
    (display (string-append "n: " (number->string n) "\n"))
    (if (= n 0)
        1
        (* n (factorial (- n 1))))))
```

Executing the function:

```
> (factorial 3)
n: 3
n: 2
n: 1
n: 0
6
```

These print outputs provide insight into the recursive steps and intermediary values, assisting in identifying mismatches or logical errors.

Effective debugging of recursive functions in Scheme leverages a thorough understanding of base cases, recursive progression, termination criteria, and intermediary states. By carefully scrutinizing each aspect, recursive functions can be designed and debugged effectively, ensuring correct behavior and performance.

9.10 Testing and Validating Scheme Code

Testing and validating Scheme code is a fundamental aspect of software development, ensuring that programs function correctly and reliably under various conditions. This section will delve into the methodologies and best practices for testing Scheme code, focusing on unit testing, property-based testing, and integration testing. Additionally, it will cover how to set up automated testing environments and interpret test results for effective code verification.

Unit Testing in Scheme

Unit testing involves isolating and testing individual components or functions of a program to ensure they work as expected. Scheme provides several libraries that facilitate unit testing; one of the most commonly used is srfi-64 (Scheme Request for Implementation). Below is an example of how to write and run unit tests using srfi-64.

```
(import (srfi 64))

(define (add x y)
  (+ x y))

(test-begin "Test add function")

(test-equal "Test adding positive numbers"
            (add 2 3)
            5)

(test-equal "Test adding negative numbers"
            (add -1 -3)
            -4)
```

```
(test-equal "Test adding zero"
            (add 0 0)
            0)

(test-end "Test add function")
```

In the above code, test-begin initializes a test suite named "Test add function". Each test-equal statement checks if the output of the add function matches the expected result. The test-end statement concludes the test suite.

Executing this snippet in a Scheme interpreter or environment supporting srfi-64 will produce output similar to the following:

```
Running "Test add function"...
Test adding positive numbers: OK
Test adding negative numbers: OK
Test adding zero: OK
All tests in "Test add function" passed.
```

Property-Based Testing

Property-based testing is a method where the properties of the output, rather than specific values, are tested against a wide range of inputs. One notable Scheme library for property-based testing is quickcheck, inspired by Haskell's QuickCheck. An example of property-based testing for the add function is shown below:

```
(import (quickcheck))

(define (add x y)
  (+ x y))

(define (prop-addition-commutative)
  (forall (x y integer)
          (= (add x y) (add y x))))

(quickcheck "Addition is commutative" prop-addition-commutative)
```

This property test checks the commutativity property of the add function, which should return the same result when the arguments are swapped. Running this test would yield:

```
*** QuickCheck: Addition is commutative.
*** Tests: 100 (100% passed)
```

Integration Testing

Integration testing examines whether different components or systems interact correctly. It is crucial when the components have already been unit tested and verified. For instance, consider two interdependent functions:

```
(define (fetch-data)
```

```
  ;; Simulated data fetching from a database
  '((1 "Alice") (2 "Bob") (3 "Charlie")))

(define (process-data data)
  ;; Process data by extracting names
  (map cadr data))

;; Integration test for fetch-data and process-data
(define (integration-test)
  (let* ((data (fetch-data))
         (names (process-data data)))
    (equal? names '("Alice" "Bob" "Charlie"))))

(if (integration-test)
    (display "Integration test passed.\n")
    (display "Integration test failed.\n"))
```

Running the integration test should display:

```
Integration test passed.
```

Automated Testing Environments

Automated testing is essential for maintaining code quality over time, especially in large projects. Continuous Integration (CI) systems can run tests automatically with each code change. Popular CI services like Travis CI or GitHub Actions can be configured for Scheme projects. Below is an example configuration for GitHub Actions, assuming tests are defined in a file named test.scm.

```
name: Scheme CI

on: [push]

jobs:
  build:
    runs-on: ubuntu-latest
    steps:
    - name: Checkout code
      uses: actions/checkout@v2
    - name: Install Chez Scheme
      run: sudo apt-get install -y chezscheme
    - name: Run tests
      run: chez --script test.scm
```

Upon each push, this CI configuration checks out the code, installs Chez Scheme, and runs the test suite. The results are displayed in the CI interface.

Interpreting Test Results

Effective interpretation of test results is paramount to debugging and refining code. Common outcomes include 'pass', 'fail', and 'error'. A passing test indicates the code works as expected. A failing test suggests a discrepancy between expected and actual results, requiring inspection of either the code or the test. Errors often signify issues in the test setup or runtime problems.

By employing a comprehensive testing strategy encompassing unit, property-based, and integration tests, along with setting up automated environments, the reliability and robustness of Scheme code can be significantly enhanced. Proper analysis and interpretation of test results further augment the development process, leading to high-quality software.

9.11 Strategies for Preventing Common Errors

Preventing common errors in Scheme programming requires a strategic approach that involves anticipating potential pitfalls, adopting best practices, and leveraging Scheme's features for robust code. Here, we discuss key strategies that can help mitigate the occurrence of common errors.

1. Write Clear and Readable Code: Clear and readable code is easier to debug and maintain. Using meaningful names for variables, functions, and parameters enhances the readability of the code. Adopting a consistent naming convention and commenting on complex sections of code provides additional clarity.

/* Example of clear and readable code */

```
(define (calculate-area radius)
  ;; This function calculates the area of a circle
  (let ((pi 3.14159))
    (* pi radius radius)))
```

2. Modularize Code: Breaking down a program into smaller, manageable functions or modules facilitates easier identification of errors. It allows individual functions to be tested independently before integrating them into the larger program.

```
(define (calculate-circumference radius)
  ;; This function calculates the circumference of a circle
  (let ((pi 3.14159))
    (* 2 pi radius)))

(define (circle-properties radius)
  ;; This function calculates both area and circumference of a circle
  (let ((area (calculate-area radius))
        (circumference (calculate-circumference radius)))
    (list area circumference)))
```

3. Use Assertions: Assertions are a useful tool for validating assumptions made in the code. They help catch logical errors by ensuring that certain conditions hold true during program execution.

```
(define (safe-divide num denom)
  ;; This function performs safe division
  (assert (not (= denom 0)) "Denominator must not be zero")
  (/ num denom))
```

4. Type Checking and Validation: Scheme is dynamically typed, and type errors can easily occur if variables are not validated. Implementing explicit type checks can prevent these errors.

```
(define (add-numbers a b)
  ;; This function adds two numbers after type validation
  (when (and (number? a) (number? b))
    (+ a b)))
```

5. Error Handling Frameworks: Consistent error handling throughout the program prevents it from crashing unexpectedly. Using constructs like guard and with-exception-handler ensures that errors are managed gracefully.

```
(define (safe-divide num denom)
  (guard (exc
         ((number-divide-by-zero? exc) 'undefined))
    (/ num denom)))
```

6. Test-Driven Development (TDD): Writing tests before coding can help identify potential errors early. It ensures that the code meets the specified requirements and performs as expected.

```
(define (test-calculate-area)
  (assert (= (calculate-area 1) 3.14159) "Test failed for radius 1")
  (assert (= (calculate-area 2) 12.56636) "Test failed for radius 2"))

(test-calculate-area)
```

7. Debugging Tools: Leverage Scheme's debugging tools, such as the integrated debugger, to step through code execution and inspect variable values. This systematic approach is essential for identifying and fixing errors.

8. Code Reviews: Regular code reviews by peers can uncover overlooked errors and provide insights into potential improvements. Collaborative reviews foster better coding practices and result in more reliable code.

9. Avoiding Common Pitfalls in Recursion: Recursive functions are prone to errors such as stack overflow and incorrect base cases. Ensuring correct base cases and termination conditions prevents infinite recursion.

```
(define (factorial n)
  ;; This function calculates the factorial of n
  (if (<= n 1)
      1
      (* n (factorial (- n 1)))))
```

Anticipating potential errors and implementing robust strategies are crucial for writing reliable Scheme programs. These preventive measures align with best practices and leverage Scheme's features to mitigate common errors effectively.

9.12 Case Studies: Debugging Real-World Scheme Programs

Analyzing real-world Scheme programs provides insights into practical debugging strategies and illustrates common pitfalls encountered during software development. This section presents several case studies to highlight the application of error handling and debugging techniques discussed in previous sections.

- **Case Study 1: Stack Overflow in Recursive Functions**

Consider a Scheme program designed to calculate factorial values using a recursive approach. The naive implementation of the factorial function may lead to a stack overflow error for large inputs.

```
(define (factorial n)
  (if (= n 0)
      1
      (* n (factorial (- n 1)))))
```

Executing (factorial 10000) results in a stack overflow error. To debug this, we need to trace the recursive calls and identify the conditions leading to excessive stack consumption.

Using the Scheme debugger, we set breakpoints at the entry and exit points of the factorial function. Scheme debuggers typically allow for stepping through code, setting breakpoints, and inspecting call stacks. By examining the call stack, we observe the extended chain of recursive calls, confirming the stack overflow origin. To rectify this, we need to refactor the code to use a tail-recursive approach.

```
(define (factorial n)
  (define (iter acc n)
    (if (= n 0)
        acc
        (iter (* acc n) (- n 1))))
  (iter 1 n))
```

The refactored version is tail-recursive, ensuring that the Scheme interpreter can optimize the recursion into iteration, mitigating the risk of a stack overflow. Verifying the updated function with large inputs, such as (factorial 10000), confirms the issue is resolved.

- **Case Study 2: Handling Unexpected Input Types**

Another common scenario is handling unexpected input types in a program. Consider a function designed to sum a list of integers. If the function encounters a non-integer element, it should signal an error.

```
(define (sum-list lst)
  (if (null? lst)
      0
      (+ (car lst) (sum-list (cdr lst)))))
```

Running (sum-list '(1 2 three 4)) results in a runtime error when attempting to add an integer to the symbol three. To handle this gracefully, we use the guard construct.

```
(define (sum-list lst)
  (guard (ex ((exn:fail? ex) (error (exn-message ex))))
    (if (null? lst)
        0
        (+ (if (integer? (car lst))
               (car lst)
               (error "Non-integer element encountered"))
           (sum-list (cdr lst))))))
```

The guard clause ensures that a meaningful error message is produced and prevents the program from terminating abruptly. Testing the function with mixed input types, such as (sum-list '(1 2 three 4)), now outputs:

```
Non-integer element encountered
```

- **Case Study 3: Debugging Performance Issues**

A program might exhibit performance issues due to inefficient algorithms or data structures. For instance, consider a function that checks for duplicates in a list using a nested loop.

```
(define (contains-duplicates? lst)
  (define (check-dups l)
    (if (null? l)
        #f
        (if (member (car lst) (cdr lst))
            #t
            (check-dups (cdr l)))))
  (check-dups lst))
```

The contains-duplicates? function performs well for small lists but becomes exceedingly slow for large lists due to its $O(n^2)$ complexity.

To debug and improve the performance, profiling tools help in identifying function call times and frequency. By profiling, we observe significant time spent in the member function. As an optimization, we can use a hash table to achieve an $O(n)$ complexity.

```
(define (contains-duplicates? lst)
  (define (iter seen remain)
    (if (null? remain)
        #f
        (if (hash-ref seen (car remain) #f)
            #t
            (begin
              (hash-set! seen (car remain) #t)
              (iter seen (cdr remain))))))
  (iter (make-hash) lst))
```

With the optimized approach, performance significantly improves. Testing with large inputs confirms the enhanced efficiency without affecting correctness.

Through these case studies, understanding the application of error handling and debugging techniques in Scheme is essential for writing robust and efficient programs.

Chapter 10

Advanced Topics in Scheme Programming

This chapter explores advanced topics in Scheme programming, including continuations, call/cc, and delimiters for controlling flow. It covers lazy evaluation, delayed expressions, and streams for handling infinite lists. The chapter delves into advanced functional programming techniques, memory management, and garbage collection. Concurrency and parallelism are examined, along with interfacing Scheme with other languages. The use of libraries and modules, advanced metaprogramming techniques, and practical applications in complex projects are also discussed, providing a deep insight into sophisticated aspects of Scheme programming.

10.1 Introduction to Advanced Topics in Scheme Programming

This section provides an overview of the advanced topics that are central to mastering Scheme programming. The concepts discussed here build upon the foundational knowledge established in earlier chapters, delving into sophisticated techniques and methodologies that enhance the power and flexibility of Scheme. This section sets the stage for the subsequent detailed exploration of continuations, lazy evaluation, streams, advanced functional programming techniques, memory management, concurrency, and interfacing with other languages.

Scheme, a dialect of Lisp, is known for its minimalist design and powerful features, making it particularly well-suited for advanced programming techniques. To fully leverage Scheme's capabilities, a deep understanding of the following advanced topics is essential:

- **Continuations**: Continuations capture the current state of a program, allowing it to resume execution at a later point. They enable advanced flow control mechanisms, such as non-linear control structures and backtracking.
- **Call/CC (call-with-current-continuation)**: A powerful feature of Scheme that provides access to the current continuation, allowing for sophisticated control flows and implementing complex behavior such as coroutines and exceptions.
- **Delimiters and Prompts**: These tools allow control over the extent of continuations, enabling modular and incremental construction of control operators.
- **Lazy Evaluation and Delayed Expressions**: Scheme supports lazy evaluation, allowing computations to be deferred until their results are needed. This can lead to efficiency gains and enable the creation of infinite data structures.
- **Streams and Infinite Lists**: Streams enable the representation of potentially infinite sequences of data, allowing for efficient and elegant handling of sources such as real-time data feeds.
- **Advanced Functional Programming Techniques**: Higher-order functions, closures, and recursion are foundational in Scheme. Mastery of these techniques is fundamental for building complex and reusable components.
- **Memory Management and Garbage Collection**: Scheme's automatic memory management requires an understanding of garbage collection mechanisms to optimize performance and manage resources effectively.
- **Concurrency and Parallelism**: Leveraging multiple processors requires knowledge of concurrency constructs and parallel execution models to build high-performance and responsive programs.

- **Interfacing with Other Languages**: Scheme's ability to interoperate with other languages, such as C or Java, extends its utility and allows for the integration of Scheme programs with existing software infrastructures.

- **Building and Using Libraries and Modules**: Modules and libraries promote code reuse and modularization, which are critical for managing large codebases and improving maintainability.

- **Advanced Metaprogramming Techniques**: Metaprogramming enables programs to manipulate other programs or themselves, allowing for powerful abstraction and extensibility mechanisms.

Continuations in Scheme

Continuations are one of the most distinctive features of Scheme, offering a unique approach to flow control. A continuation represents the state of a computation at a specific point in the program. By capturing a continuation, the program can save its current execution context and resume from that point at a later time.

Scheme provides the call-with-current-continuation, or call/cc, as a built-in mechanism to capture the current continuation. The following example illustrates the basic use of call/cc:

```
(define (test-call-cc)
  (call/cc
    (lambda (k)
      (display "Before continuation\n")
      (k 'continuation-called)
      (display "After continuation\n"))))

(test-call-cc)
```

In this example, the lambda function passed to call/cc captures the current continuation in the variable k. When k is invoked with the argument 'continuation-called, the program state is restored to the point of the call to k, and the execution continues from there, effectively bypassing the subsequent display call.

The output is as follows:

```
Before continuation
```

Lazy Evaluation

Lazy evaluation is a strategy where expressions are not evaluated until their values are actually needed. This can lead to performance gains by avoiding unnecessary calculations and can also enable the definition of infinitely large data structures. Scheme provides primitives like delay and force to support lazy evaluation.

To create a delayed expression, use the delay macro:

```
(define lazy-value (delay (+ 1 2)))
```

The expression (+ 1 2) is not evaluated immediately. When the value is needed, the force procedure forces its evaluation:

```
(define result (force lazy-value))
(display result) ; Outputs: 3
```

Streams and Infinite Lists

Streams in Scheme are a powerful abstraction for dealing with sequences of data that are potentially infinite. A stream is essentially a delayed list, where the head of the list is an actual value and the tail is a delayed computation. This allows the program to generate elements of the sequence on demand.

The following code defines a simple stream and demonstrates how to operate on it:

```
(define (stream-cons hd tl)
  (cons hd (delay tl)))

(define (stream-car str)
  (car str))

(define (stream-cdr str)
  (force (cdr str)))

(define (stream-from n)
  (stream-cons n (stream-from (+ n 1))))

(define naturals (stream-from 0))
```

The function stream-from generates an infinite stream of natural numbers starting from n. You can access elements of the stream as follows:

```
(display (stream-car naturals)) ; Outputs: 0
(display (stream-car (stream-cdr naturals))) ; Outputs: 1
```

Understanding these advanced topics in Scheme lays the groundwork for exploring more complex concepts and techniques. Each topic builds upon the foundational principles of functional programming and extends Scheme's capabilities to handle sophisticated programming tasks effectively.

10.2 Continuations and Their Uses

Continuations in Scheme represent the rest of the computation from a given point in a program. They are powerful constructs providing a means to capture the current continuation—essentially, the state and control flow of a program—and can be used to jump to or manipulate that captured continuation at will.

Continuations are created and manipulated using the call/cc (call-with-current-continuation) function. This function captures the current continuation as a procedure, which can then be invoked to return control to the point of capture. Understanding and effectively utilizing continuations requires a deep comprehension of control flow and state in programming.

To illustrate the basic usage of continuations, let us consider a simple example using call/cc:

```
(define (example-continuation)
  (call/cc
   (lambda (k)
     (display "Before continuation\n")
     (k 'exit)
     (display "After continuation\n"))))
(example-continuation)
```

In this code, the call/cc function is called with a lambda function that takes a single argument k, representing the continuation. The message "Before continuation" is displayed, then the continuation k is invoked with the argument exit, which immediately returns control to the point just after the call/cc call, effectively preventing the "After continuation" message from being displayed.

```
Before continuation
```

Continuations have several practical uses:

1. Early Exits: Continuations can be used to provide an escape mechanism similar to exceptions in other languages. This allows a procedure to exit early based on some condition.

```
(define (search lst target)
  (call/cc
   (lambda (exit)
     (for-each
      (lambda (item)
        (if (equal? item target)
            (exit #t)))
      lst)
     #f)))
(search '(1 2 3 4 5) 3) ; Returns #t
```

```
(search '(1 2 3 4 5) 6) ; Returns #f
```

The search function uses call/cc to create an exit continuation that terminates the search early if the target is found, returning #t. If the target is not found, it returns #f.

2. Backtracking: Continuations enable non-linear control flows like backtracking, often used in algorithms like depth-first searches or constraint solvers.

```
(define (find-combination lst target)
  (call/cc
   (lambda (success)
     (letrec ((search
               (lambda (lst current-sum)
                 (cond
                  ((null? lst) (success '()))
                  ((= (+ current-sum (car lst)) target)
                   (success (list (car lst))))
                  (else
                   (search (cdr lst) (+ current-sum (car lst)))
                   (search (cdr lst) current-sum))))))
       (search lst 0)
       'not-found))))

(find-combination '(1 2 3 4 5) 7) ; Returns (3 4)
(find-combination '(1 2 3 4) 10) ; Returns not-found
```

This example searches for a combination of numbers in the list that sum up to the target. It uses call/cc to return the first valid combination found. The success continuation captures the state where a solution is found and returns immediately, preventing further search.

3. Cooperative Multitasking: Continuations can be employed to implement coroutines, enabling cooperative multitasking. This allows multiple routines to yield control to each other without preemption.

```
(define coroutine1 #f)
(define coroutine2 #f)

(define (start-coroutines)
  (call/cc
   (lambda (k)
     (set! coroutine1 k)
     ((lambda () (call/cc
                  (lambda (k)
                    (set! coroutine2 k)
                    (coroutine1 'resume))))))))

(define (run-coroutines)
  (display "Coroutine 1: Step 1\n")
  (coroutine2 'resume)
  (display "Coroutine 1: Step 2\n"))

(define (run-coroutine2)
  (display "Coroutine 2: Step 1\n")
```

```
  (coroutine1 'resume)
  (display "Coroutine 2: Step 2\n"))

(start-coroutines)
(run-coroutines)
(run-coroutine2)
```

This setup initializes two coroutines. start-coroutines captures the current continuation for each coroutine. When run-coroutines and run-coroutine2 are called, they repeatedly yield control to each other using the previously captured continuations.

```
Coroutine 1: Step 1
Coroutine 2: Step 1
Coroutine 1: Step 2
Coroutine 2: Step 2
```

Understanding continuations and their uses is crucial for harnessing the full potential of control structures and flow manipulations in Scheme. By mastering continuations, programmers gain a robust tool for managing complex control flows and enhancing the expressiveness of their code.

10.3 Understanding and Using Call/CC

The concept of continuations is a powerful feature in Scheme that allows for advanced flow control in programs. One of the core constructs that utilize continuations is call-with-current-continuation, abbreviated as call/cc. This section will elucidate the mechanics and applications of call/cc.

Mechanics of call/cc

call/cc captures the current continuation (i.e., the rest of the program computation) and makes it available as a first-class object. To understand its operation, consider the following simple example:

```
(define (example)
  (call/cc
    (lambda (k)
      (display "Before continuation call\n")
      (k 'done)
      (display "This will not be printed\n"))))
```

When example is invoked, it produces:

```
Before continuation call
```

Here, call/cc takes a single argument, which is a function. This function receives the current continuation k as its parameter. The function first displays "Before continuation call", then the continuation k is called with the argument 'done. At this point, the current continuation captures the rest of the computation, meaning all future instructions within this scope are discarded. Thus, "This will not be printed" is never executed.

Passing Continuations

Continuations can be stored and invoked later, allowing for non-local exits and implementing control structures like loops, exceptions, and coroutines.

Consider a scenario where a continuation is stored for later use:

```
(define saved-cont #f)
(define (test-call/cc)
  (call/cc
    (lambda (k)
      (set! saved-cont k)
      (display "Continuation saved\n")))
  (display "After call/cc\n"))

(test-call/cc)

; use the saved continuation
(if saved-cont ((saved-cont 'again)))
```

Execution gives:

```
Continuation saved
After call/cc
After call/cc
```

Initially, call/cc captures the continuation, which is saved in saved-cont. After the first invocation of test-call/cc, the program prints "Continuation saved" and "After call/cc". Invoking the saved continuation prints "After call/cc" again, as the continuation stores the execution state.

Implementing Control Structures

call/cc can be used to create custom control structures. One such example is implementing an escape operator similar to catch/throw in other languages.

```
(define (escape-example)
  (call/cc
    (lambda (escape)
      (for-each
        (lambda (x)
```

```
        (display x)
        (newline)
        (if (= x 3) (escape 'exit)))
      '(1 2 3 4 5 6))
    'complete)))

(display (escape-example))
```

This outputs:

```
1
2
3
exit
```

In this code, call/cc establishes an escape function. Upon encountering the condition (= x 3), the escape function is invoked, terminating the loop prematurely and returning 'exit. This demonstrates a controlled exit from computation.

Advanced Applications of call/cc

Beyond simple flow control, call/cc is instrumental in advanced applications, such as implementing coroutines and multi-threading.

Coroutines can be created using call/cc for cooperative multitasking:

```
(define (coroutine f)
  (call/cc
    (lambda (yield)
      (f (lambda () (call/cc yield))))))

(define coro1
  (coroutine
    (lambda (yield)
      (display "Coro1 - part 1\n")
      (yield)
      (display "Coro1 - part 2\n")
      (yield))))

(define coro2
  (coroutine
    (lambda (yield)
      (display "Coro2 - part 1\n")
      (yield)
      (display "Coro2 - part 2\n"))))

(coro1)
(coro2)
(coro1)
(coro2)
```

This leads to:

```
Coro1 - part 1
Coro2 - part 1
Coro1 - part 2
Coro2 - part 2
```

Each coroutine uses yield to suspend its execution and pass control. The successive invocation of coro1 and coro2 illustrates how computation alternates between coroutines.

Practical Considerations

While call/cc provides flexibility and power, it should be used judiciously. Misuse can lead to convoluted and difficult-to-maintain code. It is advisable to utilize continuations for well-justified scenarios and follow best practice coding standards to ensure clarity.

As we conclude our exploration, it is evident that understanding and using call/cc facilitates mastery in sophisticated flow control and advanced Scheme programming techniques.

10.4 Delimiters and Prompts with Continuations

In advanced Scheme programming, understanding how to utilize delimiters and prompts with continuations is crucial for mastering control flow. Delimiters and prompts are essential for managing the extent and capturing behavior of continuations, especially when working with non-local exits and complex logical flows.

Continuations, as covered earlier, represent the rest of the computation at any given point in a program. Delimiters help manage these computations by delimiting the scope within which a continuation can be captured and invoked. This technique is particularly useful when precise control over continuation capture and invocation is required, often in cooperative multitasking, generators, or backtracking algorithms.

Delimited Continuations allow fine-grained control over which parts of a program's continuation are captured. The two primary constructs for working with delimited continuations are reset and shift. The reset operator delimits the continuation, while the shift operator captures the continuation up to the nearest enclosing reset. The syntactic forms are typically represented as:

```
(reset E)
```

```
(shift k E)
```

reset establishes a scope boundary, and shift captures the continuation up to that boundary and binds it to the variable k. The following example illustrates a basic use of these constructs:

```
(define result
  (reset
   (+ 1 (shift k
             (k (k 2))))))
```

Here, reset sets up a boundary for the continuation. The shift operator captures the continuation from that point, binding it to k. Invoking k effectively replays the continuation. Evaluating this example step-by-step reveals that result will evaluate to 5, illustrating the captured continuation's impact.

Prompt and control are other constructs for working with delimited continuations. They operate similarly to reset and shift, but with nuanced differences useful for certain advanced scenarios.

Additionally, handling prompts allows us to establish dynamic boundaries for continuations. The following pseudocode demonstrates this interplay:

```
(let ((p (make-prompt)))
  (prompt p
   (print (+ 1 (control p
                        (lambda (k)
                          (k (k 2))))))))
```

This code shows the use of make-prompt to create a prompt, prompt to delimit the continuation scope, and control to capture and manipulate the continuation within that delimited scope.

Captured continuations can be invoked as regular procedures, reinstating saved execution states. This enables significant flexibility, such as suspending and resuming computations or implementing cooperative multitasking, which is a form of context switching.

Understanding how prompts interact with multiple nested continuations is also instructive. Consider a more complex scenario involving nested reset and shift:

```
(define nested-result
  (reset
   (reset
    (+ 1 (shift k1
               (k1 (reset
                     (+ 10 (shift k2
                                (k2 20))))))))))
```

Here, multiple reset and shift pairs interact to capture and manipulate nested continuations. Validation of the evaluation order and the resulting computation demonstrates intricate control flow.

Leveraging delimiters and prompts with continuations empowers developers to construct robust, non-linear control structures within Scheme programs. This mastery fosters the creation of sophisticated, performance-tuned applications capable of leveraging the full potential of advanced Scheme programming paradigms.

10.5 Lazy Evaluation and Delayed Expressions

Lazy evaluation is a technique that delays the evaluation of an expression until its value is actually needed. This approach can lead to improved performance and reduced memory usage in scenarios where not all computed values are required immediately or might not be required at all. Delayed expressions, also known as promises, are a fundamental component of lazy evaluation in Scheme.

In Scheme, the delay and force constructs enable lazy evaluation. The delay construct defers the computation of an expression, creating a promise that can be forced later to obtain its value. The force construct, on the other hand, triggers the evaluation of a delayed expression.

Consider the following example where we use delay and force to manage the computation:

```
(define delayed-exp (delay (+ 1 2 3)))
(display "The promise has been created, but not yet evaluated.\n")

(define forced-exp (force delayed-exp))
(display "Now the promise is forced and the result is: ")
(display forced-exp)
```

Executing the above code would produce the following output:

```
The promise has been created, but not yet evaluated.
Now the promise is forced and the result is: 6
```

In this scenario, (+ 1 2 3) is wrapped by the delay construct, which creates a promise. The expression within a promise will not be evaluated until force is called on it. When force delayed-exp is executed, the delayed computation is performed, returning the sum of 1, 2, and

3, which is 6.

Lazy evaluation can be particularly advantageous when dealing with potentially infinite data structures, such as infinite lists. An infinite list, or stream, is a sequence of data elements that can be computed incrementally. Scheme's support for lazy evaluation allows for elegant manipulation of such sequences without incurring the overhead of computing and storing unneeded parts of the list.

Using lazy evaluation to handle infinite sequences can be illustrated with the example of generating an infinite list of natural numbers:

```
(define (integers-from n)
  (cons n (delay (integers-from (+ n 1)))))

(define integers (integers-from 0))
```

Here, integers-from is a function that takes an integer n and returns a pair (cons) where the first element is n and the second element is a delayed computation (delay (integers-from (+ n 1))) of the succeeding integers.

To access the elements of this infinite list, we use force as follows:

```
(define first-integer (car integers))
(define rest-integers (force (cdr integers)))

(display first-integer) ; Prints 0
(display (car rest-integers)) ; Prints 1
```

By delaying the computation of subsequent integers, we construct an infinite list we can traverse and process without evaluating the entire list at once.

Let's examine a practical use case: implementing an infinite stream of Fibonacci numbers using lazy evaluation.

```
(define (fib-gen a b)
  (cons a (delay (fib-gen b (+ a b)))))

(define fibs (fib-gen 0 1))
```

In this example, fib-gen is a function that generates pairs where each number is the sum of the two preceding ones. The flexibility of lazy evaluation allows handling this infinite sequence efficiently.

To retrieve Fibonacci numbers from the stream, we perform:

```
(define first-fib (car fibs))
(define rest-fibs (force (cdr fibs)))
(define second-fib (car rest-fibs))
```

```
(display first-fib) ; Prints 0
(display second-fib) ; Prints 1
```

Lazy evaluation combined with delayed expressions not only optimize resource usage but also provide a powerful abstraction for working with large or infinite data structures. This advanced technique fits well within the functional programming paradigm, fostering declarative and concise code that emphasizes what the program should accomplish over how it achieves that outcome.

10.6 Streams and Infinite Lists

In Scheme, streams provide an elegant mechanism for handling potentially infinite lists. Unlike traditional lists, streams are lazily evaluated, meaning that their elements are computed only as needed. This system allows for efficient computation and can handle data sources or sequences that are conceptually infinite.

Streams are represented as pairs where the head is a first value, and the tail is a thunk (a function with no arguments) that computes the rest of the stream when called. This lazy evaluation is crucial for managing performance and memory usage, particularly when working with large or infinite data sets.

To define a stream in Scheme, we start by creating a procedure that returns such a pair. The following example demonstrates how to create a stream of natural numbers starting from a given number n.

```
(define (stream-start-n n)
  (cons n (lambda () (stream-start-n (+ n 1)))))
```

In this example, stream-start-n takes a number n and returns a stream where the head is n and the tail is a thunk that generates the next number by recursively calling stream-start-n with n+1.

To fetch elements from a stream, we define functions to access the head and tail of a stream:

```
(define (stream-head stream)
  (car stream))

(define (stream-tail stream)
  (force (cdr stream)))
```

Here, stream-head fetches the first element (car) of the stream, and stream-tail evaluates the thunk holding the rest of the stream (cdr) with the force procedure.

Consider an example of utilizing these definitions:

```
(define natural-numbers (stream-start-n 1))

(display (stream-head natural-numbers)) ; displays 1
(display (stream-head (stream-tail natural-numbers))) ; displays 2
(display (stream-head (stream-tail (stream-tail natural-numbers)))) ; displays 3
```

The example above demonstrates generating and accessing the first three natural numbers from our stream.

A key operation in working with streams is mapping a function over a stream to transform its elements. Here is how we define a map function for streams:

```
(define (stream-map proc stream)
  (cons (proc (stream-head stream))
        (lambda () (stream-map proc (stream-tail stream)))))
```

The stream-map function takes a procedure proc and a stream, applies proc to the stream-head, and constructs a new stream where each element results from applying proc to the corresponding element of the original stream.

Next, consider generating a stream of squares using stream-map:

```
(define square-stream (stream-map (lambda (x) (* x x)) natural-numbers))

(display (stream-head square-stream)) ; displays 1
(display (stream-head (stream-tail square-stream))) ; displays 4
(display (stream-head (stream-tail (stream-tail square-stream)))) ; displays 9
```

This ability to lazily compute the elements becomes especially valuable when dealing with infinite sequences. Some operations and algorithms, like the Sieve of Eratosthenes for generating prime numbers, can naturally benefit from the laziness of streams.

To construct the Sieve of Eratosthenes using streams, we can follow these steps:

1. Generate an initial infinite stream of natural numbers starting from 2. 2. Take the head of the stream as a prime number. 3. Filter the rest of the stream to remove multiples of the prime number. 4. Recursively apply these steps to the filtered stream.

Here is the implementation of primes using streams:

```
(define (sieve stream)
  (cons (stream-head stream)
```

```
    (lambda ()
      (sieve (stream-filter (lambda (x)
                              (not (= 0 (modulo x (stream-head stream)))))
                            (stream-tail stream))))))

(define primes (sieve (stream-start-n 2)))

(display (stream-head primes)) ; displays 2
(display (stream-head (stream-tail primes))) ; displays 3
(display (stream-head (stream-tail (stream-tail primes)))) ; displays 5
```

In this example, sieve filters out non-prime numbers from the stream of natural numbers. The stream-filter function operates similarly to stream-map, producing a stream with elements that satisfy the given predicate.

Streams provide powerful abstractions for sequences and make it possible to elegantly handle infinite lists. By leveraging lazy evaluation, Scheme programmers can work with large or unbounded data structures efficiently.

10.7 Functional Programming Techniques

Functional programming in Scheme leverages higher-order functions, pure functions, immutability, and recursion to create concise and expressive code. This section extends the fundamental concepts introduced earlier, delving into advanced techniques that facilitate powerful and flexible problem-solving capabilities in Scheme.

One essential functional programming technique is the use of higher-order functions. Higher-order functions are functions that take other functions as arguments or return them as results. This feature allows for a high degree of modularity and code reuse. Common higher-order functions like map, filter, and fold enable operations on lists and other data structures.

```
;; Define a simple function that will be used as an argument.
(define (square x)
  (* x x))

;; Using map to apply 'square' function to a list.
(map square '(1 2 3 4 5))
;; Output: (1 4 9 16 25)

;; Using filter to select only even numbers from a list.
(define (even? x)
  (= (modulo x 2) 0))

(filter even? '(1 2 3 4 5 6 7 8 9 10))
;; Output: (2 4 6 8 10)
```

```
;; Using fold (also known as reduce) to sum elements of a list.
(fold + 0 '(1 2 3 4 5))
;; Output: 15
```

Pure functions are another key concept; they return the same result given the same arguments and cause no side effects. Scheme encourages the use of pure functions to maintain consistency and predictability.

Next, immutability is a pivotal aspect of functional programming, ensuring that once a data structure is created, it cannot be modified. Instead, new data structures are generated with the required changes. This trait prevents unintended side-effects and makes concurrent programming more manageable.

```
;; Original list
(define my-list '(1 2 3 4 5))

;; Instead of modifying 'my-list', create a new list.
(define new-list (append my-list '(6 7 8)))

;; my-list remains unchanged: '(1 2 3 4 5)
;; new-list is: '(1 2 3 4 5 6 7 8)
```

Recursion, an essential mechanism in Scheme, allows functions to call themselves to solve problems incrementally. Scheme optimizes tail-recursive functions, making recursion an efficient method for iterating processes.

```
;; A tail-recursive function to calculate factorial.
(define (factorial n)
  (define (iter product counter)
    (if (> counter n)
        product
        (iter (* product counter) (+ counter 1))))
  (iter 1 1))

(factorial 5)
;; Output: 120
```

Understanding closures is crucial for mastering functional programming in Scheme. A closure is a function that retains access to its lexical scope, even when the function is invoked outside that scope. This capability enables functions to maintain state across invocations.

```
;; Function that returns a closure.
(define (make-counter)
  (let ((count 0))
    (lambda ()
      (set! count (+ count 1))
      count)))

(define counter1 (make-counter))
```

```
(define counter2 (make-counter))

(counter1) ;; Output: 1
(counter1) ;; Output: 2
(counter2) ;; Output: 1
(counter2) ;; Output: 2
```

Scheme also supports lazy evaluation, deferring the computation of expressions until their values are needed. Using delay and force, we can implement lazy evaluation for creating potentially infinite data structures.

```
;; Delayed computation of a value.
(define delayed-value (delay (+ 1 2)))

;; The computation is not performed until 'force' is called.
(force delayed-value)
;; Output: 3
```

Streams are infinite sequences, an extension of lazy evaluation, allowing the definition of infinite lists while only computing elements when needed. This technique can optimize memory usage and performance when working with large or infinite datasets.

```
;; Helper functions for streams.
(define (stream-car stream) (car stream))
(define (stream-cdr stream) ((cdr stream)))
(define (stream-cons head thunk)
  (cons head thunk))

;; Creating an infinite stream of natural numbers.
(define (naturals n)
  (stream-cons n (lambda () (naturals (+ n 1)))))
(define natural-numbers (naturals 0))

;; Accessing the first few elements of the stream.
(stream-car natural-numbers) ;; Output: 0
(stream-car (stream-cdr natural-numbers)) ;; Output: 1
```

These functional programming techniques enable efficient and elegant implementations of complex algorithms. By leveraging higher-order functions, immutability, recursion, closures, lazy evaluation, and streams, Scheme programmers can write code that is both flexible and robust. Understanding these advanced concepts is essential for mastering Scheme and applying functional programming principles effectively.

10.8 Memory Management and Garbage Collection

Memory management is a critical aspect in Scheme programming, particularly as programs grow in complexity and size. Efficient management of memory ensures optimal use of system resources, prevents memory leaks, and maintains program stability. In Scheme, memory management is often abstracted away from the programmer, thanks to the powerful garbage collector. This section delves into the intricacies of memory management and the functioning of garbage collection in Scheme.

Dynamic Memory Allocation

Scheme employs dynamic memory allocation, meaning that memory is allocated at runtime rather than at compile-time. This flexibility is a double-edged sword: while it allows for dynamic data structures and efficient use of memory, it also requires vigilant management to avoid issues such as fragmentation and memory leaks.

Consider the following example, where lists are dynamically allocated:

```
(define list1 (list 1 2 3))
(define list2 (cons 4 list1))
```

In this snippet, list1 and list2 are dynamically allocated in memory. The use of cons constructs a new pair, pointing to list1, effectively creating a new list that shares memory with the previous list.

Automatic Garbage Collection

Scheme utilizes automatic garbage collection to manage memory. Garbage collection is the process of identifying and reclaiming memory that is no longer in use by the program. This is achieved without explicit instructions from the programmer, helping prevent memory leaks and other issues related to manual memory management. The garbage collector automatically frees the memory occupied by objects that are unreachable.

Call graph tracing is a common garbage collection method used in Scheme. This process involves identifying live objects by tracing their references from a set of root objects, typically the global variables and the stack. Any objects not reachable from the root objects are considered garbage and are collected.

```
(define (create-list n)
```

```
  (if (zero? n)
      '()
      (cons n (create-list (- n 1)))))

(define my-list (create-list 10))
(set! my-list '())
```

After the set! operation, the previous list created by create-list is no longer referenced by my-list, making it eligible for garbage collection.

Mark-and-Sweep Algorithm

A widely-used approach in garbage collection is the mark-and-sweep algorithm. This method involves two phases: marking and sweeping. During the marking phase, the garbage collector traverses the object graph, starting from the root objects, and marks all reachable objects. In the sweeping phase, it scans through memory and collects unmarked objects.

Algorithm 5: Mark-and-Sweep Garbage Collection Algorithm

```
Data: Root Objects, Heap Memory
Result: Memory is cleaned
begin
    Mark Phase
    - Initialize a stack with root objects
    - While the stack is not empty:
    – Pop an object from the stack
    – If the object is not marked:
    — Mark the object
    — Push all references of this object onto the stack
    Sweep Phase
    - Loop through all objects in heap memory
    - If an object is not marked:
    – Deallocate the object
end
```

The mark-and-sweep algorithm ensures that all memory not in use is reclaimed, preventing memory leaks.

Generational Garbage Collection

Generational garbage collection is another optimization technique that Scheme implementations frequently use. It is based on the observation that most objects have a short lifespan, and a small percentage of objects survive multiple garbage collection cycles. Generational garbage collection segregates objects by age and applies different collection strategies to each generation.

Objects are initially allocated in the young generation. Since most objects die young, frequent collections are performed on this generation. Surviving objects are promoted to the old generation, where collections occur less frequently. This approach reduces the overhead of garbage collection by focusing on the areas of memory that are more likely to contain garbage.

Memory Management Best Practices

While garbage collection in Scheme reduces the burden on the programmer, it is still crucial to write memory-efficient code. Here are a few best practices:

- **Avoid Unnecessary Allocations**: Minimize the creation of short-lived objects.
- **Release Unneeded References**: Clear references to large data structures when they are no longer needed.
- **Profile and Optimize**: Use profiling tools to detect memory usage patterns and optimize accordingly.
- **Use Efficient Data Structures**: Prefer more memory-efficient data structures when possible.

By adhering to these practices, programmers can ensure that their Scheme programs run efficiently and utilize memory resources effectively, leveraging the full potential of the garbage collector.

10.9 Concurrency and Parallelism in Scheme

Concurrency and parallelism are critical concepts in high-performance computing and modern software design. They enable multiple processes to execute simultaneously, thereby optimizing resource utilization and execution times. In Scheme, several constructs and libraries facilitate concurrent and parallel programming, which we will explore extensively in this section.

Scheme supports concurrency through various paradigms. We will discuss threads, synchronization mechanisms, and message-passing interfaces. Meanwhile, parallelism is achieved by distributing computational tasks across multiple processors or cores.

Threads in Scheme

Threads allow multiple sequences of operations to be interleaved, providing the illusion of simultaneous execution. Scheme's thread model is typically based on the POSIX thread (pthread) standard, which enables thread creation, synchronization, and management. Below is an example of simple thread creation and execution in Scheme:

```
(define (thread-function)
  (display "Thread is running\n"))

(define thread (thread-start! thread-function))
```

In the example above, we define a function thread-function that prints a message. We then create and start a thread using thread-start!. The thread variable holds the thread object, which can be managed or synchronized as needed.

Synchronization Mechanisms

Thread synchronization is crucial in concurrent programming to avoid race conditions and ensure data consistency. Scheme offers several synchronization primitives, such as mutexes (mutual exclusions) and condition variables. Mutexes prevent multiple threads from concurrently accessing shared resources, while condition variables allow threads to wait for certain conditions to be met.

Creating and using a mutex in Scheme can be illustrated as follows:

```
(define my-mutex (make-mutex))

(mutex-lock! my-mutex)
;; Critical section: Shared resource access
(mutex-unlock! my-mutex)
```

Here, make-mutex creates a new mutex. We lock the mutex with mutex-lock! before entering the critical section and unlock it with mutex-unlock! after completing the operations on shared resources.

Condition variables allow threads to wait for and signal conditions. An example usage of condition variables is:

```
(define my-cond (make-condition-variable))

(mutex-lock! my-mutex)
(condition-wait! my-cond my-mutex)
;; Code executed after condition is met
(mutex-unlock! my-mutex)
```

```
;; In another thread
(mutex-lock! my-mutex)
(condition-signal! my-cond)
(mutex-unlock! my-mutex)
```

In this example, a thread waits for a condition by calling condition-wait!, and another thread signals that condition using condition-signal!. The mutex ensures exclusive access to the shared condition variable.

Message-Passing Interface

Message-passing is a paradigm where threads or processes communicate by sending and receiving messages. This approach is particularly useful in distributed systems where threads or processes might not share memory. Scheme supports message-passing through channels or queues.

Here's how we can implement message-passing using channels in Scheme:

```
(define chan (make-channel))

;; Sender thread
(thread-start!
 (lambda ()
   (channel-send! chan "Hello from sender")))

;; Receiver thread
(thread-start!
 (lambda ()
   (let ((message (channel-receive! chan)))
     (display message))))
```

In this example, make-channel creates a new communication channel. The sender thread sends a message through the channel using channel-send!, while the receiver thread retrieves the message with channel-receive!. This mechanism ensures that data is safely passed between concurrent threads.

Parallelism in Scheme

Parallelism in Scheme involves executing tasks on multiple processors or cores. This can be achieved using libraries like 'parallel' and constructs like futures and promises.

Futures allow expressions to be evaluated concurrently in the background, and their results can be retrieved when needed. This is particularly useful for tasks that can be executed in parallel without dependencies. An example of using futures in Scheme is provided below:

```
(define future-result (future (lambda () (expensive-computation))))
```

```
;; The future-result is computed in the background
(display (touch future-result))
```

In this snippet, future initiates the concurrent execution of expensive-computation. The touch function retrieves the result, blocking if the computation is not yet complete.

Another efficient parallel construct is promises, which represent values that will become available later. Promises can be used to coordinate parallel tasks, and their values are computed when first accessed.

A practical illustration of promises in Scheme is shown below:

```
(define my-promise
  (promise (lambda ()
             (delayed-computation))))

;; The computation is triggered when the promise is forced
(force my-promise)
```

In this example, promise sets up delayed-computation to be evaluated later. Accessing the promise's value using force triggers the computation.

Parallelism can also be achieved by explicitly creating parallel tasks and managing their execution. Libraries like SRFI 18 (Standard Scheme Request for Implementation) provide standard interfaces for parallel processing.

```
;; Example parallel execution using SRFI 18
(let ((task1 (thread-start! (lambda () (expensive-task-1))))
      (task2 (thread-start! (lambda () (expensive-task-2)))))
  ;; Wait for both tasks to complete
  (thread-join! task1)
  (thread-join! task2))
```

This script demonstrates parallel execution by creating and starting two threads, each performing different tasks. The thread-join! functions ensure that the main thread waits for both tasks to finish.

The constructs and paradigms discussed here significantly enhance Scheme's capacity for handling concurrent and parallel computations, making it adaptable for complex and high-performance applications.

10.10 Interfacing with Other Languages

Interfacing Scheme with other programming languages enhances its utility by allowing developers to leverage the strengths of multiple languages within a single application. This interoperation is particularly useful for integrating Scheme's powerful symbolic computation features with systems and languages optimized for tasks like numerical computation or low-level hardware control. This section discusses methods and considerations for effectively interfacing Scheme with languages such as C, C++, and Python.

Foreign Function Interface (FFI)

The Foreign Function Interface (FFI) is a standard mechanism for calling functions written in another language from within Scheme. This interface allows Scheme programs to invoke routines defined in languages like C and C++ directly.

```
int add(int a, int b) {
    return a + b;
}
```

To call this C function from Scheme, one typically relies on an FFI provided by the Scheme implementation. Here's an example using Gambit Scheme's FFI capabilities:

```
(define add (c-lambda (int int) int "add"))
```

In this example, the c-lambda form is used to declare the types of the input and output parameters, effectively linking the Scheme function add to the C function add.

Using SWIG for Scheme

SWIG (Simplified Wrapper and Interface Generator) is a powerful tool that simplifies the creation of FFIs for various languages, including Scheme. Consider a C++ class:

```
class Rectangle {
public:
    Rectangle(int w, int h) : width(w), height(h) {}
    int area() { return width * height; }
private:
    int width, height;
};
```

To interface this with Scheme using SWIG:

1. Create a SWIG interface file describing the C++ class:

```
%module rectangle
%{
#include "Rectangle.h"
%}
class Rectangle {
public:
```

```
    Rectangle(int w, int h);
    int area();
};
```

2. Generate the wrapper code using:

```
swig -scheme rectangle.i
```

3. Compile the wrapper and link against your library.

After these steps, you can use the Rectangle class in Scheme:

```
(define rect (new Rectangle 10 20))
(display (area rect)) ; Output: 200
```

Interfacing with Python

Though Scheme and Python are both high-level languages, it might be necessary to interface with Python to utilize its extensive libraries. Various tools enable this, such as clojure-py or custom Scheme FFI bindings designed specifically for CPython.

One common approach for Python integration is to use the built-in os.system or more sophisticated methods like cffi for calling C functions in Python, which can in turn call Scheme functions using SWIG-generated wrappers.

Here's a small example using ctypes in Python to call a Scheme function:

1. Assume a Scheme function is provided that calculates a factorial:

```
(define (factorial n)
  (if (<= n 1) 1 (* n (factorial (- n 1)))))
```

2. Compile this Scheme code to a shared library (*.so).

3. Use Python's ctypes to load and call the Scheme function:

```
import ctypes

# Load the shared library
scheme_lib = ctypes.CDLL('./libfactorial.so')

# Define the signature of the function we will call
factorial = scheme_lib.factorial
factorial.argtypes = [ctypes.c_int]
factorial.restype = ctypes.c_int

# Call the Scheme function
result = factorial(5)
print(f"Factorial of 5 is {result}") # Output: 120
```

Considerations for Interfacing

When integrating Scheme with other languages, several considerations must be addressed:

- **Data Type Mismatches**: Ensure that data types are correctly mapped between Scheme and the foreign language. For instance, numeric types in Scheme should be matched with appropriate C types.
- **Memory Management**: Handle memory allocation and deallocation carefully to avoid memory leaks or segmentation faults. When passing data structures (like strings and arrays), consider who owns the memory.
- **Error Handling**: Provide mechanisms for error propagation between languages. For example, exceptions in Python or error codes in C should be translated into appropriate Scheme error handling constructs.
- **Performance Overhead**: Inter-language calls can introduce significant overhead. Minimize the frequency of these calls, and profile performance to identify bottlenecks.

Interfacing Scheme with other languages opens up a vast array of possibilities, making it feasible to combine the expressive power of Scheme with the specialized capabilities of other environments. Understanding and effectively utilizing these mechanisms can significantly enhance the robustness and flexibility of your applications.

10.11 Building and Using Libraries and Modules

In Scheme programming, modularity and code reuse are crucial for managing complexity, promoting maintainability, and enhancing collaboration. Libraries and modules play an essential role in achieving these goals. This section will cover the creation, management, and use of libraries and modules in Scheme, along with practical examples to clarify these concepts.

Creating Libraries

A library in Scheme is a collection of procedures, macros, and data structures that can be used by multiple programs or other libraries. Libraries are defined using the library form. The general syntax for defining a library is as follows:

```
(library (library-name)
  (export exported-identifiers)
  (import imported-libraries)
  body...)
```

Let's create a simple library called math-lib that provides basic arithmetic operations:

```
(library (math-lib)
  (export add subtract multiply divide)
  (import
   (only (scheme base) + - * /))

  (define (add a b)
    (+ a b))

  (define (subtract a b)
    (- a b))

  (define (multiply a b)
    (* a b))

  (define (divide a b)
    (/ a b)))
```

In this library, we use the import statement to import the necessary symbols from the base language. The export statement makes the specified identifiers available to clients of the library.

Using Libraries

To use a library in a Scheme program, we use the import form. Suppose we want to use the math-lib we defined earlier:

```
(import (math-lib))

(define a 10)
(define b 5)

(define result-add (add a b))
(define result-subtract (subtract a b))
(define result-multiply (multiply a b))
(define result-divide (divide a b))

(display result-add) ; Prints 15
(newline)
(display result-subtract) ; Prints 5
(newline)
(display result-multiply) ; Prints 50
(newline)
(display result-divide) ; Prints 2
(newline)
```

Modular Program Design

Core principles of modularity include encapsulation, abstraction, and separation of concerns. Well-designed modules expose only the necessary interface while hiding the implementation details. This separation allows for easier updates and maintenance since changes to the implementation do not affect modules that depend on the interface.

To illustrate, let's create another library for more advanced mathematical operations that builds upon math-lib:

```
(library (advanced-math-lib)
  (export power factorial)
  (import (math-lib)
          (only (scheme base) expt))

  (define (power base exponent)
    (expt base exponent))

  (define (factorial n)
    (define (iter acc n)
      (if (<= n 1)
          acc
          (iter (multiply acc n) (subtract n 1))))
    (iter 1 n)))
```

The advanced-math-lib library imports math-lib and the expt procedure from the base library. This demonstrates how libraries can build upon each other, providing more complex functionality while maintaining modularity.

Library and Module Management

Scheme implementations provide tools for managing libraries and modules. Typically, libraries are stored in specific directories and files follow a naming convention based on their library name. For instance, the math-lib might be saved in a file named math-lib.scm in a designated library directory.

When a Scheme program imports a library, the implementation searches predefined library paths to locate the corresponding file. Configurations for library paths can generally be customized, allowing for flexibility in project organization.

Practical Usage

Consider a practical example where we construct a program that calculates the combinations of two numbers using our libraries:

```
(import (math-lib) (advanced-math-lib))

(define (combinations n k)
  (let* ((numerator (factorial n))
         (denominator (multiply (factorial k) (factorial (subtract n k)))))
    (divide numerator denominator)))
```

```
(define n 5)
(define k 2)

(display (combinations n k)) ; Prints 10
(newline)
```

This example showcases how the combination of multiple libraries results in a more complex yet modular program.

Best Practices

When developing libraries and modules in Scheme, adhere to the following best practices for optimal results: 1. Maintain clear and concise interfaces. Export only what is necessary. 2. Document the purpose and usage of each library and its procedures. 3. Write unit tests for each library to ensure correctness and facilitate maintenance. 4. Follow consistent naming conventions and coding standards to enhance readability and maintainability. 5. Use version control to manage and track changes in libraries systematically.

These practices contribute to creating robust, reusable, and maintainable codebases, driving efficiency and collaboration in Scheme programming projects.

10.12 Advanced Metaprogramming Techniques

Metaprogramming in Scheme refers to the practice of writing programs that generate or manipulate other programs or themselves. This allows for greater flexibility, code reusability, and abstraction. Scheme's minimalist syntax and powerful macro system provide an ideal platform for metaprogramming. This section explores advanced techniques in Scheme's metaprogramming capabilities, including macro systems, quasi-quoting, syntactic closures, and code walkers.

Metaprogramming enables the creation of new syntactic constructs in a high-level manner. The primary feature that Scheme offers for this purpose is its macro system. Scheme macros operate on the syntactic structure of the code during compile-time.

Hygienic Macros

Scheme emphasizes the use of hygienic macros, which ensure that macros do not accidentally capture free variables or cause naming conflicts. Hygienic macros in Scheme are typically defined using syntax-rules.

```
(define-syntax when
  (syntax-rules ()
    ((_ test body ...)
     (if test
         (begin body ...)))))
```

In the above definition, the when macro simplifies conditional expressions where the else part is not needed. The hygienic nature ensures that the variable bindings inside the macro do not interfere with those outside it.

Quasi-Quoting

Quasi-quoting, enabled by the backtick ‘ character, allows for the construction of code templates with evaluated embedded expressions using the comma , operator. This technique is useful for generating code dynamically.

```
(define (generate-adder n)
  `(lambda (x) (+ x ,n)))

(define add5 (generate-adder 5))
(add5 10) ; Evaluates to 15
```

The above example demonstrates how quasi-quoting is utilized to create a lambda expression that adds a given number to its input dynamically.

Syntactic Closures

Syntactic closures are an advanced macro technique that allows parts of a macro to be evaluated in the environment where the macro is used, rather than where it is defined. This can be particularly useful for ensuring context-sensitive transformations.

```
(define-syntax let*
  (syntax-rules ()
    ((_ () body ...)
     (begin body ...))
    ((_ ((var expr) bindings ...) body ...)
```

```
    (let ((var expr))
      (let* (bindings ...) body ...)))))
```

In the above let* macro definition, syntactic closures ensure that each binding can refer to the previous ones sequentially, emulating the behavior of nested let expressions.

Code Walkers

Code walkers are tools that traverse and transform code structures. They provide capabilities for recursive manipulation of syntactic forms. An important concept here is writing a macro expander to recursively expand all macros in a piece of code.

```
(define (expand-all x)
  (cond
    ((pair? x)
     (let ((macro (syntax-local-value (car x))))
       (if macro
           (expand-all (apply macro (cdr x)))
           (cons (expand-all (car x)) (expand-all (cdr x))))))
    (else x)))

(expand-all '(when (> 3 2) (display "Hello")))
```

The expand-all function processes each expression, expanding macros recursively. Here, syntax-local-value retrieves the macro associated with a syntactic keyword.

Macro Libraries

Scheme supports macro libraries to encapsulate macro definitions and reuse them. Various SRFI (Scheme Requests for Implementation) provide collections of macros standardized for common tasks.

```
(import (srfi 26)) ; Import SRFI-26 for cut and cute macros

(define (add-three-numbers a b c)
  (cut +
       (cut + a <> <>)
       (cut - <> c)))
```

In this example, SRFI-26 provides the cut and cute macros, which create partially applied functions. The cut macro enables concise and flexible functional composition.

Mastering advanced metaprogramming techniques in Scheme offers significant leverage in writing concise, reusable, and high-level abstractions, thereby enhancing the comprehensibility and maintainability of the codebase.

10.13 Case Studies: Advanced Scheme Applications

To gain a comprehensive understanding of the advanced topics in Scheme programming, we now investigate several practical case studies. These applications showcase the power and flexibility of Scheme in solving complex computational problems. Each case study will draw upon the techniques and concepts discussed throughout this chapter, providing concrete examples of how these can be applied to real-world scenarios.

Case Study 1: Implementing a Simple Web Server

A simple yet powerful example of Scheme's capabilities is the implementation of a minimal web server. We will utilize continuations and concurrency features to handle multiple client connections efficiently.

```
(define (start-server port handler)
  (let ((listener (socket-listen port)))
    (let loop ()
      (call/cc (lambda (k)
        (let ((client (socket-accept listener)))
          (thread (lambda ()
                    (handler client)
                    (k)))
          (loop)))))))
```

This code defines a function start-server that takes a port and a request handler as arguments. The socket-listen function creates a listening socket on the specified port. The server enters an infinite loop where it accepts incoming client connections using socket-accept. A new thread is spawned for each connection, allowing multiple clients to be served concurrently. By using call/cc, the server can retain the loop's continuation, ensuring that new connections are handled appropriately without blocking.

The handler function for processing incoming requests might look like this:

```
(define (request-handler client)
  (let ((input (socket-receive client))
        (output (socket-send client)))
    (write-line "HTTP/1.0 200 OK" output)
    (write-line "Content-Type: text/html" output)
```

```
    (write-line "" output)
    (write-line "<html><body><h1>Hello, Scheme!</h1></body></html>" output
        )
    (close output)
    (close input)))
```

In this handler, the request is read from the client socket, and a simple HTTP response is sent back. The server responds with a basic HTML page containing the text "Hello, Scheme!". The sockets are then closed to complete the request/response cycle.

Case Study 2: Creating a Lazy Evaluator

The second case study illustrates the creation of a lazy evaluator in Scheme. By delaying evaluation until the value is actually needed, we can handle potentially infinite data structures. This technique is highly beneficial for computations involving large or infinite sequences.

```
(define (delay exp)
  (lambda () exp))

(define (force delayed-exp)
  (delayed-exp))
```

The delay function wraps an expression in a lambda to defer its evaluation, while force triggers the evaluation of the delayed expression. For practical use, we can construct infinite sequences like the list of natural numbers.

```
(define (integers-from n)
  (cons n (delay (integers-from (+ n 1)))))
```

```
(define (take n delayed-stream)
  (if (zero? n)
      '()
      (cons (car delayed-stream)
            (take (- n 1) (force (cdr delayed-stream))))))
```

The integers-from function generates an infinite lazy list starting from a given number. take is used to extract the first n elements from a lazy list. By forcing the evaluation of the stream's tail, we ensure that each element is computed only when needed.

Case Study 3: Parallel Fibonacci Computation

To demonstrate concurrency and parallelism, we implement a parallel version of the Fibonacci sequence calculation. This implementation leverages Scheme's threading capabilities to compute Fibonacci numbers more efficiently.

```
(define (fib n)
```

```
  (if (< n 2)
      n
      (+ (future (fib (- n 1)))
         (future (fib (- n 2))))))
```

```
(define (future expr)
  (let ((result-ref (make-promise expr)))
    (lambda () @result-ref)))
```

```
(define (make-promise expr)
  (let ((result #f)
        (computed #f))
    (thread
     (lambda ()
       (set! result (expr))
       (set! computed #t)))
    (lambda ()
      (if computed
          result
          (begin
            (thread-yield)
            (@ make-promise expr))))))
```

The fib function recursively computes Fibonacci numbers. Each recursive call is made in parallel using the future construct. The future function creates a computation that runs in the background, returning a promise. The promise evaluates the expression asynchronously, and its value is accessed only when needed. This approach enables parallel computation of Fibonacci numbers, significantly improving performance for large values of n.

Case Study 4: Building a Domain-Specific Language (DSL)

Our final case study involves building a domain-specific language (DSL) for arithmetic expressions. This example showcases advanced metaprogramming techniques, allowing users to define and evaluate custom expressions intuitively.

```
(define-syntax rule
  (syntax-rules ()
    ((rule (op . args) body)
     (define (op . args) body))))

(rule (square x) (* x x))
(rule (sum-squares x y) (+ (square x) (square y)))
(rule (eval-expr expr)
  (if (symbol? expr)
      expr
      (apply (car expr) (map eval-expr (cdr expr)))))
```

The rule macro simplifies the definition of new DSL operations. For instance, square and sum-squares can be defined easily using this macro. The eval-expr function recursively evaluates an arithmetic expression represented as a list. It checks if the expression is a symbol and returns it as-is; otherwise, it applies the operator (car) to the evaluated arguments (cdr).

```
(eval-expr '(sum-squares 3 4))
```

Output: 25

The expression (eval-expr '(sum-squares 3 4)) results in 25, demonstrating the DSL's capabilities. This approach can be extended to support more complex operations and features, highlighting Scheme's strength in metaprogramming.

These case studies illustrate the versatility and power of Scheme for implementing advanced applications, leveraging the various concepts and techniques covered in this chapter. Through practical examples, we have seen how to apply these advanced features to build efficient, high-performance programs in Scheme.

Made in United States
Cleveland, OH
10 November 2026

48114698R00165